363.5809 Barak, Gregg.
BAR
        Gimme shelter.

$39.95

DATE			

Gimme Shelter

Gimme Shelter

A SOCIAL HISTORY OF HOMELESSNESS IN CONTEMPORARY AMERICA

Gregg Barak

 PRAEGER

New York
Westport, Connecticut
London

Library of Congress Cataloging-in-Publication Data

Barak, Gregg.
    Gimme shelter / Gregg Barak.
      p. cm.
    Includes bibliographical references and index.
    ISBN 0–275–93320–2 (alk. paper)
      ISBN 0–275–94401–8 (pbk. : alk. paper)
      1. Homelessness—United States. 2. Homeless persons—Services
  for—United States. I. Title.
    HV4505.B37 1991
    363.5'8'0973—dc20   90–24567

British Library Cataloguing in Publication Data is available.

Library of Congress Catalog Card Number: 90–24567
ISBN: 0–275–93320–2
      0–275–94401–8 (pbk.)

First published in 1991
Paperback edition 1992

Praeger Publishers, One Madison Avenue, New York, NY 10010
An imprint of Greenwood Publishing Group, Inc.

Printed in the United States of America

(∞)™

The paper used in this book complies with the
Permanent Paper Standard issued by the National
Information Standards Organization (Z39.48–1984).

10 9 8 7 6 5 4 3 2

Copyright Acknowledgment

The author and publisher gratefully acknowledge permission to use the following copyrighted materials:

Table from Deborah Judith Devine, "Homelessness and the Social Safety Net," Doctoral Dissertation, 1988 (Ann Arbor, MI: University Microfilms, 1989).

Tables from Stephen Crystal, Susan Ladner, and Richard Towber, "Multiple Impairment Patterns in the Mentally Ill Homeless," *International Journal of Mental Health*, Vol. 14, no. 4. Reprinted by permission of M. E. Sharpe, Inc., Armonk, New York 10504.

Selections from Francine Rabinowitz, "What Shall Be Done." Published by permission of Transaction Publishers, from SOCIETY, Volume 26, No. 4. Copyright © 1989 by Transaction Publishers.

In
Memory
of
Mitch Snyder

Contents

Preface

During the last 15 years of his life, homeless activist Mitch Snyder—who committed suicide in July 1990—struggled valiantly on behalf of the nation's homeless, destitute, and powerless. There were pray-ins, eat-ins, cage-ins, jump-ins, and, yes, laugh-ins. But most of all, there were Snyder's fasts; the danger of his condition and the size of his risk had captured the hearts and minds of the American people. There was even a TV movie made about his life with the homeless. As part and parcel of this human struggle, Snyder "pricked our conscience about a group of people Americans didn't see, and didn't want to see" (Rader, 1986: ix).

Conservatives will contend in contradictory fashion that the protests by Snyder and the Community for Creative Non-Violence (CCNV) were too confrontational. However, had Snyder, CCNV, and others not adopted the tactics that they did for resisting homelessness in the United States, does anybody think in these times of "modest expectations"—as Mitch used to call them—that literally every branch of the U.S. government would respond to the short-term (as opposed to long-term) needs of the homeless as they have? Without Snyder and company we would not have the few, inadequate pieces of federal legislation on homelessness and housing that we do.

I would agree with the assessment of homeless activist Robert Hayes, founder of the National Coalition for the Homeless, who said following the news of Snyder's death that he "created, almost single-handedly, a movement" on behalf of homeless people (Keil, 1990: 4A). There is no doubt about it, homelessness and the efforts by Snyder and others had put the homeless on the agenda, during the 1980s, at a time when the Reagan administration was busy counting catsup as a vegetable in the federally funded lunch programs for the nation's millions of poor children.

Snyder was also the person responsible for making Ronald Reagan act contrary to what he really believed in (helping the rich get richer) while he was president, when Reagan and his chief of staff, James Baker, eventually capitulated to Snyder's hunger strike demands that the administration do something to shelter Washington, D.C.'s homeless. With the stroke of the pen, the District of Columbia had the promise of a shelter to house a thousand homeless Washingtonians, and Reagan could not be portrayed by the Democrats in the upcoming 1984 election as mean and indifferent to the plight of the homeless in his own backyard.

Immediately following Snyder's death, themes in both print and electronic journalism focused attention on the "internal strife and apparent decline in public support" for the homeless (DeParle, 1990: 6A). Some media pundits were even wondering if Snyder's death had not indicated the beginning of the end of the homeless movement in the United States. The problem with these kinds of mass-mediated analyses of the life and times of contemporary America is the typically superficial coverage of the media itself. Regarding homelessness and Mitch Snyder over the last decade, the media had reinforced the latter's dominance in the homeless movement. By singling him out, the media quickly made Snyder into one more celebrity for mass consumption.

The real point, however, should have been that though Snyder would indeed be missed, the future of the homelessness movement did not rest on the shoulders of its earliest leaders, including the famous, the infamous, or the unknown. Many of the unsung heroes and heroines of the homelessness movement are still quite active, some have moved on to other things, but many more have yet to take the stage in this human tragedy that is far from over. As for the internal strife in the movement to resist homelessness, that should have been reported as politics as usual and as being very characteristic of social movements and organizational development in general.

Concerning the so-called news of a decline in public support for the homeless, public opinion polls taken in the late 1980s consistently showed otherwise. One should not, for example, have confused the various political setbacks in the struggle against homelessness at the turn of the decade with having had any relationship to popular support. In fact, the most recent national survey that I am aware of was conducted in 1989 by Kane, Parsons and Associates. It revealed that 80 percent of the respondents believed that homelessness dramatically symbolized one of the most tragic inequities of U.S. society, and that the majority of those respondents were willing to have their taxes raised so that more could be done on behalf of the homeless.

The losses that the homeless have recently experienced at both the national and local levels has had more to do with power politics than with any decline in the movement's cause or appeal. In other words, one should assume as we enter the early 1990s that the prevailing interests of local, national, and multinational business elites, responding to the real needs in the competitive markets of global capitalism, have not been particularly excited about passing any legislation or supporting any judicial decisions obligating the government or the private sector to provide (mandate) permanent housing for all people in the United States.

While I differ with some advocacy people who believe that a backlash against the homeless has begun, it is certainly clear that there have already been municipal cuts in aid to the poor as well as the passing of ordinances criminalizing homeless behavior. More and more homeless are being evicted from public places, and more and more beggars are being harassed and prohibited from public and private spaces. Sympathetic or nonsympathetic to the needs of the homeless, very few people have ever really wanted them around. Nevertheless, the vast majority of people living in the United States in 1990 have not abandoned the homeless cause. In fact, historically speaking the homeless of 1990 are regarded in a far more humane, compassionate, and understanding way than they were just ten short years ago. Back then, people were denying that the homeless existed, and if they did, it was because of their own doing. At that time many cities, led by their local Chambers of Commerce, were doing all they could to drive the homeless out of their communities.

Although we may not have heard the last from Snyder's legacy and its relationship to the homelessness movement, in the not-too-distant future, his memory will disappear while the homeless situation will continue to become firmly entrenched in the American conscience. For the record, while Snyder may not have been a saint, he was a genuine shepard of the poor. In the future the United States will need more activists like Mitch Snyder because in the 1990s, unfortunately, assuming that domestic federal policy does not change its current course, the number of homeless persons in this country is going to swell considerably. For instead of addressing the underlying sources and changes in both society and the larger world that have been primarily responsible for this growth, our various governmental bodies have appeared destined simply to continue to expand another system for warehousing homeless people similar in purpose and design to the expanding "correctional" system for warehousing street criminals.

The study of homelessness that you are about to read is grounded in those perspectives that can be traced to the disciplines of critical criminology and victimology. More fundamentally, this treatise is a social history in the tradition of elucidating the material social relations that structure the real world of power and exploitation in the United States. Accordingly, when discussing homelessness in "America," we will not be referring to homelessness in Central or South America, nor to our neighbors to the north in Canada. This does not mean, however, that we do not recognize that homelessness is not a worldwide phenomenon. On the contrary, the forthcoming analysis is grounded in an appreciation of the forces of globalism and the internationalization of capital. Finally, my work is informed by critical social theory and discourse theory. In terms of historical and dialectical materialism, however, language has meaning essentially because of its context. Herein lies the goal of struggling, not only to interpret the world objectively, but to change it as Karl Marx once declared. In the case of homelessness in America, the point is to first understand why we have it, and then to eliminate it.

REFERENCES

DeParle, Jason. 1990. "Advocates for homeless debate how to continue cause." *Sunday Montgomery Advertiser*, July 8.

Keil, Richard. 1990. "Friend to the homeless dead of apparent suicide." *The Montgomery Advertiser*, July 6.

Rader, Victoria. 1986. *Signal Through the Flames: Mitch Snyder and America's Homeless*. Kansas City, MO: Sheed & Ward.

Acknowledgments

Unlike the struggle to eradicate homelessness, the struggle to write this book was a relatively simple one. The words as well as the various pieces of the contemporary homeless story seemed to almost write themselves. It was as though I had become obsessed or perhaps "possessed" with the telling of what I hoped would become the first truly comprehensive overview and analysis of the homelessness problem in the United States. This book, of course, would never have been actually produced had it not been for the emergence and development of the homelessness movement and its intersection with my own personal history and experience.

In this regard I must thank the relatively few homeless persons and homeless activists whom I have personally known. More important, I must acknowledge the millions of homeless persons and thousands of homeless advocates who provided me with the inspiration to write this book. I also want to thank too many people to mention, residing inside and outside of the third ward in Aurora, Illinois, who provided me with the opportunity, from 1982 to 1985, to become deeply involved and immersed in the related struggles of the abused, the hungry, and the homeless. In particular, I want to acknowledge Joan Little, Homero Basaldua, Rosemarie Lorentzen, and Betty Barr. I learned so much from my Auroran experience; many thanks to my allies and adversaries alike.

Throughout the course of my research on homelessness and long before, during, and after my initial writings on the homeless, there were a number of people who supported, assisted, influenced, or critiqued my thinking on the history of social problems in general, especially as it related to my various perspectives on and analyses of homelessness. In this regard I wish to acknowledge Leon Anderson, Nicholas Astone, Lillian Barak, Robert Bohm, Renee Brown-Mills, William Chambliss, Francis Cullen, Walter De-Keseredy, Christina Johns, Dragan Milovanovic, Charlotte Pagni, Harold Pepinsky, Tony Platt, Katheryn Russell, Herman and Julia Schwendinger, David Spinner, Paul Takagi, and Robert Thomson.

I would also like to acknowledge a significant debt that I owe to the authors of five doctoral dissertations completed during the late 1980s on the subject of homelessness: Marjorie Bard, Joel Blau, Deborah Devine, Kim Hopper, and Pearl Werfel. Each of these persons in her or his own way has exemplified not only the value of being actively engaged in the phenomenon under investigation, but of applied social science research more generally. Their works provide excellent examples of the kinds of social and behavioral research that can make a difference in the real world.

Finally, acknowledgment is given to the research support made possible by a grant from Alabama State University during the summer of 1989.

PART I

The Problem of Homelessness

1 Introduction

In the United States of the early 1990s there is probably less controversy, more frustration, and about the same confusion surrounding the homelessness condition as there was during the decade of the 1980s. While public attitudes regarding the homeless are still divided, more and more people, about two to one—or 54 percent to 27 percent—"believe people become homeless for circumstances largely beyond their control than said homelessness is due to a person's own negligence or irresponsible behavior" and a full 80 percent of respondents to the national survey[1] said that "homelessness dramatically symbolizes some of the tragic inequities in American society" (New York [AP], 1989: 5a).

The beliefs about the homeless in the United States have become demystified, in part, as a reflection of the actions of the homeless themselves, as well as the actions of those people organized on behalf of the various homeless populations. As far as social movements are concerned, the one to abolish homelessness during the contemporary homeless crisis is relatively sophisticated and well along in terms of development; it expresses itself at both the indigenous, grass-roots, local level and at the state and national levels. In a sense, the movement to reform the U.S. response to the homelessness conditions has, at least, minimally raised people's consciousness regarding the plight of the homeless. It has also served to prick the body politic regarding the so-called ethic and shame of the 1980s decade of "me and greed." In another more important sense, however, the public policy response to homelessness has yet to confront the situation with a serious long-term plan.

As for the opinions, analyses, and approaches to the causes and solutions of the homelessness condition, there are a lot of disagreements. With respect to a changing domestic picture, especially as it relates to the poor and homeless, there is of course the traditional political resistance or lack of will to examine candidly the underlying social policy question of our time and possibly of the next century, namely: "What is the role of the population as a whole, as represented by government, in regulating economic behavior and in evening out economic inequities among its members?" (*American Journal of Public Health*, 1986: 1085). Or stated differently, what is the state's democratically appropriate role in dealing with poverty, social control, and liberty for all?

In relation to these undiscussed problems or questions in the United States, it has been the competing ideologies of liberalism and conservatism that have propelled public policy. The liberals favor active regulation of economic behavior, some kind of developed welfare state, and minimal intervention into personal freedom. The conservatives argue on behalf of little or no regulation of the economy and no government-run income redistribution programs, while at the same time they call for a great deal of personal behavior control.

While there is still some debate on the size of the homelessness population, with low estimates around 300,000 and the higher estimates around 3 million,[2] there is nevertheless general agreement as reported by emergency shelter providers, housing advocacy organizations, and local governments with respect to the following conditions:

- homelessness is a growing problem across the nation, inflicting small rural communities to big urban cities;
- the shortage of affordable housing is always identified as a factor in the expanding homelessness rates;
- among the fastest growing sector of the homeless population are families with children (75 percent of which are single-parent);
- minorities—African-Americans and Hispanics in particular—are highly overrepresented among the homeless;
- special-needs populations—the most significant including the mentally ill, the substance abuser, and the AIDS sufferer—are among the homeless who require supportive services in addition to affordable housing (National Coalition for the Homeless, 1989).

In short, by the beginning of this decade the U.S. condition of homelessness counted among its victims of societal violence[3] the following: men, women, and children of all racial and ethnic backgrounds; the urban and rural working and nonworking poor; displaced and deinstitutionalized persons; alcoholics, drug addicts, mentally ill, and those inflicted with AIDS; physically abused mothers and their babies, throwaways and runaways, sexually abused adolescents, and neglected older people; migrants, refugees, and Vietnam War veterans. As for the near future, a 1988 congressionally funded study by the Neighborhood Reinvestment Corporation informs us that unless immediate action is taken to preserve and expand the supply of affordable housing in the United States, then by the end of the century there could be as many as 19 million homeless residents. Concomitantly, it is argued by many homeless advocates that the 1980s trend, which saw federal spending for low-income housing slashed by 77 percent, or $25 billion per year since 1981, has to be reversed in the 1990s or the housing/homelessness crisis will only deepen (HOUSING NOW! 1989).

ON THE "OLD" VAGRANCY AND THE "NEW" VAGRANCY

Since the emergence of vagrancy statutes in early modern Europe during the sixteenth century and as far back as the earliest enacted vagrancy laws (ca. 1349) in England, their enforcements, punishments, and appellations have changed frequently and dramatically (Adler, 1986; Chambliss, 1964). The vagueness of vagrancy statues throughout their long disreputable history may have, as a practical matter, been put to legal rest by the U.S. Supreme Court ruling in *Papachristou et al. v. City of Jacksonville* in 1972 (Chambliss and Seidman, 1982). However, "there is reason to believe that the Supreme Court is modifying the stand that it took in *Papachristou*. A number of statutes and ordinances forbidding loitering or disorderly conduct have been upheld on various grounds, principally the fear that peace, order, or public safety are threatened" (Leiser, 1988: 123). Perhaps more importantly, there are the cultural and mental legacies associated with the ominous presence of the "new" and "old" vagrants that still persist in the imaginations of many people. The "new" vagrancy also poses familiar and unfamiliar threats to our contemporary social order than say the "old" vagrancy of colonial America or Elizabethan England did to their respective social orders. Today, most people talk about the "new" and the "old" homeless, but as this book will reveal throughout, it makes more sense to realize that we are actually discussing the "old" and "new" vagrancy as defined by Anglo-American legal tradition:

English law, for example, at times defined vagrants as unemployed workers. At other times, it expanded the definition of vagrancy to include "lusty rogues," shiftless beggars, jugglers, minstrels, and thieves. [In the United States] vagrancy codes have included "characters" ranging from paupers to recalcitrant former slaves, prostitutes, "pigeon droppers," and "players at dice" (Adler, 1989: 209).

When referring to the "old" or the "new" vagrancy, *Roget's International Thesaurus* (3rd ed., 1962) provides such nouns and adjectives as:

vagrant, vagabond, bum, tramp, hobo, waif, stray, beggar, loafter, gamin

wandering, drifting, roaming, deviating, devious, aberrant, wanton, wayward, transient, undisciplined, unrestrained, twisted, freakish, maggoty

As for *Roget's* treatment of the meaning of homeless and homelessness:

homeless, forlorn, abandoned, deserted, desolate, friendless, helpless, defenseless, indigence, pauperism, destitution, privation, neediness, beggary, impoverishment, destitution

One can see from our language (and from our practice) that while perhaps the meaning and terminology used to describe the homeless is less degrading and more sympathetic than that used to describe the vagrant, the unambiguous common denominator unifying homelessness and vagrancy has been poverty. As Hoch and Slayton (1989) have argued, since the same sources—poverty and shelter deprivation—account for the problems confronted by the old and new homeless alike, there is really very little difference between the two. However, as treated in this book, an essential distinction is made between the old and new vagrancy/homelessness in the United States. Such a distinction is grounded in the sociohistoric reality that the sources of poverty and shelter changed significantly during the decade of the 1980s. This distinction further assumes that poverty and shelter deprivation are symptoms of a developing political economy and public policy rather than the causes of homelessness per se.

Since settlers first came to the New World there have been homeless people here. Homelessness is certainly not new to the American experience, but a fundamental distinction can be made between those people in colonial times, the homeless people from the turn of the century, including the swelled population of the homeless during the Great Depression, those homeless persons of the decades since the 1950s, and those of the 1990s. To put it simply, while their histories and experiences share much in common, their social production is different. The homelessness characteristic of the period 1880–1980 was typically the product of a depressed, industrial economy struggling with the underproduction and experiencing a labor surplus. On the other hand, homelessness as characteristic of the new poverty that emerged in the 1980s is a product of the transition from an industrial-based capitalist economy to a postindustrial capitalist service economy within the context of internationally developing global relations. The problems of the contemporary U.S. economy as expressed in the crises in poverty and homelessness involve underconsumption and a surplus of technically unskilled workers. Hence, since the ultimate sources of homelessness differ, the appropriate solutions to poverty and shelter deprivation should vary from place to place and time to time as the nature of the vagrancy condition changes in relation to the developing political economies, locally and globally. In a nutshell, the problem with the current response to the new vagrancy is that the policy assumptions are still grounded in the political economy of the old vagrancy.

Homelessness is both a condition of being and a state of mind. For example, there are those homeless people who are not only strong in body and spirit, but who in spite of all of the adversity are striving to achieve a sense of friendship and community. There are also those victims of homelessness who have lost their sense of purpose and worth, their sense of identity, and their will to live. Taken as a whole, homeless people in the 1990s, regardless of their personal condition, find themselves struggling to cope with the numerous indecencies, indignities, and obscenities that envelop their daily existences. On top of these burdens, today's homeless people are in the position of having to resist further victimization by other homeless persons, by traditional street criminals, and by the more impersonal forces of alienation and detachment.

In brief, when discussing global capitalism and its relationship to the new vagrancy of a postindustrial economy, and while focusing attention on the material deprivation of the homeless have-nots of the affluent U.S. society, one should not ignore or dismiss the psychological, physical, and social violence that enshrouds the homelessness condition.

RESPONSES TO THE NEW HOMELESSNESS: THE DESERVING VERSUS THE UNDESERVING POOR

The way we respond to the new homeless today cannot be removed or separated from the ideology and practice of social welfare that has been developing in the United States for the past century. Stated differently, the treatment of the new vagrancy is related to the treatment of the old vagrancy. Since the last quarter of the nineteenth century, one legacy has been the ideology of Social Darwinism and the practice of distinguishing between the "deserving" and "undeserving" poor. As applied to the homeless and to homelessness, the prevailing ideology of the post–Civil War period was that of the Charity Organization Societies who maintained that " 'indiscriminate almsgiving' and personal faults were viewed as the main causes of vagrancy" (Blau, 1987: 32). This ideology helped to transform all able-bodied beggars, voluntary or involuntary, into the criminal class of tramping vagrants. Reform Darwinism, the ideology of the Progressive Era, which was introduced at the turn of the century, despite its somewhat kinder judgments of the poor, reinforced the practices of centralizing services and discriminating among homeless clients. The policies advocated were for two different kinds of labor colonies—one "forced" and one "freed," one for the "recalcitrant" and one for the "blameless victim" (Blau, 1987).

Social and Reform Darwinism's concerns or fears are still alive as we approach the twenty-first century: namely, that indiscriminate relief or welfare, or giving something for nothing, is still a prerequisite for encouraging begging, vagrancy, homelessness, and criminality. However, as pointed out in the opening of this chapter, a large percentage of the American people today also recognize that the new homelessness is a product not only of individual circumstances but, more importantly, of institutional and structural arrangements. However, the distinction between the deserving and the undeserving homeless is still in place as evidenced in the shift of giving away from the shelterless and near shelterless in San Francisco to the displaced property-owning "homeful" victims of the October 1989 Bay Area earthquake. Such shifting responses to homelessness in San Francisco resulted in area homeless and shelter advocates taking to the airwaves to make the situation known by late January 1990.

Consequently, during the 1980s and I suspect the 1990s too, we will continue to witness public and private, individual and community, statewide and national responses to both the homeless and the homelessness condition that are reflective of ambivalent and contradictory feelings. In short, U.S. policy responses to the new homelessness represent dissonant ideological and political pressures that we can expect to continue to range from extreme cruelty and inhumanity to extreme kindness and compassion. Most people, however, will continue to respond with indifference or neglect to the plight of the homeless.

The two homelessness response scenarios that follow provide a sense of the extremes on a response continuum. In the first or "repressive" scenario, the homeless are viewed as underserving vagrants/criminals who receive punitive forms of intervention from people trying to rid themselves and their environs of spoiled goods. In the second or "nonrepressive" scenario, the homeless are viewed as deserving, unfortunate people in need of human services who receive caring intervention by concerned citizens attempting to struggle with the homelessness condition.

Repressive Scenario

In perhaps fewer and fewer communities, but with notable exceptions persisting in the smaller and larger towns across the nation, the homeless are still looked upon as being more fully responsible and, therefore, they are regarded with less empathy and more scorn. In these rural areas of the country, if friends and family have abandoned the homeless, then it is time for these people to disappear literally and figuratively. The homeless in these communities can become victims of citizens' beatings and bashings or they can become objects of law enforcement, subject to criminalization and incarceration. In these typically poor communities, where emergency assistance is not usually available, where few if any shelter beds or soup kitchens exist, and where official and unofficial policies are to run the homeless out of town, these vagrant people have been verbally harassed and physically abused.

Thus, far away from the more conspicuous sights of the urban homeless, on the rural roads of the corporate agrieconomy of the United States, are thousands of the hidden homeless doing their best to stay out of the way of local citizens and police who may arrest and charge them for criminal trespassing, squatting, panhandling, or loitering. In more than a few incidences, these homeless persons have been arrested for merely trying to feed themselves. In other words, in the sparsely populated regions of the Middle West and the South, it is quite common to find recently bankrupted and marginal farmers who have been forced off the land joining the ranks of other migrant workers in search of unskilled work. Criss-crossing the country, these members of a new migrant class, with and without their families, spend varying periods of time traveling the state highways and byways in their mobile homes if they are lucky, and with their packs strapped on their backs if they are not. If they are fortunate, they sleep in their cars and trucks; if they are not, they sleep at rest stops, all-night truck stops, in plowed fields, or on the side of the road.

Nonrepressive Scenario

In many more communities, including medium-sized cities as well as the urbanized metropolitan areas, a sizable majority of the homeless population remain, if not hidden, relatively invisible. That is to say, most of the urban homeless populations are warehoused out of sight. In part, this situation is a result of governmental assistance and programs; it is also a result, in part, of the private efforts of concerned citizens and groups, especially church-related assistance. In these communities, temporary or emergency assistance is available through bureaucracies operating at all levels of government. At the same time, public and private armories and shelters—some for whole families, some for couples only, some for single women, and some for battered women and their infants—protect these homeless groups from physical elements, at least during the night. There are also the various secular and religious efforts to provide the homeless, the hungry, and the near destitute with day shelters, soup kitchens, clothes closets, and food pantries. Without this array of programs to regulate the behavior of the new poor and homeless, these members of society's relatively harmless "social junk" would quickly become members of society's "social dynamite"—or threatening classes that call into question established political and economic arrangements (Spitzer, 1975). The sheer numbers of tens of thousands of homeless people roaming the urban streets in search of food and shelter would certainly contribute to widespread victimization and social disorder.

Despite these programs and other services, such as city policies that require police to pick up homeless individuals and drive them to one of the nearby community shelters on those cold nights when the temperatures often drop below zero, dozens of Americans still manage to freeze to death every winter. As for the homeless of the communities who do not or cannot avail themselves of the various forms of social welfare, most do not quickly perish. But even in the most caring and compassionate urban communities, where people do not necessarily look out of the way as they step over or around homeless persons, after a while even those unfortunate souls who can be found sleeping in doorways, in metal trash receptacles, and in home-made cardboard shelters become invisible, like so many other homeless people who are congregated in such out-of-the-way places as city alleyways, subways, train depots, and bus stations.

While these two scenarios of responding to the needs of the homeless are not meant to be exhaustive of the vagaries of homelessness, they do serve to underscore the dominant ideological values in this country with respect to such fundamental questions as the meaning of individualism, community, and human nature. In the first scenario, the more conservative Social Dar-winist orientation with its repressive or punitive responses to the homeless, is reflective of the nineteenth-century ideologies of laissez-faire capitalism and rugged individualism. The treatment of the homeless as members of the underserving poor exemplifies the same types of responses that members of the old vagrancy and other victims of surplus and marginal labor have always experienced during the past five centuries of commercial and indus-trial capitalism. In the second scenario, the more liberal or interventionist orientation, ascribing to the ideological values of reformation and change, is reflective of the emergence and development of the twentieth-century welfare state and the Judeo-Christian ethic that recognizes the needs for peace and security among all of God's "deserving" and "forgiving" poor.

CONCEPTUALIZING THE HOMELESSNESS PROBLEM: THE 1980s AND BEYOND

How people respond to the homeless and to the condition of homelessness depends on how they view the world and how they personally and politically conceptualize social problems generally. In certain respects, therefore, the forthcoming analysis of homelessness and how our society has responded to it could be applied to other critically related problems such as health care, domestic violence, and street crime. The common or unifying theme that informs each of these (and other social problems) has historically always revolved around the way in which specific societal groups and class interests define or create the very social issue in the first place. This book is essentially about understanding how the processes of socially constructing the homeless and the homelessness condition shape the production and reproduction of the problem.

When most people, for example, think personally about the homeless, rarely do images come to mind of the realities of teenage runaways, lacking marketable skills and financial resources, selling their bodies to the highest urban bidders. Similarly, people do not often think about homeless children, most of them abused or neglected, as sleeping in abandoned buildings with-out heat, electricity, and running water. Finally, most people hardly, if ever, think about homeless mothers exchanging sexual services for roofs over their children's and their own heads as preferable alternatives to other shelter opportunities where the chance of losing their children to foster care or an adoption agency is a distinct possibility.

Our conceptualizations of homelessness and the homeless are also influenced by and inseparable from other political and economic considerations. Traditionally in the United States, whether the condition of vagrancy was viewed as the product of individual weakness, public policy design, structural push or pull, institutional crisis, or some combination, the vagrants (homeless) have always been discussed primarily in terms of the problems that they have presented for themselves and the larger society. Even though the decade of the 1980s closed with a majority of the people recognizing the structural nature of the homelessness condition, we are still buying into an ideology of "blaming the victim" (Ryan, 1971) and we are still approaching the problem without historical perspective.

In this book, rather than viewing the homeless exclusively in terms of their real or imaginary characterological problems (e.g., mental depravity, genetic inferiority, cultural deprivation), of their social threats to the welfare of the larger community (e.g., crime, contamination, demoralization), and of their material costs of survival (e.g., shelter, food, clothes), the argument is developed that a more realistic and appropriate analysis of the new vagrancy should be grounded in the historically informed view that understands the new homelessness to be an expression of the more fundamental change in the global political economy as related to the whole panoply of domestic policy decisions, including those specifically involving health care, education, housing, and law and order. At the same time, this analysis does not ignore the conflicting and often contradictory social views that people express about homelessness and the homeless or the ambivalent personal feelings and attitudes that most of us share toward the new vagrancy. It follows that ambivalent attitudes and feelings make for ambivalent policies. Caught between warehousing thousands of New York City's homeless in a few large central facilities versus the creation of decentralized smaller community-based shelters in the mid–1980s, former Mayor Ed Koch came down strongly in favor of the less humane and more efficient warehousing. In 1985 Koch could be heard bragging, on the one hand, how New York City had done more for the homeless than any other city. On the other hand, he could be heard boasting that the only way neighborhood shelters would be opened throughout the city, as called for by the city's advocates for the homeless, would be over his dead body.

To put it more directly, the homeless make us uncomfortable; they "evoke our pity and a tangle of other disquieting emotions: anger, frustration, fear, and a lingering malaise" that the American dream may be starting to fade away (Hope and Young, 1986: 28). To put it as bluntly as he could, in an essay for *Harper's Magazine*, Peter Marin (1987: 47) captured the darker side of our psychic relationship with the homeless: "for many of us, the homeless are shit, and our policies toward them, our spontaneous sense of disgust and horror, our wish to be rid of them—all of this has hidden in it, close to its heart, our feelings about excrement."

Located within these various conceptual perspectives on homelessness have been the social policy discussions of the 1980s, dominated by the traditional liberal-conservative debates about the proper role and responsibilty of the welfare state. Such conceptualization during the 1980s had, for the most part, confined the examination of homelessness to three types of questions: What is the actual size of the homeless population? To what extent is homelessness a condition of free will? Should the homeless be helped, punished, or left alone? While these may be interesting and important questions to explore, they fail to address the more fundamental questions confronting the changing realities of our postindustrial informational society, which appears to be slowly but surely transforming us into a society of haves and have nots. With the question of the ever-widening gap between the rich and the poor in mind, the rest of this section provides a brief review and critique of the conventional debates.

First, there is the debate over the number of homeless persons and whether the population is growing out of control. Those who cite lower estimates argue that the problem of homelessness is exaggerated. It has even been seriously suggested by those who prefer the smallest estimates that the homeless crisis of the 1980s was a manufactured tale of two advocates: Mitch Snyder, a former Vietnam protester and founder of the Community for Creative Non-Violence, and Robert Hayes, an attorney who represented New York's homeless populations in class action suits against the city: "It becomes clear that homelessness has become an issue in American life largely because of the efforts of two charismatic lobbyists—a Washington adman and a New York City lawyer" (Wooster, 1988: 106). Followers of this viewpoint on homelessness see the problem as manageable with a modest expansion of the number of shelter emergency beds, combined with some specialized assistance for the mentally ill. They argue in classic Social Darwinian language that the bloating of the welfare state—free food, free housing, free electricity—will not solve the problem but, on the contrary, will only exacerbate the problem by providing incentives for people to become homeless.

On the other hand, those who favor the larger estimates on the number of homeless and who believe that the homeless are growing significantly, argue that homelessness is a very serious problem that requires the introduction of policies that go way beyond the provision of temporary shelters with or without various human service programs. Advocates for the homeless, in fact, maintain that the welfare state under the custom of social contract is obligated to provide the homeless with the basic resources necessary for human survival. This liberal reformist position of entitlements moves beyond the exclusive rights of private property to include the inclusive economic rights to a living wage and affordable housing. These liberal interventionists contend that

shelters and soup lines do not offer those presently homeless, or those who risk falling through the "safety net" to the streets, a basis for recreating their lives. At best, these services only temporarily halt the physical, emotional and intellectual deterioration of the homeless person. If the needs of the homeless, chronically unemployed or temporarily unemployed are to be met, then economic entitlement must be expanded or advanced, not diminished (Fabricant and Kelly, 1988: 104).

The second debate revolves around the interrelated issues of "communal responsibility," "voluntarism," and "existentialism" as each of these interacts with the homelessness condition. In the spirit of rugged individualism, free enterprise, and laissez-faire, there are those viewpoints which argue that society (or community) has virtually no responsibility for or obligation to the able-bodied poor and homeless. The fact that these homeless people are here and in need is not enough:

Like many so-called human rights, those fundamental "rights" claimed by the poor (including those to food, drink, clothing, and shelter) are of imperfect obligation. They are pleas or requests directed to the good nature, the kindness, the compassion, the charity of those who find themselves in more fortunate circumstances. Thus it does not follow that *this* community, where the poor persons happen to be located, has the obligation to provide them their needs. Nor does it follow that the poor have a special claim upon the members of that community, or that they have a special moral obligation to fill those needs, just because the poor happen to be among *them* (Leiser, 1988: 125).

This position is grounded in the sanctity of private property, and the concomitant rights of one to deny admission to anybody and to enhance one's property value. Adherents of the exclusive property argument go so far as to call for the reinstatement of vagrancy statutes as a means of protecting public property and resisting threats to peace, order, or public safety:

When parks, streets, and sidewalks are converted into temporary residences, there can be no doubt of the deleterious impact upon the local community. The stench of human excrement fills the air. Benches intended for the enjoyment of local residents are occupied by sleeping vagabonds. Grounds become littered with the refuse left by persons who use them for purposes for which they were neither intended nor designed. Passersby and householders are intercepted and importuned by beggars and panhandlers, and the peace of the community is disrupted by the influx of strangers, not all of whom are determined to find an honorable way of satisfying their needs (Leiser, 1988: 124).

On the other hand, the late Justice William O. Douglas, who was strongly opposed to vagrancy statutes and the manner in which they were enforced, appealed to both the populist and libertarian sides of the discussion when he wrote, perhaps accurately but a bit too romantically, in 1960 about the old vagrancy, "my old friend Carl Sandburg, whom America loves, feels warm inside when I address him as Fellow Hobo. The term implies independence, a restless spirit, the quest for a better life, rebellion against submission to orthodoxy" (quoted in Leiser, 1988: 122). While the first position is more concerned about economic conformity and the second position with political freedom, both are situated within the framework or spirit of rugged individualism.

A third position, depicting both the social reality of victimization and the existential sides of homelessness, recognizes that there are two kinds of homeless people: the majority who have been marginalized against their will and who wish to regain their place in society; the minority who have voluntarily taken a leave of absence and who wish simply to be left alone. This middle-ground position not only argues against repressive punishments for the homeless, but it argues for the moral obligation to aid the involuntary marginal on the assumption that "the world of the homeless has its roots in various policies, events, and ways of life for which some of us are responsible and from which some of us actually prosper" (Marin, 1987: 41). At the same time, this position argues existentially (or anarchistically) that the freely marginal should be allowed a place to exist.

The third conventional debate revolves around the question of coercive intervention, especially as it pertains to the homeless population of mentally ill persons. While this debate had been a loud and controversial one, part of the discussion has been put to rest. I am referring to what had been an important issue concerning whether the upsurge of homelessness in the 1980s was simply a question of inadequate care for the mentally ill or whether the mentally ill had become a convenient scapegoat for the problem of homelessness. Most would agree today with the facts and the conclusion reached by Morse and Hopper (1988: 138) that "there are clearly people with psychiatric disorders among the homeless poor [but] that doesn't explain contemporary homelessness."

The more important question concerning this debate has to do with the issues of how to address the needs of the homeless mentally ill in a humane fashion and without violating the civil liberties of these people. On one side of this very complicated issue are those who argue that the forced treatment of the homeless mentally ill will not help because resources will not be made available. For example, they claim that "the expanded use of involuntary hospitalization will not help non-dangerous disordered persons, because we will not spend the money necessary for adequate care and treatment of increased numbers of inmates" (Morse and Hopper, 1988: 135). Instead of sweeping the streets clean through reinstitutionalization, these advocates for the mentally ill call for the allocation of sufficient resources to provide community-based housing with supportive services (Kanter, 1989) as a preferable alternative to the new "warehousing" movement. These defenders of civil liberties and proponents of community-based treatment argue that the discomfort that the homeless may cause us is insufficient moral or legal justification for the infringement of liberty that involuntary hospitalization represents for nondangerous disordered people.

On the other side of the debate are those who argue that those homeless persons who are suffering from mental illness should be forced to receive treatment against their will. One such proponent is Washington, D.C. psychiatrist E. Fuller Torrey, who runs a shelter for homeless women and maintains that

liberty and cruelty have become confused. The laws need to be changed so that obviously disabled individuals can be hospitalized and treated before they become a danger to themselves or others. If they are gravely disabled and refuse help because they can't understand their illness, then psychiatric staff or police should be allowed to take them—involuntarily—to a hospital for evaluation. Release from a hospital should be made contingent upon the patients' agreeing to continue to take medication. If the patients stop taking their medication (as determined by blood tests) then they can also be returned to the hospital (Torrey, 1988a: 133).

As suggested earlier, for the most part these three debates about or conceptualizations of the problem of homelessness are grounded in assumptions about our society that do not reflect the growing realities of a postindustrial or an electronically based economy. Like the presidential debates of 1988, most debates on the nature of homelessness in the United States have not come to grips with the altered world underpinnings of the new vagrancy. Following the lead of Bush and Dukakis, who either could not comprehend or who chose more or less to ignore the obvious changes taking place at home and abroad, most discussions of homelessness have similarly failed to grasp the significance of a changing system of global capitalism. Such changes in the developing political economy call for radically different public and private policies to address the problems of the new poor and homeless. To put it succinctly, the older practices of forced and contract labor, and their modern counterparts of "workfare" and "learnfare" are simply no longer appropriate, if they ever were.

A case in point was the Welfare Reform Act that was signed into law by President Reagan in October 1988. This act, which received substantial bipartisan support, had been lauded as the first major overhaul of the nation's welfare system since it was created during the Great Depression. While the president and others may have believed that the new welfare plan posed an alternative to life on welfare and a means for welfare recipients to take responsibility for their lives and the lives of the children they bring into this world, it was destined to fail before it even began. The failure was not necessarily because of some of the regressive or progressive features of the law, but because it simply did not appreciate the gravity of the situation confronting young families today, especially those without some kind of higher education. Simply expressed, the shifting economic landscape reveals more than a few signs that the current (1980s) generation, at various socio-economic levels, not just the growing poor, will end up becoming the first generation in U.S. history to experience a decline in its standard of living and to be worse off financially than their parents.

In sum, the situation calls for fundamental changes in our prevailing economic and social priorities as these relate to the problem of the poor and the homeless. Whether talking about welfare reform in general or the problems of housing affordability and homelessness in particular, the time has arrived to opt for alternative strategies to those that were formulated in the orderly 1950s or in the hopeful and relatively affluent 1960s. The new order of an emerging global capitalism demands that the old ways of doing things under the passing order of national monopoly capital give way. If worldwide problems such as hunger and homelessness are to be conquered, then all nations must learn to share power as well as the planet's resources. In other words, a significant reduction in the distribution of wealth and inequality worldwide is a fundamental prerequisite for the international elimination of poverty and homelessness. Finally, as demonstrated throughout the course of this book, the overcoming of homelessness and violence in human affairs "requires transformations of work, exchange, and distribution in accordance with egalitarian, democratic, humanistic and ecological values in order to eliminate obstacles to human development" (Gil: 1989: 39).

ORGANIZATION OF THIS BOOK

Gimme Shelter is divided into two parts: "The Problem of Homelessness" and "Confronting the Problem." In the remaining three chapters of Part I, the various realities of both the homeless and the homelessness condition will be elaborated. Representative myths associated with the stereotypes of the old homeless—including the inebriated and disheveled bums, the paranoid and deluded mentally ill, and the shopping bag ladies—will be placed into social perspective. This type of demystification of the homeless in America also extends to the alleged and underlying causes of homelessness.

Chapter 2 through 4 address different aspects of the fundamental nature of homelessness in the United States. Chapter 2—"The Changing Nature of Homelessness"—adds to those realities of the homeless portrayed in this chapter by providing a demographic profile of the different homeless populations. By including a picture of the regional distribution of homelessness in America as well as a breakdown of the homeless according to age, sex, race, marital status, and so on, two basic questions are raised for discussion:

First, to what degree has homelessness actually changed with respect to the old and new homeless distinctions? Second, to what extent has the new homelessness actually expanded during the decade of the eighties?

Chapter 3—"The Political Economy of the New Vagrancy"—critically evaluates the causes of homelessness that have been articulated in both popular and scholarly U.S. discussions. At the same time, careful attention is given to identifying those explanations that confuse or do not distinguish between symptom and root causes of homelessness. Explanations or interpretations of the homeless have typically fallen into four groupings: individual characteristics such as alcoholism, mental illness, and lack of marketable skills; family disruptions involving domestic violence, runaway children, or elderly persons who lose family support; institutional policies affecting dependent populations such as AIDS victims or the deinstitutionalization of the chronically mentally ill; and market forces related to housing affordability such as tightening of the low-income housing pool, rising mortgage interest rates, declining relative wages, or job shortfalls. Contrary to these conventional analyses, I will argue both implicitly and explicitly throughout this book that the more important changes underpinning homelessness today can be found in the emerging relations of global capitalism as these are expressed domestically in competing class interests, social policy formations, and individual versus collective rights of justice for all.

Chapter 4—"The Crime of Homelessness Versus the Crimes of the Homeless"—explores the violent nature of homelessness by focusing attention on both the victimization and criminalization of the homeless. An examination of the homeless is provided, which demonstrates that whether we are talking in terms of narrowly defined crimes against the law or the more broadly defined crimes against humanity, the homeless are not only often criminalized but they are more commonly victimized. While generalizations are not easy to make, the available findings do strongly suggest that the homeless do not pose a serious or dangerous threat to society. On the contrary, the homeless tend to belong more to a class of vulnerable people than to one of hard-core habitual offenders.

Part II of the book provides a detailed analysis of the U.S. response to homelessness and to the homeless during the 1980s. Chapters 5–7 specifically examine the programs for the homeless, the movement against homelessness, and the legal developments that have occurred regarding the status of marginal and homeless people. In Chapter 5—"Responding to Short-Term Homeless Needs"—extensive discussion and criticism of the various temporary or short-term responses to homeless are provided. Both governmental and private programs are surveyed; lists of services available are included, as well as the presentation of some program "up-closes" in order to help describe the various experiences of human service delivery. Although public and private responses and the resources, facilities, and agencies involved in the delivery and provision of programs for the homeless are often viable and humane for an emergency, the long-term value of the usual short-term "warehousing" approach to homelessness is seriously questioned. Finally, the case is made that the provision of temporary, emergency, and transitional services for the homeless without the development of long-range permanent strategies to confront the structural nature of homelessness is not only costly in both financial and human terms, but it is politically incorrect in light of the changing political economy.

Chapter 6—"Resisting Homelessness"—provides a history of the recent emergence and development of the movement against homelessness and on behalf of the homeless. Attention is focused on the movement as a whole and with respect to various groups and organizations that formed during the 1980s on behalf of the homeless. Particular scrutiny is given to the movement's efforts and struggle to make homelessness a national issue and a priority of the domestic agenda.

Chapter 7—"The Rights of the Homeless"—picks up where Chapter 6 ends by examining the related judicial decisions rendered or pending as well as the passed and proposed legislation that affects the homeless. In light of the growing and what appears to be the permanent condition of homelessness in the United States, the fundamental question raised throughout this chapter is whether or not the increased national awareness and understanding of homelessness has resulted in the kind of public policy demanded by the nature of the problem.

In Chapter 8—"Social Change and Homelessness: Past and Future"—a summation of the general arguments developed about homelessness and the U.S. response to the homeless is located in the relationships of the restructuring of the world economy under an emerging global capitalism, on the one hand, and in the relationships of the new social realities of homelessness that have accompanied the emergence of the Third World peripheral classes in the core of the global cities of the First World, on the other hand. It is argued, therefore, that U.S. domestic policy in general and homelessness/housing policy in particular must be transformed to reflect these changes in global capitalism. Otherwise, the trends of increasing marginality and homelessness as we have known them for the past decade will continue unabated into the twenty-first century. Unless the institutional and societal violence perpetrated daily against our most vulnerable populations is recognized for what it is—a crime against humanity—then the problems associated with homelessness and the homeless will continue to grow.

Finally, based on our ten-year experience of inadequately responding to the new vagrancy and situated within an international context, a preventive strategy to resist homelessness is suggested as part of a new domestic policy grounded in a willingness to confront the underlying structural nature of the problem. In other words, the necessary social policies for eliminating homelessness in America cannot be limited to questions of shelter and housing alone. These policies must also address questions of power, justice, and democracy as they relate to the status quo of inequality and privilege in the United States and the world. Sooner or later, we must recognize the bankruptcy of both the conservative and liberal policies that have prevailed in this country for the past century. In their place, our domestic policies must confront the necessity of creating noncapitalist spheres of economic and social activity, and of decommodifying certain goods and services such as housing and education for the working and nonworking poor.

NOTES

1. The telephone survey interview of 1,000 randomly sampled adults was conducted in late April and early May 1989 by Kane, Parsons and Associates. The margin of error was/is plus or minus 3.1 percent.

2. The highest figure that I have seen is 6 million homeless, which appeared in an issue of the national communist biweekly *People's Tribune*. However, there was no substantiation for the figure. See Chapter 2 for a fuller discussion of the magnitude of the problem.

3. David Gil (1989: 40) has done a nice job of describing the nature and the importance of *societal violence*:

The concept societal violence refers to systemic obstructions to human growth, development and self-actualization inherent in a society's institutional order, its policies, practices and human relations, its circumstances of living and quality of life, and its values and ideology. Societal violence inhibits the unfolding of people's innate potential, their spontaneous drive to become what they are capable of becoming, by interfering with the fulfillment of their biological, psychological, and social needs. Simple illustrations of societal violence are such aspects of "normal" social life in the United States as unemployment, poverty, hunger, homelessness, and overt and covert discrimination by race, sex, age and class.

REFERENCES

Adler, Jeffrey S. 1986. "Vagging the Demons and Scoundrels: Vagrancy and Growth of St. Louis, 1830–1861." *Journal of Urban History*, 13 (November).

———. 1989. "A Historical Analysis of the Law of Vagrancy." *Criminology*, 27, no. 2: 209–229.

American Journal of Public Health. 1986. Editorial "On Homelessness and the American Way," 76, no. 9: 1084–1086.

Blau, Joel S. 1987. The Homeless of New York: A Case Study in Social Welfare-Policy." Doctoral Dissertation. Ann Arbor, MI: University Microfilms International (1989).

Chambliss, William J. 1964. "A Sociological Analysis of the Law of Vagrancy." *Social Problems*, 12 (Summer): 67–77.

Chambliss, William J. and Robert B. Seidman. 1982. *Law, Order and Power*, rev. ed. Reading, MA: Addison-Wesley.

Fabricant, Michael and Michael Kelly. 1988. "The Problem of Homelessness Is Serious." In William Dudley, ed., *Poverty: Opposing Viewpoints*. St. Paul: Greenhaven Press. Reprinted from "No Haven for Homeless in a Heartless Economy," *Radical America*, 20, nos. 2 & 3, 1986.

Gil, David G. 1989. "Work, Violence, Injustice and War." *Journal of Sociology and Social Welfare*, 16, no. 1: 39–53.

Hoch, Charles and Robert A. Slayton. 1989. *New Homeless and Old: Community and the Skid Row Hotel.* Philadelphia: Temple University Press.

Hope, Marjorie and James Young. 1986. *The Faces of Homelessness.* Lexington, MA: Lexington Books.

HOUSING NOW! 1989. "Homeless Fact Sheet." April.

Kanter, Arlene. 1989. "Homeless but Not Helpless: Legal Issues in the Care of Homeless People with Mental Illness." *Journal of Social Issues*, 45, no. 3: 91–104.

Leiser, Burton M. 1988. "Society Should Protect Its Own Interests." In William Dudley, ed., *Poverty: Opposing Viewpoints.* St. Paul: Greenhaven Press. Reprinted from "Vagrancy, Loitering, and Economic Justice," in Kenneth Kipnes and Diana Meyers, eds., *Economic Justice.* (Totowa, NJ: Rowman and Allanheld, 1985).

Marin, Peter. 1987. "Helping and Hating the Homeless: The Struggle at the Margins in America." *Harper's Magazine*, 274 (January): 112–120.

Morse, Stephen J. and Kim Hopper. 1988. "Forced Treatment of the Homeless Mentally Ill Will Not Help." In William Dudley, ed., *Poverty: Opposing Viewpoints*, St. Paul: Greenhaven Press. Reprinted from Morse's "From Mean Streets to Mental Hospital Is No Cure for Homeless," *Los Angeles Times*, August 25, 1987 and Hopper's "Homeless Choose Streets Over Inhuman Shelters," *The Guardian*, November 11, 1987.

National Coalition for the Homeless. 1989. *American Nightmare: A Decade of Homelessness in the United States.* New York: NCH.

New York (AP). 1989. "Poll: Most Would Help Homeless." *The Montgomery Advertiser*, October 18.

Ryan, William. 1971. *Blaming the Victim.* New York: Pantheon.

Spitzer, Steven. 1975. "Towards a Marxian Theory of Deviance." *Social Problems*, 22, no. 5: 638–651.

Torrey, E. Fuller. 1988. "The Homeless Mentally Ill Should Be Forced to Receive Treatment." In William Dudley, ed., *Poverty: Opposing Viewpoints.* St. Paul: Greenhaven Press. Reprinted from "Finally, a Cure for the Homeless," *The Washington Monthly*, September 1986.

Wooster, Martin Morse. 1988. "The Problem of Homelessness is Exaggerated." In William Dudley, ed., *Poverty: Opposing Viewpoints.* St. Paul: Greenhaven Press. Reprinted from "The Homeless Issue: An Adman's Dream," *Reason Magazine*, July 1987.

2 The Changing Nature of Homelessness

What distinguishes the fine contemporary studies of homelessness that began to emerge in the mid–1980s (Werfel, 1985; Blau, 1987; Hopper, 1987; Bard, 1988; Devine, 1988) from most of those studies that appeared between 1880 and 1980 is the emphasis on the homelessness condition rather than on the homeless per se, and on the relationship between the former and the latter as well as between homelessness and the changing nature of the global political economy and U.S. society. For example, Hopper's ethnographic analysis of homeless men in New York City and Blau's policy analysis of New York's social welfare state and the homeless combine to capture, among other things, the structure of the "new vagrancy" by recognizing the fundamental relationships involved with both vagrancy/homelessness and the demands of the labor market: the "dimensions of homelessness today are rooted in changes in the ecology and economy of the city—in the labor and land markets especially" (Hopper, 1987: Abstract). In turn, this kind of understanding has helped to demystify both the scholarly and more popularly believed stereotypes and misconceptions of the old and new homeless, portraying them as roaming idlers and shirkers; alone, alienated, and disaffiliated.

In brief, the days of the expanding and developing industrial society that gave birth to "tramping" and "hoboing" at the turn of the century, to the demographic trend of migratory workers in search of employment that may have peaked at a couple of million homeless during the Great Depression, are no more. In this postindustrial, technically skilled, and service-oriented economy the demographics of the homeless populations have changed considerably, so too have the migratory patterns of the homeless, which is not to argue that there is no overlap between the old and new. For example, it can generally be defended that most members of the old and new homeless populations have wanted to and did work whenever and wherever possible. But more fundamentally these important changes raise the larger question about whether or not there will become a permanent underclass of sheltered and unsheltered homeless persons in the United States.

Despite the obvious demographic-historical relationship between changes in the political economy of labor discipline and social control and in the nature, size, and composition of homelessness populations, until the 1980s all of the serious writing on twentieth-century American homelessness had been mostly devoid of making any connections. Instead, the focus had been on problems of the homeless, on their deviant behavior, and on the imagined and real threat posed by the homelessness condition. Not only has the proliferation of writing by social scientists and others on the homeless, especially during the downturns of the economy over the past century, failed to consider the more fundamental changes in the political economy, but along with other interested private and governmental parties, they have also ignored these relationships in attempting to develop strategies for responding to the varying crises in U.S. homelessness.

Nevertheless, as Chapter 1 has already suggested, the history of opinion on the homeless has been quite diverse. Between the late nineteenth century and the mid–1980s, Blau (1987: 30) has chronologically identified ten highly differentiated and distinct categories of literature on the homeless:

1. Social Darwinism and the homeless
2. Progressivism and the first empirical studies
3. the on-the-road genre in Britain and America
4. studies of homelessness during the depression
5. the functionalist sociological classics
6. the nonfunctionalist critiques
7. the advocacy writing of the 1980s
8. literature on the homeless mentally ill
9. government reports
10. independent commentary

As Blau (1987: 75) emphasized throughout his dissertation, "in each historical period, people have made of homelessness what they *needed* to make of homeless. This need has, in turn, shaped and been shaped, by political and economic institutions." Without going into too much detail, the next section provides an overview of 100 years of mainstream thinking about the socio-demographic character of the homeless.

THE SOCIAL CONSTRUCTION OF THE HOMELESS: HOMOGENEITY, DISAFFILIATION, AND MARGINALITY

In the wake of the depression of 1873–75 there were some 3 million unemployed and many more poor people. Yet in an address before the

Conference on State Charities, Francis Wayland (1877) divided the poor into three categories: (1) those reduced to poverty by physical or medical infirmities, the permanent paupers; (2) people entitled to outdoor relief as a result of temporary difficulties—war, famine, and natural disasters; and (3) able-bodied persons without homes who are either unable or unwilling to work. What about those displaced homeless people who became so in response to the downturn in the economy? By the turn of the century in one of the earlier books on the homeless, Solenberger (1911) had concluded that there were four distinct classes of homeless men:

1. self-supporting, who work all or most of the year;
2. temporarily dependent, runaway boys or victims of industrial accidents;
3. chronically dependent, who used to belong to the first or second group but must now continuously rely on public charity; and
4. the parasitic, whether able-bodied or defective, who make a living off the public.

In a similar portrayal of what has become the first classic in the sociological study of Chicago's homeless population, Nels Anderson's *The Hobo* (1961, originally published in 1923) listed some six reasons why people became homeless: (1) seasonal work and unemployment, (2) an inability to work due to physical handicaps, (3) defects of personality, (4) crises in the life of the person, (5) racial or national discrimination, and (6) wanderlust. In these and the earlier empirical studies of the late teens, the Progressives understood the diversification of the homeless populations, at least during those depressed periods of economic development and industrial expansion, but they nevertheless typically resorted to explanations of individual deviance or nonconformity. As Anderson (1961: 230) concluded about the hobo, he was "an individualistic person. Not even the actors and the artists can boast a higher proportion of egocentrics. They are the modern Ishmaels who refuse to fit into the routine of conventional social life. Resenting every sort of social discipline, they have "cut loose" from organized society."

It appears that the themes of disaffiliation and nonconformity were used primarily to describe the homeless majority of single men. But among the many Depression-era studies of the homeless, there was at least one with a radically different theme. Edwin Sutherland, at one time president of the American Sociological Association and the first so-called dean of American criminology, and a colleague, Harvey Locke, in 1936 published the second classic in the study of Chicago's homeless men. In answering the question, "Why does a person choose to become a shelter man," Sutherland and Locke (1971: 17) responded:

He does not choose to enter the shelters but is forced to do so because he is destitute and homeless. Destitution and homelessness, to be sure, are formal conditions of eligibility to the shelters and a large proportion—probably three-fourths—of the men are destitute and homeless when they first apply to the shelters for relief. But there are persons equally destitute and homeless who do not enter the shelters but adopt such alternatives as suicide, making a living by crime or by begging.

What set Sutherland and Locke's analysis apart from most of the other U.S. studies on homelessness was their ability to draw out the relationship between the individual characteristics that differentiated the homeless man from the nonhomeless and the historical or structural changes that were occurring in the commercial and industrial orders:

> These forms of personal inefficiency may in turn be traced in many instances to the general disorganization in modern society. . . . While [these homeless men] were compelled to be mobile in order to meet the demands of industry, no provision was made by industry or by the general society to counteract the demoralizing effects of mobility. . . . Thus we find that modern society has not been organized or planned for the satisfaction of the basic needs of a great mass of the population, from which the homeless men in the shelters have come as representative (Sutherland and Locke, 1971: 48–49).

In the 1950s and 1960s, and to a lesser degree during the 1970s, the literature on the homeless reflected the conservative concerns of the dominant ideologies of functionalist sociology, concentrating its attention on the alienated, disaffiliated, and caucasian male. Following the sociology of Durkheim, Parsons, and Merton, studies of the homeless involved subjectless agents, living outside or marginal to society, and retreatist in their orientation. It was also argued that subcultures of homelessness (i.e., skid row bums, boxcar tramps) preferred transient life-styles, lacked ambition, and were socially maladaptive or maladjusted. In short, the homeless were regarded as residing somewhere beyond the system, not because they were either poor or free, but because they did not participate. Consequently, it was argued that the homeless did not possess any stake in the continuity of the existing order, and therefore they presented themselves not only as a threat to but also as a reminder of the fact that the system could some day come apart (Bahr and Caplow, 1973).

The 1970s brought with them a critique of the functional approach, initially grounded in theories of labelling, existentialism, and symbolic interaction, but later by a more radical or fundamental criticism of the system, grounded in both institutional and structural analyses. Finally, by the 1980s the proliferation of writing on or about the homeless came to be dominated by three types of advocacy research: (1) those that rejected personal deficiency models of the homeless, favoring models that asserted instead that there was simply not enough low-income housing to go around, especially in urban America, thus forcing people into an involuntary state of homelessness (Hopper and Baxter, 1981; Hopper et al., 1982); (2) those that examined public policies, the shelterization process, and political responses to homelessness (Hombs and Snyder, 1983; National Coalition for the Homeless, 1983 and 1986; Hopper and Hamberg, 1985); and (3) those that studied one of the several subgroups within the homeless population such as the mentally ill, which has often had the effect of stigmatizing most if not all of the other homeless persons (Bassuk, 1984; Hope and Young, 1984).

The advocates' bottom lines called for food, shelter, and treatment to be circulated unconditionally as basic human rights. The writings of the advocates generally can be "characterized by outrage, sharp social criticism, and a faith in power of language to prod people out of their indifference" (Blau, 1987: 60). In contrast, the governmental reports of the 1980s were much more subdued, but they too carried with them political agendas. The primary message was to reassure the people that if everything was not exactly as it should be, then it soon would be. The trickle-down theory would take care of everybody, including the truly needy and marginal of society.

Early on in the Reagan administration, when catsup was being counted as a vegetable in school children's lunches, there was an attempt to dismiss the problem of homelessness, followed by efforts to minimize the size of the homeless population, and finally by the reluctant admissions that something should be done about the problem. Typically, governmental reports tended to isolate the problem of housing/homelessness from other social problems. Most of these reports were primarily descriptive, lacking the structural kinds of analysis found in the advocacy literature. Certainty, the most controversial of the major government documents produced during this period was *A Report to the Secretary on the Homeless and Emergency Shelters* (U.S. Department of Housing and Urban Development (HUD), 1984).

Among the report's findings, there were only some 250,000 to 350,000 homeless persons in the United States. Unlike the portraits presented by most of the other contemporary literature, private or governmental, HUD's methodology yielded the following conclusions about homelessness: it is temporary, involves few formerly middle-class people, and has no relation with the 1981–82 recession. In response to the national outcry leveled against HUD's findings by homeless experts, a congressional inquiry was held on May 24, 1984, concerning the study's methodology. Of course, this discussion raised a host of questions surrounding the meaning of homelessness and the measuring of the number of homeless persons.

NO ONE KNOWS HOW MANY ARE HOMELESS: THE PROBLEMS OF DEFINITION AND MEASUREMENT

The debate over how the homeless should be defined or classified and the related discussion about the appropriate measurements to be used in

counting the homeless resulted in the federal government not even attempting to officially count the nation's homeless during the 1980s. The 1990
Bureau of the Census report is attempting the "difficult task of counting the
homeless, a population that often must remain hidden in order to survive"
(Safety Network, 1988: 2). The Census will not actually provide an official
count of the number of homeless per se nor will it even provide an official
definition of homelessness. Nevertheless, it does aim to provide demographic, social, and economic data on selected groups and aspects of the
homeless population, making its findings known to data users trying to construct homeless counts for a variety of purposes. The problems posed by the
definitional/measurement issues are not superficial ones, and it makes good
theoretical and practical sense to use multiple meanings and techniques for
gathering information about homelessness. At the beginning of the 1990s I
believe that the debate has lessened and that people are using definitions
of the homeless and employing methods that fit their particular political
strategies or needs. The social reality of the 1980s was different, but it
remained the case that people were divided: "government officials, university researchers, charitable organizations and advocacy groups" could not
agree upon adequate definitions of the homeless problem (Ludlow, 1988:
10A).

How a person defines and counts the homeless can certainly account for
the wide schism between the lower and higher estimates that are often
quoted and tossed about. For the purposes of this discussion, think of the
estimates as based on tightly or loosely constructed definitions of the homeless and homelessness. One proponent of the tighter or narrower definition
has been Peter Rossi of the University of Massachusetts. Rossi and his
investigators conducted a study of Chicago's "literal homeless" on two nights,
between the hours of one and six A.M., in the fall of 1985 and the spring
of 1986. Rossi (1987) believes that it's important that some kind of author-
itative number be reached, and he further believes that the most appropriate
way of counting the homeless is to include only those people who are actually
without shelter on a given night. Favoring the less restrictive and more open
definition of the homeless is Louise Stark of Arizona State University and
former president of the National Coalition of the Homeless. She argues that
when counting the number of the homeless people the "almost homeless"
should be included. Stark queries: "What about the people who are doubled
and tripled up in substandard housing? What about the people who receive
[welfare] checks and run out of money for a week or so? And the people in
detox programs who will just return to the streets? The people who camp
in the parks?" (Ludlow: 1988: 10A). There are also those middle positions
that argue that the homeless counts should include both the sheltered and
unsheltered homeless populations.

A succinct overview of the various definitions and classification schemes of the homeless that were used during the 1980s is now provided as a way of doing justice to this complicated subject.

Definitions

To begin with, there are two of the more common or traditional meanings associated with the homeless and homelessness. The homeless are "those persons who lack resources and community ties necessary to provide for their own adequate shelter" (U.S. General Accounting Office, 1985: 5). As for homelessness, the International Encyclopedia of Social Sciences designates disaffiliation as the salient characteristic: "Homelessness is a condition of detachment from society characterized by the absence or attentuation of the affiliative bonds that link settled persons to a network of internnected social structures" (quoted in Devine, 1988: 38).

Kim Hopper, who has done as much for the homeless movement as any single individual and who has probably written more on the subject than anybody else, refers to homelessness in the strict and unstrict senses. Recognizing the need for both, he identifies the homelessness condition as referring to those "people who claim as their usual nighttime residence either emergency shelters and drop-in centers, or the interstices of public space—the streets, parks, alleyways, abandoned buildings, and other out-of-the-way sanctuaries, known only to their users" (Hopper, 1987: 11). At the same time, Hopper points out that the homeless represented by this definition are restricted to a specific group or class, which is by no means inclusive of those people experiencing homelessness. Hence, homeless refers only to those people officially labelled as such and therefore eligible as clients to receive services. Following Simmel, he continues that the homeless label is not created by the interactions of its members or by their organized interests, but rather by an ascribed status or public recognition brought about by the "collective attitude which society as a whole adopts toward it" (quoted in Hopper, 1987: 12).

In other words, below the surface of the homeless there may also be the hidden or invisible homeless, the prehomeless people, the renters and even the home owners at risk, or people who are without a fixed domicile. Of course, until these people are appropriately labelled as suffering from homelessness or from some social problem, they are not regarded as entitled to human service delivery and must continue experiencing with relative public indifference the societal violence of impoverishment. More encompassing definitions of homelessness, therefore, are encouraged as well as the stricter definitions. With regard to the more inclusive definitions, we would add the following to the homeless already identified: persons facing release from jail or prison without a residence; anyone "without an address which assures them at least 30 days' sleeping quarters which meet minimal health and safety standards" (Caro quoted in Hopper, 1987: 19); and "an undomiciled person who is unable to secure permanent and stable housing without special assistance" (Hopper, 1987: 19). As Hopper (pp. 20–21) concluded in his lengthy discussion on the subject,

homelessness in the most encompassing sense of the term has to do with various kinds and degrees of residential uncertainty and instability. In the absence of secure and stable dwelling, people have devised makeshifts that span everything from shared (and overcrowded) living arrangements to a nomadic life on the streets. Officially, only those makeshifts that are on display in public spaces, and the need that declares itself to public or charitable authorities, are classified as "homelessness." Up to that point, hardship may exist, but it exists as "coping," or in "at risk" populations, or as "unmet need." *But the official definition is not the only one.* The precise dimensions of the problem and the kinds of makeshifts that are to be sanctioned as legitimate "homelessness," are contested matters (emphasis added).

As I will argue in Part II of this book, in terms of policy considerations, especially long-term strategies aimed at addressing the new vagrancy, more encompassing definitions of homeless eligibility are required if the United States is ever realistically going to confront the problem of homelessness as an expression or manifestation of poverty amid a society of affluence, rather than merely the expression of some form of individual pathology.

Classifications

When it comes to classification schema of the homeless, one can obviously break down the population into subpopulations (e.g., families versus individuals, men, women, etc.). Some of the differentiation is quite objective demographic material that will be taken up later in the chapter. Some of the differentiation involves more subjective material, such as dividing the homeless subgroups based on a history of their homelessness into the "intermediate," "episodic," and "chronic" homeless, or "homeless for the first time," "multiple episodes of homelessness," and "continuously homeless for more than one year." Utilizing this classification scheme, Putchat (1988: abstract) concluded in her study of "the personal and interpersonal resources of 286 homeless 18–65 year olds residing in emergency shelters in comparison to 81 never homeless rooming house residents," that the homeless were a very heterogeneous group:

Subgroups based on homeless history differed in terms of life events experienced, coping behavior, social support and locus of control. The episodically homeless were found to have the highest incidence of psychopathology and the greatest support need. The homeless as a group differed from the never homeless rooming house on most variables. Adaptive and maladaptive MMPI [Minnesota Multiphasic Personality Inventory] personality types were identified.

More generally, other attempts to classify the homeless have included those based on differences in mobility and means of support or those such as the HUD report that used precipitating factors like chronic disabilities, personal crises, and economic conditions. In discussing mental health, mental illness, and homelessness, of course, the schema of clinical psychology naturally dominates with its preferred reliance on disaffiliation. Working within such a framework, for example, Fischer and Breakey's (1986) typology of homeless persons includes four subgroups: (1) the chronically mentally ill, (2) street people, (3) chronic alcoholics, and (4) the situationally distressed. Regardless of the categories used, the message conveyed is that something is fundamentally different about the homeless and the nonhomeless. Whatever external factors may be involved with homelessness, ultimately, it is still a function of individual weakness, choice, disease, or personal background. Fischer and Breakey (1986: 11–12) inform us that: *the chronically mentally ill* as a subgroup of the homeless is made of "mentally disabled people who in some cases have been recently deinstitutionalized, but in others have been in and out of the ambulatory mental health system without ever having had a significant history of hospitalization"; *the street people* consist of "bag ladies" and "grate men" whose "bizarre appearance make them particularly visible" and contributes to the apparent reality that these people, both men and women, "elect to live relatively isolated from others to the extent that they are reputed to shun shelters in favor of choosing their own places to sleep and eat," finally "from field observations, it appears that the prevalence of mental disorder may be high among street people"; *chronic alcoholics* refer to the hard-core skid-row "chronic, deteriorated alcoholics whose life-style centers around the procurement and consumption of alcohol," and "who have acquired their homeless state through mobility, disaffiliation, and alcoholism, usually reporting personal histories that reflect a working-class background and low educational levels and inadequate employment skills"; *the situationally distressed* include many drawn from the "new poor who have recently become unemployed, evicted, or ejected from home following a domestic quarrel, or are traveling in search of work," but who are nevertheless thought of in their existing misfortune to have somehow been responsible due to "personality disorder, impaired capacity, and/or substance abuse."

The definition of the homeless (and homelessness) preferred in this book departs from those analyses that are primarily grounded in notions of disaffiliation. It also parts company with those definitions that regard homelessness as a property of persons—settled or unsettled—rather than a condition of subsistence. From an anthropological point of view, Hopper correctly reminds us that homelessness is not a trait, or an impairment, or even a social deficit. It is rather a circumstance, arising from a variety of causes, that presents a problem to be solved: "where to stay that night?"

Measurement

Although homelessness expresses itself differently and the condition encompasses a wide spread of behaviors and circumstances, the need of housing remains fundamental to the homeless. When it comes to measurement there are at least two basic questions: "whom do you count as homeless?" and "how do you count or collect your data/information about homelessness?" Related questions include those involving methodological calculations that are subject to wide variation, depending on whether the discussion revolves around those homeless with high visibility or those with marginal invisibility.

Blau (1987: 22) has argued that there are three primary subpopulations of homeless: the population "served" (in shelters); the population "in need" (in the streets); and the population "at risk" (residing temporarily with friends or family, or those people paying more than 50 percent or more of their income on housing). When it comes to estimating the number and characteristics of these subgroups of homeless, the incidence of homelessness is reported in terms of the per capita rate of homelessness for a metropolitan statistical area (typically an urban/suburban area with a population of 250,000 or more). The actual incidences refer to those persons using emergency shelters or public spaces for their evening habitat. Devine (1988) identifies emergency shelters and public spaces:

Emergency Shelters	Public Spaces
armories	streets
schools	parks
church basements	subways
government buildings	bus terminals
former firehouses	railroad stations
hotels	airports
motels	abandoned buildings
apartments	cars
boarding houses	trucks
	bridges/aquaducts

Typically left out of official counts, therefore, are the "at risk" populations— an oversight that I believe is significant especially in light of trends and long-term social policy.

Table 1 represents the medians for the visibly homeless for 42 metropolitan

Table 1
Estimates of the Number of Homeless Persons and Per Capita Rates in Different Metropolitan Areas

Place	Number Homeless	Per Capita Rate
Albuquerque	543	.00164
Atlanta	3000	.00154
Baltimore	700	.00037
Baton Rouge	155	.00035
Birmingham	1000	.00350
Boston	3000	.00334
Charlotte	225	.00047
Chicago	3750	.00048
Cincinnati	925	.00063
Cleveland	550	.00025
Colorado Springs	100	.00033
Davenport	312	.00095
Dayton	238	.00031
Detroit	5250	.00125
Fort Wayne	475	.00154
Grand Rapids	110	.00023
Hartford	500	.00047
Honolulu	800	.00105
Houston	5000	.00186
Kansas City	275	.00061
Las Vegas	1500	.00340
Little Rock	300	.00079
Los Angeles	30000	.00367
Louisville	620	.00070
Miami	4500	.00167
Minneapolis	500	.00023
New York	18050	.00154
Pittsburgh	1500	.00069
Phoenix	1155	.00011
Portland	2000	.00164
Philadelphia	2100	.00051
Raleigh	225	.00080
Richmond	350	.00064
Rochester	90	.00010
San Diego	1900	.00217
Salt Lake City	489	.00071
San Francisco	1670	.00177
Scranton	75	.00016
Seattle	2250	.00113
Syracuse	425	.00078
Tampa	500	.00087
Worcester	900	.00249

Source: Devine, 1988: 189-90.

areas with populations of 250,000 or more. The per capita rates of homelessness among these areas vary from a low of .00010 in Rochester, New York, to a high of .00367 in Los Angeles. Two other sunbelt cities—Las Vegas, Nevada, and Birmingham, Alabama—have rates similar to that of Los Angeles. The number of homeless ranging from a low of 75 in Scranton, Pennsylvania, to 30,000 in Los Angeles.

Most studies, in order to eliminate the pitfall of duplication (counting the same homeless person twice), have typically resorted to one-night or two-night counts spaced months apart and designed to take the weather into account. By the end of the 1980s, there had been only two attempts made to come up with national estimates of the new homelessness. The U.S. Department of Housing and Urban Development set out to determine a "reasonable" estimate on a single night in early 1984. Politically speaking, HUD wanted to challenge a November 1983 report by the U.S. Department of Health and Human Services, which had concluded that there might be as many as 2 million homeless Americans. HUD's "snapshot" count came up with an estimated figure of some 250,000 to 350,000 (U.S. Department of HUD, 1984). As mentioned above, these findings stirred up national controversy among the homelessness advocacy community and resulted in the United States refraining from any more attempts to define or precisely count the homeless until the 1990 Census. The second attempt was in 1985 by Freeman and Hall (1986), who came up with a national figure similar to HUD's, 350,000. However, the dubious methods involved in extrapolating street-to-shelter ratios in New York City and generalizing those findings across the country have been subjected to much criticism (Lee, 1988).

The argument is generally made that it is dangerous to generalize nationally because in doing so, one tends not to give recognition to the trends and countertrends in the homeless populations that may be related to changes in the geographically specific socioeconomic formations. In the context of the methodological criticisms raised, the two national estimates on homeless Americans still seem to underscore much public discussion and policy. But as the National Coalition for the Homeless stated in its Newsletter, the main issue is "not the numbers themselves, but the uses to which they will be put—to either help or harm homeless Americans" (Safety Network, 1988: 2).

With respect to certain types of demographic information, on the other hand, the characteristics of the visibly homeless have been gathered and analyzed for 45 metropolitan areas (Devine, 1988). This kind of data or information, unlike the snapshot accounts, is based on an extended period. Hence, there are built-in biases of overpresentation of the episodically homeless. In other words, such characterizations of the homeless tend to distort the picture in the direction of the old as opposed to the new homelessness.

Accordingly, Deborah Devine examined five variables among the homeless: disability status, household composition, sex, age, and transiency. In combining the disabling categories of mental disability and alcohol/substance abuse, she found that place-to-place variation in the percentage of the population that is disabled is enormous, ranging from less than 7 percent in Louisville to 100 percent in Atlanta. With respect to the homeless population who are single or are made up of families, Devine found that the proportion of homeless population consisting of family members range from a low of 7 percent in Austin, Texas, to a high of 76 percent in St. Louis. Devine also discovered that the distribution of the adult population by sex varied from a low of 40 percent in Seattle to a high of 95 percent in San Diego; and that the modal age range varied from a low of 18–29 in Providence, Rhode Island, to a high of 41–68 in Minneapolis. Finally, Devine found that the percentage of the homeless populations that consist of transients, including both those from different states and countries, ranges from a low of 7.6 percent in Richmond, Virginia, to a high of 98 percent in Phoenix.

THE NEW VAGRANCY: PORTRAITS OF THE NEW HOMELESS

Whatever the precise magnitude, scenes of men and women foraging in garbage cans, conversing earnestly with unseen companions, catching catnaps along the well-lit lanes of public commerce and transport, or simply lumbering along, tattered parcels of belongings in tow, have become almost clichéd items of the urban prospect. Its insistent, obtrusive presence in the rhythms and avenues of everyday life, together with the marked heterogeneity of the population, more than anything else signal what is distinctive about homelessness today (Hopper, 1987: 9).

What virtually every study, analysis, or survey of the homeless of the past decade revealed was a picture of street people who did not fit the stereotyped images of the hobos, tramps, and migrants of an era gone by. What has characterized the condition of homelessness over the past decade has been its total disregard for the older geographical boundaries that had confined the homeless to those areas traditionally designated as skid row. In other words, the old vagrancy, except during times of recession and especially during times of depression, remained hidden or out of sight. By contrast, the new vagrancy, which had sustained itself throughout the recovery and during the prosperity of the 1980s, was and still is very visible despite the hidden magnitude of the problem today. Several relationships come into play in the production of the new vagrancy, including among others the spreading geography of relief and the simple press of expanding numbers of people in need of affordable shelter (Momeni, 1989; Walker, 1989).

While Chapter 3 will develop a political economy of homelessness, for now suffice it to say that changes in the political-economic conditions have dispersed people beyond the boundaries of the old vagrancy. The new vagrancy has also consisted of subgroups (subpopulations) of homeless people who did not exist in significant numbers to be responded to or even counted prior to the fundamental changes in the global economy that started to emerge back in the 1970s. In the context of both commonness and uniqueness, the experiences, problems, or special struggles of four homeless groups will be profiled in order to gain a better sense of the heterogeneity of the new homelessness.

Before turning to the four portraits, however, some of the data and information collected by the Task Force for the Homeless of Atlanta, Georgia, are provided as an "up-close" portrayal of the sheltered homeless in the largest metropolitan area of the New South. While one cannot generalize from this profile, it is suggestive of the characteristics of many of today's new homeless. It is included here because these kinds of demographic data are typically used to construct breakdowns of the homeless. The Task Force gathered its statistics during the months of February and March 1988. The "intake" data were collected from 639 individuals who were living in Atlanta area shelters at the time. As the Task Force (1988) noted on the flyer disclosing the information, the "number of males and females reflects the kind of shelters open at the time, not necessarily the breakdown among the entire homeless population."

Among some of the more revealing Atlanta findings were those pertaining to education and work: 40 percent had graduated from high school, 8 percent from college, and another 24 percent had some college or technical school. Some 39 percent of those surveyed were working at the time and, of those, 61 percent were working part-time and 47 percent were working in labor pools. With respect to those working, the average income for males was $716 per month and for females, $472. Meanwhile, the average cost of "last housing" for men was $314 per month and for women, $304. Thus, the average male was paying 44 percent of his income for housing while the average female was paying 69 percent. Finally, it is interesting to note that 23 percent of the homeless had been homeless before. With respect to where these homeless people had previously lived, only 36 percent had been living in an apartment or a house, while nearly 67 percent had been living in some kind of temporary arrangement.

Table 2 presents a breakdown of Atlanta's sheltered homeless by age, sex, race, education, birthplace, residence for last five years, amount of time in shelters in year, and where they lived before the shelter.

The Rural Homeless

Amid the frozen farm fields of Iowa, Judy Shelly answered a cry for help from a small wooden garage. Huddled inside were a mother and three children. They'd lost almost everything—including their home.

They had blankets, bed, a few sticks of furniture and a hot plate, but no bathroom or refrigerator. No money either. Forced off their farm, abandoned by husband and father the family was struggling to survive (Cohen, 1988: F1).

Table 2
Demographics of Atlanta's Sheltered Homeless, 1988

AGE	
17–29	33%
30–59	62%
60–over	5%

SEX	
Male	75%
Female	25%

RACE			AMOUNT OF TIME IN SHELTERS IN PAST YEAR	
Black	63%			
White	31%			
Hispanic	3%		0-3 months	55%
Oriental	1%		3-6 months	19%
American Indian	2%		6-12 months	26%

EDUCATION			WHERE DID YOU LIVE BEFORE THE SHELTER	
1-6 yrs.	4%		House or apartment	36%
7-11 yrs.	33%		With friends/rel.	28%
High School Grad.	40%		Another shelter	18%
Some College	14%		Street	10%
College Grad.	8%		Hotel/motel	8%
Tech. School	10%		Car	3%

BIRTHPLACE	
Atlanta	19%
Other Georgia	15%
South (Not Georgia)	28%
Other	38%

LIVED LAST FIVE YEARS	
Atlanta	43%
Other Georgia	10%
South (Not Georgia)	19%
Other	28%

Source: Flyer distributed by the Task Force for the Homeless, 363 Georgia Ave. South East, Atlanta, Georgia 30312.

During the 1980s, a growing number of rural folks joined the ranks of the nation's homeless. Although nobody has ever attempted seriously to count the rural homeless, estimates are that the rural areas comprise about 10 to 20 percent of the total homeless populations. The rural homeless are generally regarded as being among the most invisible homeless because "they don't wander the streets of small-town America. . . . They leave or they somehow hide themselves or hide their problems. They don't want anyone to know" (Cohen, 1988: F1). Typically, those among the new rural homeless were working poor and former farm families, dependent on two incomes in order to make ends meet, when a troubled business or industry went under or a farm was foreclosed. No longer able to afford the rend or the mortgage, these people found themselves to be members of the new homeless, whether they were actually or nearly shelterless. As advocates for the rural homeless have been quick to point out, people living in ramshackle houses, shanties, and shacks without heat, water, or toilets who are too proud to ask for assistance should be counted among the rural homeless. Even if they did ask, however, the rural homeless were usually in the position of receiving much less help. There are, after all, fewer shelters, fewer soup kitchens, and less money from charities in rural areas.

The hard times experienced in the heartland came about as farmers were losing their land, small-town factories were closing their doors, and housing costs were rising. In other words, rural homelessness has been tied to the economics of decline in small-town America: "the slump in the timber, agriculture, mining, meat and energy industries, the loss of manufacturing jobs, farm foreclosures and the ripple effect on Main Street" (Cohen: 1988: F4). Hence, one cannot separate the growing rural homelessness during the 1980s from the farm crisis of that period. For the period between 1980 and 1988, the U.S. government has estimated that the number of farms that disappeared was 271,000. For the same period, the number of people living on farms dropped from 6 million to 5 million. Meanwhile, the Public Voice for Food and Health Policy, a Washington consumer education and research group, has determined that the number of rural people living in poverty, between 1978 and 1986, increased by one-third to 9.7 million (Cohen, 1988).

Among some of the more selective findings on the rural Midwest homeless populations of the 1980s are:

- In 1987 more than three-quarters of community agencies responding to a Housing Assistance Council survey reported increases in rural homelessness from 1981–82 to 1986–87, and 38 percent reported the increases to be significant.
- A 1985 study in Ohio reported that the proportion of women among the rural homeless was twice that of urban homeless populations.
- The percentage of married people among the rural homeless is higher than the percentage of married urban homeless, 18.5 and 6.7, respectively.
- The 1988 study by the Minnesota Coalition for the Homeless reported a 24 percent employment rate among urban Minneapolis adults living in shelters and transition living conditions as compared to a 36 percent employment rate among Minnesotans statewide.
- An Iowa study found that one of the larger groups in danger of losing homes was farm widows, many of whom were living on just a few hundred dollars a month (Cohen, 1988).

Day Labor Pools and the Homeless

Racism and exploitation of labor are the two basic problems of homelessness, believes Billy Hands Robinson, co-originator of the CORE Service concept. "The perception the community at large has of homeless people is a group of alcoholics, ne'er-do-wells and complainers. It simply is not the truth. Homeless people work, those who are capable of it. But they work out of these labor pools and they don't make enough to have a place to stay" (Williams, 1988: 29).

Day labor pools provide daily work for men and women able to do heavy labor. Day labor pools commonly refer to those temporary services businesses that specialize in providing manual laborers for construction and industry. While no formal definition of temporary employment exists, it generally refers to the impermanency of the employment, the hazards in or undesirability of the work, the absence of fringe benefits, and limited governmental protection (Williams, 1988). In the context of the growing and expanding service economy, it can be argued that two central trends have included the increased use of temporary employment and homeless laborers:

Already day labor pools are an integral part of American urban life, and they continue to grow rapidly. Yet, the issues of both public policy and personal conscience which the labor pools raise [especially as related to homelessness] have been recognized by only a small band of social activists and, of course, the workers who endure the labor pools' practices (Williams, 1988: 3).

As Williams and the Southern Regional Council (SRC) pointed out in *Hard Labor*, the 1988 report on labor pools and temporary employment, neither the U.S. Department of Labor nor any other governmental body keeps data on day labor pools. It also has been the case that virtually nothing has been written in professional and academic literature on the subject. And in the SRC's review of 30 daily newspapers during the late 1970s and the 1980s, only a handful of articles turned up that addressed the various issues raised in *Hard Labor*.

In an effort to place day labor pools on the political agenda, or at least to raise the public awareness of the problems involved in temporary employment, the SRC and Randall Williams (1988:3) set out not only to establish a fundamental understanding of the phenomenon, but to help "end a misguided system of employment before it damages the lives of a great many and the future of us all." The SRC study focused on urban areas with special attention given to the South because of its recent economic growth. More specifically, analysis occurred of temporary employment agencies in 37 U.S. cities, and it covered the major cities in the 11 Southern states. By population size, the ten larger cities in declining order were: Chicago, Dallas, Houston, Cleveland, St. Louis, Baltimore, Atlanta, Miami, Phoenix, and Kansas City. Of particular concern to the SRC study was an understanding of how the growth of the temporary industry was affecting the poorest of the temporary labor force, a group that usually included a substantial percentage of the homeless.

In fact, what the SRC study found was consistent with the findings of the three estimates of employed homeless people by the U.S. Conference of

Table 3
Employment Levels of the Homeless in Selected Cities

Location	Percent Working
Atlanta	40
Boston	25
Chicago	30
Cleveland	06
Kansas City	35
Louisville	10
Nashville	28
New Orleans	15
Phoenix	20
San Antonio	54

Source: Randall Williams, 1988:21.

Mayors in the 1980s: 19 percent, 22 percent, and 35 percent for the respective surveys conducted in 1986, 1987, and 1988. For example, the SRC's survey of shelter directors found that 85 percent had labor pools recruiting from the homeless residing at their shelters. This is also consistent with the employment level of the homeless in selected cities (see Table 3) and with such trends as those that saw the number of not full-time employees for the 37 cities studied increase from a total of 1.5 million persons, including 900,000 in the Southern cities, to a total of 4.4 million part-time workers and 2.6 million in the South, by 1980.

Historically, temporary labor is not new. Since the turn of the century various forms of temporary migrant labor have been part of agricultural production and rural existence. In the South, especially with the decline in the plantation and sharecropper systems, there was the systemization of day labor. As for the larger cities of both the North and South, "hiring corners," have always been a part of the urban landscape and casual labor market during most of this century. Even big employers such as the U.S. Postal Service or the Internal Revenue Service have relied on temporary workers as a matter of policy for limited periods of time throughout the year. For a partial listing of those employers who use manual labor pools, see Table 4.

By 1983 the *The Wall Street Journal* was estimating the total number of day laborers or temporary employees in the United States to be 2 million. During the 1980s the fastest growing sector within this expanding labor pool had been in the area of manual labor (Williams, 1988). Most day laborers earn the minimum or slightly above the minimum wage and receive no benefits to speak of. At best, they earn what amounts to as a subsistence income for a single person. If one is able to work a full eight-hour day, one is able to take home (if he has one) about $20–25 a day. Most day laborers, however, do not work more than two or three days a week, typically taking "home" less than $100 per week. As Robinson comments: "the abuses of the labor pool are many . . . if you work out of a labor pool, you have no say, no control, no nothing. Your humanity is gone. You become a product in the labor pool" (quoted in Williams, 1988: 29). Being "a product in the labor

Table 4
Businesses and Institutions Who Are Customers of Manual Labor Pools

Ace Worldwide Movers	3M Company
A.G. Ray Company	Mercy Hospital
Baltimore Gas and Electric	Motorola
B.F. Goodrich	North American Van Lines
Borden Dairy	Northern Telecom
Burroughs Wellcome	Orlando Bottling
Coca-Cola	Pendleton Woolen Mills
College of Charleston	Pepsi-Cola Company
Dallas Semiconductor	Procter and Gamble
Estech, Inc.	Revlon
Federal Home Loan Bank	Royal Crown Cola
Frank Moving and Storage	Sacramento Airport
General Electric	Sears
Gilbert Engineering	State of Arizona
Grass Busters	Tenneco
Harcourt, Brace, Jovanovich	Texas Department of
HDL Corporation	Human Services
Helene Curtis	Towson State University
Hills Brothers Coffee	7-Up Bottling Company
Honda USA	U.S. Railroad
IBM	U.S. Sprint
Johns Hopkins Hospital	Walmart
Kimberly-Clark	Wells Fargo
Maryland Science Center	Westinghouse
McGraw Hill	W.R. Grace Co.

Source: Randall Williams, 1988:31.

pool," of course, benefits all of the employers using temporary labor services, not to mention the services themselves. As one business entrepreneurship, Industrial Labor Service (ILS) of Atlanta, has already discovered, the assets to be derived from combining the needs of the homeless with the needs of business for cheap and temporary labor can be worked out quite nicely. ILS has already developed a business that brings housing together with its labor halls

in a unique method of covering its overhead and making sure it has a steady pool of laborers, especially for night work. ILS employees and van drivers visit bus stations and homeless shelters to hand out cards good for a "free night" in ILS dormitories. "Need a place to stay," say the cards. "Come to the Bunk Haus." These are barracks in which 50 to 100 men live for one day to several months. The rent is $6.50 a night and people staying in the bunkhouses are given first priority at jobs in the ILS labor hall (Williams, 1988: 30).

The Mentally Ill Homeless

Although few would probably disagree that there are significant numbers of homeless persons suffering from mental disorders, the prevalence or incidence of mental illness within the homeless population has not been clearly established. In the not-too-distant past, when it came to the size of the estimates and the characterization of the mentally ill homeless, both had been substantially distorted. By the mid- to late 1980s, a number of studies about mental illness and the homeless should have reduced the number of the homeless mentally ill and changed the characterization that associated most homeless people with mental illness. One study by Snow et al. (1986) of 1,000 unattached homeless adults in Texas has done as much to delegitimate the traditional arguments that had successfully stereotyped the majority of the homeless (with some guesses as high as 90 percent) as mentally ill. Conventional wisdom of the 1980s was trying to claim that the streets of urban America had become the asylums of the 1980s; a response, it was argued, because of deinstitutionalization of the mentally ill in the late 1960s. But since the so-called community mental health movement that provided the ideological justification for displacing the mentally ill onto the streets had peaked by the mid–1970s, its impact on the homelessness problem of the 1980s had been highly overstated. There is, however, still disagreement about the revised lower ends of the most realistic figure, ranging from a low of 15 percent (Snow et al., 1986) to highs of 30 to 45 percent (Wright, 1988). As Snow et al. (pp. 421–422) concluded:

> Without denying that there is a disturbingly significant number of impaired and dysfunctional individuals among the homeless, we would argue that their face is not the most common one on the street. Instead, we suggest that the modal type among the homeless is a psychiatrically non-impaired individual trapped in a cycle of low-paying, dead-end jobs which fail to provide the financial where-withal to get off and stay off the streets. . . . To the extent that this picture from one city can be generalized throughout the country, it is demeaning and unfair to the majority of the homeless to focus so much public attention on the presumed relationship between mental illness, deinstitutionalization, and homelessness.

These facts do not deny that there are homeless people with mental difficulties who require a range of supportive care, including protective long-term residential facilities as well as a variety of multiple services to address their special needs. However, "it is still unclear whether the homeless condition and/or the effects of mental illness lead to shrinkage of the networks [of affiliation] or, conversely, whether the lack of adequate networks may cause people to become homeless and/or exacerbate the affects [sic] of mental illness" (Fischer and Breakey, 1986: 22). Answering such questions as "does mental illness precipitate homelessness?" or "does homelessness precipitate mental illness?" requires that samples of the psychiatric and nonpsychiatric clients of shelters be gathered from multiple shelter sites and from relatively large populations. One such study was conducted by Crystal, Ladner, and Towber (1986).

Crystal et al. collected data from a large system of public shelters in New

Table 5
Percent of Shelter Users with Indications of Mental Problems, by Sex and Racial Group

	Percent with mental problems	Number
Black	22.9	4748
Male	20.3	3828
Female	35.3	915
White	30.6	1215
Male	26.9	807
Female	38.0	408
Hispanic	23.9	1220
Male	21.9	1074
Female	39.0	146
Total	24.9	7578
Male	21.5	5935
Female	37.1	1635

Source: Crystal et al., 1986.

York City between November 1, 1982, and December 31, 1983. Their total sample included the intake of 8,061 men and women over the age of 18. Comparative characteristics for psychiatrically and nonpsychiatrically identified populations were 1,885 and 5,693. The other 483 homeless persons who had entered the 14 shelters during the study were eliminated from the sample for failing to answer all the appropriate questions. The findings of this study were discussed in terms of age, gender, and race; substance abuse; residential history; and financial benefits received.

A very interesting finding was that the average age of shelter clients, with or without indications of mental problems, was virtually the same, 35.8 for the psychiatric group and 35.5 for the nonpsychiatric group. As Table 5 indicates, mental illness/disorder is more prevalent among women in each racial group, and among whites than either blacks or Hispanics. When it came to substance abuse, as Table 6 reveals, those in the psychiatric group (34.1%) were slightly more likely to have problems than the nonpsychiatric group (32%).

Sizable percentages of both the psychiatric (51%) and nonpsychiatric (39%) groups had previously stayed in a shelter for the homeless. With respect to different psychiatric care experiences, prior shelter stays were reported by 46 percent of those who were currently under outpatient psychiatric treatment and by 52 percent of those with a history of inpatient psychiatric care. Table 7 indicates that women in both psychiatric and nonpsychiatric groups were more likely than men to have lived independently (apartment, rooming house, single-room occupancy) prior to their shelter admission; men in both groups were more likely than women to have lived in institutions (nursing

Table 6
Substance Abuse among "Psychiatric" and "Nonpsychiatric" Shelter Users

Substance Abusers, %

Substance	Psychiatric Group	Nonpsychiatric Group	Total
Alcohol	24.5	22.2	22.7
Heroin	19.2	15.4	16.3
Other Substances	2.6	1.5	1.7
Any Substances Abuse	34.1	32.0	32.6

Source: Crystal et al., 1986.

Table 7
Residence Patterns among Shelter Users, by Sex and Mental Health Status

Usual Residential Setting in Past 3-6 Months	Psychiatric Group, %		Nonpsychiatric Group, %	
	Male	Female	Male	Female
Independent living	36.6	42.8	37.9	43.1
Friends/Relatives	35.0	36.5	42.1	44.4
Institution	21.8	18.0	15.1	11.5
Street	7.0	2.7	5.0	1.0
Total	100.0	100.0	100.0	100.0
Number	1123.0	551.0	4190.0	946.0

Source: Crystal et al., 1986.

homes, hospitals, jails) or on the streets before entering the shelter. During a one-day study conducted at three New York City shelters in January 1984, the authors also collected data on the length of shelter residence. It was revealed that 28 percent of those in the psychiatric group compared with 15 percent of the nonpsychiatric group reported shelter residence of a year or higher.

Regarding financial benefits, Crystal et al. (1986: 68) found that "women (29.9%) in both groups were more likely than men (15.2%) to be currently receiving" money from the state. When it came to the psychiatric groups, they generally received more from Social Security, Veterans Administration, and Public Assistance than the nonpsychiatric groups did. For example, 15 percent of the psychiatric clients but only 3 percent of the nonpsychiatric clients were receiving Supplemental Security Income benefits.

Finally, based on the nonpsychiatric and psychiatric classification scheme used by Crystal et al. (p. 69), two very different portraits emerge of New York City's homeless sheltered populations. One has to do with the structural changes in the job market. As the authors reflect, "according to our data, the modal New York City public shelter client is a young (mid–30s), black male who lived in an apartment of his own or with family during the three to six months before entering the shelter. His inability to find a job has been the major barrier to employment." The other has to do with the feminization of psychiatric disorders, especially as related to formerly nonmarginal women. The authors informed us that the psychiatric problem looks different. "This profile is of a white woman (also in her mid–30s). She most probably lived independently, and is more likely than her nonpsychiatric counterpart to be receiving financial entitlements and to have stayed for more than a year in a shelter.

AIDS and Homelessness

Peter Smith, president of the Partnership for the Homeless (PH), at the close of the 1980s warned that "unless something is done, New York City will be called the 'City of Death,' because we will literally be stepping over and around people who are homeless and dying" of AIDS or AIDS-related illnesses (Harney, 1981: 1). PH, a New York City advocacy group, estimated in 1989 that the city streets were home to some 90,000 people, and that at least 5,000 of them had AIDS, tested positive for HIV antibodies, or had some AIDS-related symptoms or complex. The problem for those people who had AIDS or AIDS-related complex (ARC) has been that once AIDS-related symptoms are exposed, they typically lose their jobs. The experience of Ralph Hernandez was (and is) not unusual.

Having lost his job and having failed to pay his rent, Hernandez was kicked out of his New York City apartment. After spending only one night at the Ward's Island Men's Shelter, he left the shelter because of the threats that he had received from other residents who had viewed his lesions in the group shower. Hernandez was forced to take to the streets in his already debilitated physical condition. He found himself living in the waiting rooms at Grand Central Station or in various building stairwells. Of course, living on the streets aggravated the lesions on his legs and made "it difficult for him to walk or stand in line—things he must do to get food, use a shower or find a change of clothing.

I was told by the V.A. hospital to keep the sores on my legs and body clean and to get plenty of rest and good nutrition. I told them that I was homeless, but they gave me no referral to a place to stay. Nor was I given any treatment or medication. Workers at the shelter never approached me about my condition or offered me assistance or advice, so I returned to the street (Hernandez quoted in Schulman, 1989: 480).

While the situation in New York City represents an extreme example of the approaching crisis, the convergence of AIDS and its potential contribution to the increasing number of homeless is rapidly becoming a national problem, especially in such urban areas as San Francisco, Los Angeles, Philadelphia, and New Haven, Connecticut. Not only are the bed spaces in shelters and hospitals difficult to come by and to sustain for those AIDS victims who are homeless, but the situation is further constrained by the way some cities (i.e., New York City) have adhered to the definition of the problem as traditionally defined by the U.S. Centers for Disease Control in the early 1980s. This definition excludes the vast majority of the homeless who might not have AIDS per se, but instead a case of ARC, HIV-positive, or tuberculosis or chronic diarrhea. The result has been that many homeless people with suppressed immune systems have been living on the streets or covertly in shelters, in either case receiving no medical attention or special services.

The composition of the growing AIDS homeless population is represented by a variety of subgroups, each experiencing common and unique problems associated with their particular situation. Five such subgroups might include: IV drug users, male homosexuals, minority group members, street prostitutes, or Vietnam veterans. Babies and children, testing positive or negative for HIV-antibodies, left behind by dying parents also call for specialized services. Finally, matters are made worse because the U.S. responses of denial or resistance to the problems of AIDS have been further aggravated by the double and triple stigmas attached to homelessness, homophobia, and racism in America.

This chapter has tried to describe the changing nature of the new homelessness in America. While I have deliberately avoided making an educated guess at the number of homeless Americans, it has been implied throughout the discussion that membership in the new vagrancy has been growing steadily during the past decade. The view from health, social service, and human resource agencies as analyzed by The Council of State Governments (CSG) and reported in *Homelessness in the States* (Walker, 1989), reveals in Table 8 the overwhelming consensus that homelessness has been increasing throughout the United States.

This chapter has also provided caution against trying to generalize about the composition or characteristics of homelessness. It has been argued that today's homeless are a cross-section of a heterogeneous society, and that particular subgroups or subpopulations will vary from locality to locality, depending on the changing socioeconomic conditions. The final evidence presented here for this argument can be found in Table 9. Respondents to questions posed by CSG survey were asked to priority rank (number shown in column) their homeless populations according to ten characteristics. Respondents could also identify any population characteristics that they believed were not covered in the CSG listing.

Finally, if there is a typical homeless person, demographically speaking, she or he is first and foremost suffering from the crime of destitution. While

Table 8
The Change in Homelessness

Homelessness is	Increasing	Decreasing	Unchanging
Alabama	*		
Alaska	*		
Arizona	*		
Arkansas	*		
California	*		
Colorado		*	
Connecticut	*		
Delaware	*		
Florida	*		
Georgia	*		
Hawaii	*		
Idaho			*
Illinois (NR)			
Indiana	*		
Iowa			*
Kansas	*		
Kentucky	*		
Louisana	*		
Maine	*		
Maryland	*		
Massachusetts	*		
Michigan	*		
Minnesota	*		
Mississippi (NR)			
Missouri	*		
Montana (NR)			
Nebraska	*		
Nevada	*		
New Hampshire	*		
New Jersey	*		
New Mexico	*		
New York	*		
North Carolina	*		
North Dakota	*		
Ohio	*		
Oklahoma	*		
Oregon			*
Pennsylvania	*		
Rhode Island	*		
South Carolina	*		
South Dakota			*
Tennessee	*		
Texas (NR)			
Utah	*		
Vermont	*		
Virginia	*		
Washington	*		
West Virgina	*		
Wisconsin	*		
Wyoming	*		

Source: Lee Walker, 1989.

Table 9
Characteristics of the Homeless State by State (NR = No Response; the key to an explanation of parenthesized letters follows the table)

	Deinstitutionalized Mental Patients	Substance Abusers	Veterans	Runaway and Abandoned Youth
Alabama (NR)				
Alaska		1	3	4
Arizona	5	6	4	8
Arkansas	5	1		6
California	2	1		
Colorado	3	5		4
Connecticut	4	5		
Delaware	3	4	7	8
Florida	5	4		6
Georgia	1	2		
Hawaii	2	1		
Idaho	6		1	
Illinois	2	1		
Indiana	1	2	7	5
Iowa	2	3	6	4
Kansas	1	3	4	6
Kentucky		4	9	8
Louisiana	6	2		8
Maine	5	4		2
Maryland	4	3		6
Massachusetts	5	3	4	7
Michigan		2		
Minnesota	3	1	6	
Mississippi (NR)				
Missouri	1	2	6	7
Montana	3			1
Nebraska			1	2
Nevada (NR)				
New Hampshire	4	3	5	6
New Jersey	4	2	8	9
New Mexico	2	6	7	8
New York	1	2		3
North Carolina	4	1	5	6
North Dakota	5	3	8	7
Ohio	3	4	6	7
Oklahoma	4	2	6	7
Oregon	4	1		8
Pennsylvania		1		6
Rhode Island	3	1	7	6
South Carolina	2	1	7	6
South Dakota	1	3	7	8
Tennessee	6	3	4	9
Texas (NR)				
Utah	4	3	2	
Vermont	2	1	5	4
Virginia	6	5	9	7
Washington	7	2		
West Virginia	9	7	11	13
Wisconsin	6	7		
Wyoming	3	6	7	4

Table 9 (continued)

	Abused Spouses	Parolees	Unemployed	Underemployed
Alabama (NR)				
Alaska	6	5		
Arizona	7	9	1	
Arkansas	2		3	4
California			3	
Colorado			1	2
Connecticut			1	2
Delaware	6	9	2	5
Florida	7		1	
Georgia		3	5	6
Hawaii			4	
Idaho	2	3	4	
Illinois	3	4	5	6
Indiana	6	4	3	8
Iowa	5		1	
Kansas	7	8	2	5
Kentucky	6	7	2	3
Louisiana	7		1	5
Maine	3		1	2
Maryland	5		1	8
Massachusetts	6		1	8
Michigan				
Minnesota	4	5	2	
Mississippi (NR)				
Missouri	5	8	3	4
Montana			2	
Nebraska	3		4	5
Nevada (NR)				
New Hampshire	7		1	2
New Jersey	3	7	5	6
New Mexico	5	9	3	4
New York	4	5	6	7
North Carolina	7	8	2	3
North Dakota	4	6	2	9
Ohio	5	8	1	2
Oklahoma	8	5	1	3
Oregon	5	7	2	3
Pennsylvania	3	7	4	5
Rhode Island	4	8	5	9
South Carolina	8	5	3	4
South Dakota	2	4	5	6
Tennessee	7	8	1	2
Texas (NR)				
Utah				
Vermont	6	7	3	8
Virginia	2	8	1	3
Washington	4		1	
West Virginia	8	12	1	10
Wisconsin	1(r)		4	5
Wyoming	5	8	1	2

Table 9 (continued)

	Families	Transients	Other (a)
Alabama (NR)			
Alaska			(b)
Arizona	3		
Arkansas			
California			
Colorado			
Connecticut			(c)
Delaware			(d)
Florida	3		(e)
Georgia			(f)
Hawaii			(g)
Idaho		5	
Illinois			
Indiana			
Iowa			
Kansas			
Kentucky			(h)
Louisiana	3	3	
Maine			
Maryland			
Massachusetts	2		
Michigan			(i)
Minnesota			
Mississippi (NR)			
Missouri			
Montana			
Nebraska			(j)
Nevada (NR)			
New Hamsphire			
New Jersey			(k)
Nex Mexico		1	
New York	8		
North Carolina			
North Dakota	10(l)	1	
Ohio			
Oklahoma			
Oregon		6	(m)
Pennsylvania			(n)
Rhode Island	2		
South Carolina			
South Dakota			
Tennessee	5		
Texas (NR)			
Utah			
Vermont			
Virginia			(o)
Washington		6	(p)
West Virginia		3	(q)
Wisconsin		2	(s)
Wyoming			

Table 9 (continued)

Key:

(a) Number that appears in parentheses alongside noted characteristic indicates priority ranking given by respondent.

(b) Mentally and physically disabled (2).

(c) Persons affected by housing shortage (3); victims of domestic violence (6); persons affected by federal program cuts.

(d) Single-parent families with children under 18 (1).

(e) New homeless (2).

(f) AFDC recipients (4).

(g) Victims of domestic violence (3); poverty (5); chosen life-style (6).

(h) Economic reasons (1); mentally ill (5).

(i) Medical (1); mentally ill (3); psychiatric hospitalization (4); disruptive behaviors (5); victims of domestic violence (6); self-destructive behaviors (7).

(j) Affordable housing (6).

(k) ADFC recipients, especially mothers with children (1).

(l) Displaced farm families.

(m) Prostitutes (9).

(n) Mentally disabled (2).

(o) Eviction (4).

(p) Recently arrived in area (3); evicted for nonpayment (5).

(q) Children whose parents are AFDC recipients (2); elderly with physical health problems (4); handicapped (5); mentally ill (6).

(r) And violence in the home.

(s) Denied, discontinued, or delayed assistance (3).

Source: The Council of State Governments, 1989.

there are all types of homeless people, poverty—the serious kind involving the truly needy—is the lowest common denominator among the varying and overlapping groups. These homeless individuals, like their homeful counterparts, may or may not have other or related problems (e.g., domestic abuse, substance abuse), but the likelihood is probably greater that those people living without permanent housing have experienced more of the other problems. Nevertheless, as we have seen, a large percentage of the homeless are working (perhaps as high as 25 to 30 percent). But whether the homeless are working or not, their common experience is the condition of impoverishment. Poverty is not an individual problem. It is a structurally established set of institutional arrangements that changes as the political economy changes.

The new homeless of the 1980s and 1990s is, in fact, different from the old homeless. Although the social experiences and society's responses to the plights of the old and new homeless have shared a great deal in common, the fundamental relations driving or shaping U.S. homelessness today have radically changed from those that drove or shaped homelessness from as far back as the last quarter of the nineteenth century. Blau (1987: 143–144) correctly identifies the changing nature of the societal relations involved in the differentiation of New York City's contemporary homeless:

Poverty has always been the first cause of homelessness, but now . . . poverty has spread. Homelessness is no longer restricted to stereotypical "Bowery Bums," but instead encompasses women, children, and families. When it is correlated with changes in the city's political economy, the spread of homelessness to these new populations is hardly surprising. During the time that the economy required physical labor from a relatively mobile and unattached workforce, it created a risk that in an economic recession, some of these workers would become homeless. Now the labor market requires a new, more educated workforce. This workforce consists of both men and women, and it has an urban underclass to match. It is from this more diverse population that the new homeless are drawn.

The demographic findings discussed in this chapter and the other types of findings to be discussed in the rest of the book challenge the reductionist research and descriptions that purport to explain homelessness. Unlike those reductionist analyses that blame homeless men and women for their disenfranchised condition, in the next chapter we turn to a political-economic analysis of homelessness that locates the new homeless in the wider context of those social, cultural, and economic forces that produce and reproduce the problem of homelessness.

REFERENCES

Anderson, Nels. 1961. *The Hobo: The Sociology of the Homeless Man.* Chicago: University of Chicago Press. First published in 1923.

Bahr, Howard and Theodore Caplow. 1973. *Old Men Drunk and Sober*. New York: New York University Press.

Bard, Marjorie Brooks. 1988. "Domestic Abuse and the Homeless Woman: Paradigms in Personal Narratives for Organizational Strategists and Community Planners." Doctoral Dissertation. Ann Arbor, MI: University Microfilms International (1989).

Bassuk, E. L. 1984. "The Homeless Problem." *Scientific American*, 25: 40–46.

Blau, Joel S. 1987. "The Homeless of New York: A Case Study in Social Welfare." Doctoral Dissertation. Ann Arbor, MI: University Microfilms International (1989).

Cohen, Sharon. 1988. "Rural Homeless: An Unseen, But Even-worsening Tragedy." *The Montgomery Advertiser and Alabama Journal*, Sunday, Dec. 18 (Associated Press Writer).

Crystal, Stephen, Susan Ladner, and Richard Towber. 1986. "Multiple Impairment Patterns in the Mentally Ill Homeless." *International Journal of Mental Health*, 14, no. 4.

Devine, Deborah Judith. 1988. "Homelessness and the Social Safety Net." Doctoral Dissertation. Ann Arbor, MI: University Microfilms International (1989).

Fischer, Pamela J. and William R. Breakey. 1986. "Homelessness and Mental Health: An Overview." *International Journal of Mental Health*, 14, no. 4.

Freeman, Richard B. and Brian Hall. 1986. *Permanent Homelessness in America?* September Working Paper No. 2013. Cambridge, MA: National Bureau of Economic Research.

Harney, James. 1989. "8,000 AIDS Homeless." *Daily News*, January 6.

Hombs, Mary Ellen and Mitch Snyder. 1983. *Homelessness in America: A Forced March to Nowhere*. Washington, DC: Community for Creative Nonviolence.

Hope, Marjorie and James Young. 1984. *The Faces of Homelessness*. Lexington, MA: Lexington Books.

Hopper, Kim James. 1987. "A Bed for the Night: Homeless Men in New York City, Past and Present." Doctoral Dissertation. Ann Arbor, MI: University-Microfilms International (1989).

Hopper, Kim and Ellen Baxter. 1981. *Private Lives/Public Spaces*. New York: Community Service Society.

Hopper, Kim, Ellen Baxter, Stuart Cox, and Lawrence Klein. 1982. *One Year Later*. New York: Community Service Society.

Hopper, Kim and Jill Hamberg. 1985. *The Making of America's Homeless: From Skid Row to the New Poor, 1945–1984*. New York: Community Service Society.

HUD. 1984. *Report to the Secretary on the Homeless and Emergency Shelters*. Washington, DC: U.S. Government Printing Office.

Lee, Barrett A. 1988. "Stability and Change in an Urban Homeless Population." Paper presented at the Annual Meetings of the Population Association of America, New Orleans.

Ludlow, Lynn. 1988. "No One Knows How Many Homeless." *The Montgomery Advertiser*, March 2 (writer for the San Francisco Examiner).

Momeni, Jamshid A. Ed. 1989. *Homelessness in the United States*, Vol. I: *State Surveys*. Westport, CT: Greenwood Press.

National Coalition for the Homeless. 1983. *The Homeless and the Economic Recovery.* New York: National Coalition for the Homeless.

———. 1986. *National Neglect/National Shame: America's Homeless—Outlook Winter, 1986–87.* Washington, DC: National Coalition for the Homeless.

Putchat, Cynthia Ray. 1988. "Stress, Coping Style, Personality, Social Network and Locus of Control in the Homeless and Homeless Mentally Ill" *Dissertation Abstracts International,* 49, no. 11 (May 1989): 5031.

Rossi, Peter H., James D. Wright, Gene A. Fisher, and Georgiana Willis. 1987. "The Urban Homeless: Estimating Composition and Size." *Science*, March: 235.

Safety Network. 1988. "1990 Census Will Attempt to Count Homeless People." *The Newsletter of the National Coalition for the Homeless.* Washington, DC.

Schulman, Sarah. 1989. "Thousands May Die in the Streets." *The Nation,* April 10.

Snow, David A., Susan G. Baker, Leon Anderson, and Michael Martin. 1986. "The Myth of Pervasive Mental Illness Among the Homeless." *Social Problems,* 33, no. 5 (June).

Solenberger, Alice. 1911. *One Thousand Homeless Men.* New York: Russell Sage Foundation.

Sutherland, Edwin H. and Harvey J. Locke. 1971. *Twenty Thousand Homeless Men: A Study of Unemployed Men in the Chicago Shelters.* New York: Arno Press and the New York Times. First published in 1936 by J. B. Lippincott.

"Task Force for the Homeless of Atlanta." 1988. Flyer.

United States General Accounting Office. 1985. *Homelessness: A Complex Problem and the Federal Response.* Washington, DC: GAO.

Walker, Lee. 1989. *Homelessness in the States.* Lexington, KY: The Council of State Governments.

Wayland, Francis. 1877. "A Paper on Tramps Read at the Saratoga Meeting of the American Social Science Association Before the Conference of State Charities." September 6, cited in Blau (1987).

Werfel, Pearl Bonnie. 1985. "Adolescent Prostitution and its Relationship to Homelessness." Doctoral Dissertation. Ann Arbor, MI: University Microfilms International (1989).

Williams, Randall. 1988. *Hard Labor.* Atlanta: Southern Regional Council.

Wright, James D. 1988. "The Mentally Ill Homeless: What is Myth and What is Fact?" *Social Problems,* 35, no. 2 (April).

3 The Political Economy of the New Vagrancy

The homelessness condition in the United States over the past decade has provided a vivid illustration of one very real scenario of the "deindustrialized" capitalist system at work. That is to say, the public policies on homelessness in this country cannot be separated from a governmental decision making that subsidizes private, profit-making, and public indebtedness, and often involves antisocial priorities and policies of austerity, typically rationalized by the ideology of "trickle down" and fictitious capital. Stated differently, the political economy of homelessness assumes that the decline in average real wages and the increase in the poverty of working people represents a systemic response to the national crisis of profitability and productivity in the mid- and post–1970s. This is not to deny the presence of ongoing class struggles, competing social ideologies, and alternative political visions. Finally, underlying this analysis of homelessness is the belief that

in the various systems of power in the world today, the control of investment, of basic economic allocations, is not the only source of domination—racism and sexism persist in all systems—but it is the single most important constituent. Those in charge of investment, will claim and get unequal treatment for themselves on the grounds that they act in the interest of the future of the entire society and must therefore have the resources to do their job. And those who are excluded from the function will be forced to pay all the social costs of decisions made on high (Harrington, 1988: 16).

It follows that the responses to homelessness require more than simply a new housing policy or social delivery system, but rather a whole new way of thinking about homelessness in relationship to how we currently view, examine, and make social investments in our society's areas of critical need.

CONSERVATIVE AND LIBERAL ACCOUNTS OF HOMELESSNESS: A CRITIQUE

Traditional explanations or conservative accounts of the homeless have tended to blame the victim for homelessness and to identify the homeless person as someone suffering from some kind of impaired capacity. Not only have the homeless been traditionally regarded as troubled and disaffiliated individuals, but they have also been portrayed as troublesome and danger-ous, especially when their members have involved ethnic and racial minor-ities. Homeless people are viewed, in other words, as strange and different from homeful people. In the minds of conservatives, the homeless are either crazies or freeloaders. Moreover, they have crossed over from occupying the symbolic position of social junk to social dynamite (Spitzer, 1975). The legacy of deviancy as Hopper (1987) has observed, characterizes the senti-ments of conservative descriptions (explanations) of the homeless. In other words, in the traditional or conservative perspective homelessness persists because people's characters have been transformed into various personality disorders.

Conservative analyses of the homeless can usually be divided into four types: (1) those "deranged street dwellers" who are the product of patho-logical individuals or policies; (2) those "disordered families" who are the product of pathological familiar relationships (e.g., single-parent children having babies out of wedlock) or dependency producing welfare policies; (3) those "subcultural homeless" who are the product of the pathologically and chronically marginal poor; and (4) those "counterfeit beggars" exploiting the opportunity of getting something for nothing (Hopper, 1987: 44–49). In sum, the traditional outlook on the homeless locates the cause of homelessness within the individual. Fundamentally the problem is one of flawed characters taking precedent over flawed policies.

By contrast, the liberal outlook on the homeless and homelessness locates its causes in the various institutional orders and in the social experiences of people. Liberals may acknowledge the prevailing political, economic, and social relations affecting the homeless populations and associated with home-lessness (e.g., the economy, scarcity of low-income housing, deinstitution-alization), but their examinations tend to emphasize the process by which people wind up homeless divorced from the larger social arrangements. For example, Redburn and Buss (1986: 55) have described their own analysis in precisely this fashion: "it is about causes, but mainly proximate rather than ultimate causes, and its focus is on the homeless individual, rather than on the larger social structures and norms that sustain, tolerate, and justify homelessness and other kinds of severe deprivation." As a result of this kind of analysis, their general conclusions about the homeless, while recognizing the larger forces at work, still wind up blaming the homelessness situation on inadequate individuals or an inadequate welfare system:

Most people become homeless not as a result of a single catastropic event, but at the end of a series of misfortunes. Homelessness is not a dramatic fall from seemingly secure middle-class life. Most had been poor and on the margin of the labor force prior to becoming homeless. Their present condition reflects not only their inability to earn income by working, but also a social welfare system that provides haphazard and often inadequate coverage of those unable to support themselves (Redburn and Buss, 1986: 77).

While this type of liberal analysis correctly describes the situation for many homeless people, it does not explain why, for example, the social welfare system does not systemically provide adequate coverage or why plant closings provide little or no compensation to those workers who have been disemployed.

Other types of liberal analyses of homelessness recognize that this condition is a function of decreased real income and increased poverty among the working poor and a decline in the supply of private and public-sponsored affordable housing. The liberal critique, for example, may rightly attack those cities that provide tax incentives for the destruction of single-room-occupancy hotels (SROs). But it fails to realize that while the SROs themselves were better than the streets, they never did qualify as decent shelter. More importantly, these types of analyses fail to explain how the various macro relations or institutional orders emerge and develop in relationship to housing displacement.

The liberal accounts typically underscore unemployment and poverty, affordable housing and urban redevelopment, and personal attributes and interpersonal conflicts. In 1988, for example, the National Academy of Sciences' Institute issued its report on homelessness in the United States. It identified the three major causes for the growing numbers of homeless as "a decreased supply of housing in the face of increased needs; more stringent criteria for welfare assistance—and declining purchasing power of benefits for those still eligible—at a time of increasing poverty; and deinstitutionalization of the mentally ill, along with non-institutionalization—not admitting people for psychiatric care except for very brief periods" (*In These Times*, 1988: 14). Similarly, the resources guide from the National Teach-in on Homelessness, October 28–30, 1987, concluded that several major societal and structural factors were

easily identifiable as the root causes of widespread homelessness in the 1980s: drastic cuts in federal housing programs and social services, housing policies that encourage urban renewal and "gentrification" without creating low-cost replacement housing, unemployment, the deinstitutionalization of mental patients without provision of much-needed community mental health services, and the breakdown of traditionally supportive social structures such as the family and community" (Coons, 1987: 5).

While the liberal perspectives have argued that the shortage of low-income housing has been the primary cause of homelessness and that the replacement of lost low-income housing is the essential step necessary for ending homelessness in the United States, simply advocating a program for decent shelter and specifying how many units is not enough.

The point is that while liberal analyses of homelessness may oppose structures and policies of the prevailing political economy, they do not call for alternative approaches or for grounding their housing reforms in the necessity of democratizing the entire process of social investment for purposes of satisfying the basic needs of life. In other words, a more critical analysis of homelessness recognizes that it is the fundamental contradictions of advanced capitalism and the prevailing distribution of power in the way that decisions are made that needs changing, if not first and foremost, then at least simultaneously. Toward this objective, for example, a housing program "would urge a planned development of racially and socially integrated communities with public spaces and facilities for new institutions of neighborhood democracy and control" connected with a national movement "uniting the homeless in a coalition with young families from the working class and middle class as well as with those seniors who do not want to be segregated on the basis of age" (Harrington, 1986: 16). Moreover, it is absolutely crucial for these various groups to recognize that the traditional policies as well as the structures of both the conservative and liberal parties are simply not capable politically of solving the housing crisis. To solve these and other social problems requires reforms in the workings of the political economy itself. To understand how a radical or political-economic analysis deepens the insights of those liberal analyses of homelessness, we must be prepared to examine the workings of advanced capitalism in relationship to the dynamics of modern mass homelessness. It also requires that we explore those theoretical and methodological questions that can provide a bona fide explanation of the ultimate causes that accounted for the growing numbers of homeless Americans in the 1980s, during a period when the U.S. economy was alleged to have been experiencing a period of prosperity.

In sum, in order to develop a critical understanding of the ultimate causes of the new homelessness, it is imperative that our analyses transcend both the conservative theories of "personality disorders" and the liberal theories of "precipitating events." We must focus our examinations of homelessness on the forces underlying the dislocations occurring in the urban and rural environments. In other words, regardless of an individual's disability or special needs, the key to making sense out of his or her homelessness lies in the ability of our analyses to explain the distinctive structural arrangements in which homeless individuals occupy special niches. As Spitzer (1975: 638) noted some time ago about traditional explanations of deviance, they "are essentially non-structural and ahistorical in their mode of analysis." The same limitations articulated by Spitzer on deviance can apply to the conventional accounts of contemporary homelessness:

By restricting investigation to factors which are manipulable within the existing structural arrangements these theories embrace a "correctional perspective" and divert attention from the impact of the political economy as a whole. From this point of view deviance [or homelessness] is *in* but not *of* our contemporary social order. Theories that locate the source of deviance [or homelessness] in factors as diverse as personality structure, family systems, cultural transmission, social disorganization and differential opportunity share a common flaw—they attempt to understand deviance [or homelessness] apart from historically specific forms of political and economic organization. Because traditional theories proceed without any sense of historical development, deviance [or homelessness] is normally viewed as an episodic and transitory phenomenon rather than an outgrowth of long-term structural change (Spitzer, 1975: 638–639).

THEORETICAL AND METHODOLOGICAL CONSIDERATIONS FOR A POLITICAL ECONOMY OF HOMELESSNESS

As Deborah Devine (1988) has critically recognized, the identification of factors related to contemporary homelessness comes primarily from the advocacy literature and consists mostly of compilations of causes lacking an explanatory framework. She continues that in report after report the same findings and the same litany of causes appear even though there may be very real differences between those cities examined with respect to both their local economies and welfare systems, not to mention in their rates of homelessness. Devine's criticism of the deficiency of liberal analyses of causation is right on target. In an attempt to formulate a theoretically informed analysis of homelessness and the social safety net, she sought a more coherent explanation of the relationships involved in the structural phenomena associated by advocates with hardship and homelessness. In a moment we will turn to Devine's analysis of homelessness and the welfare state, but first there are still a couple of questions and a related analysis of social welfare policy that I would like to introduce.

Joel Blau (1987: 26) has concluded that two of the most relevant questions to be asked about homelessness are: "in what way does homelessness in [the United States] merely reflect an old and seemingly unresolvable debate about work and dependency, and in what way is it unique to this time and place?" The answers are that it is both because, on the one side, it has been addressed by every capitalist social order to date and, on the other side, it depends on the specific sociohistorical formations of the changing political economy. Locating the homeless within the changing contexts of subsistence, then, Blau attempted to discover the common threads of social policy underlying New York City's response to homelessness. With respect to the evolution of its policies and within the context of the political and economic functions of the welfare state, Blau concerned himself with four kinds of questions: (1) What social policies were developed in response to the growing homeless population in New York City? (2) Why did New York choose these particular policies while foregoing others? (3) How does the pattern of these choices demonstrate the city's management of the relationship between the underclass and the working poor? (4) How is this relationship connected to the evolution and current role of the modern welfare state?

Blau concluded that the city had developed a dual strategy of reducing the cost of maintaining the homeless and seeking to help find work for those who were employable. The net result of such policy was that the costs of the homeless populations were minimized while the uses of the homeless were maximized. Structural analyses of homelessness like Blau's and Devine's make substantial contributions toward the development of a political economy of homelessness as they proceed to make the necessary connections between homelessness and the economic restructuring of the cities and the nation in which it occurs. To do less is to provide merely "a tribal picture [of homelessness], shorn of the context needed to make it intelligible" (Hopper, 1987: 61).

In one of the most theoretically and methodologically ambitious studies of the dominant relations involved in the structural causes of homelessness, Devine (1988) attempted to explain the interrelationship between the various conditions (e.g., social ideologies, economic development, population migration, welfare efforts, and housing programs) associated with homelessness. Before reviewing Devine's analysis, it is important to underscore her theoretical and methodological criticism of the limitations of liberal-advocacy type analyses: "At the level of explanation, while the welfare system, the economy, the private housing market and the medical delivery system are named as prime causes of homelessness, it is unclear which among them are independent and which intervening causes and how they are linked" (Devine, 1988: 41). For example, she points out that there has been no attempt to explain the causal link between economic and welfare system inadequacies as contributors to homelessness. Hence, while the advocacy-liberal literature of the 1980s had identified the failures of the welfare system as a cause of homelessness, it had not explained where in the social systems such failures had originated. More importantly, it had not explained why we have the type of welfare system we have in the first place as opposed to other alternative systems or models of welfare.

Theoretically, Devine wanted to test three competing theories or explanations of social service delivery provided in the welfare state literature. Each of the theories—convergence, social control, and self-regulatory—leads to different predictions with respect to the relationships between development and underdevelopment. Convergence theory (Wilensky, 1975) argues for a linear-evolutionary or paralleled perspective on social welfare. What is good for development, economic and technological, is good for reducing poverty and hardship. In other words, development implies a fostering of welfare efforts or an enhancement of benefits. Convergence theories of state social welfare predict a reduction in homelessness. In contrast, social control theory (Piven and Cloward, 1971) argues that the ideology of laissez-faire and the marketplace of the free-enterprise system regulates the other institutional orders. Individualism is encouraged while welfare is discouraged. When times are relatively good, social welfare contracts; when times are relatively bad, social welfare expands. Therefore, social control theory predicts that homelessness could increase during periods of prosperity and decrease during periods of depression. In dialectical fashion, self-regulatory theory (Janowitz, 1976) argues that economic development (or the lack of) and competing ideologies influence welfare policy. Hence, self-regulatory theory predicts that homelessness could rise or decline depending on the dominant ideology in the context of the more general economic picture.

Unlike most analyses of homelessness that have failed to operationalize the problem by incorporating indicators that allow causal assertions to be tested, Devine does precisely that. Methodologically, using regression and path analysis she tested three primary (and several other) hypotheses about homelessness. Her sample included 42 metropolitan areas in the United States. The three hypotheses tested were:

H_1 social as opposed to laissez-faire ideologies lead to increased welfare efforts, which in turn lead to reduced homelessness;

H_2 increased economic development leads to reduced welfare efforts, which in turn lead to increased homelessness;

H_3 increased population stimulated by economic development leads to increased homelessness.

Devine's findings produced mixed results.

Devine (1988: Abstract) concluded that "as hypothesized, economic development does lead to decreased welfare effort and increased homelessness, indicating that convergence theory does not adequately explain welfare effort or hardship." For example, economic growth could have led to increased homelessness because new jobs were not compatible with the skills of those individuals at the bottom of the labor pool. New enterprises or economic development had also had a tendency to encroach on land and housing resources that had been vital to preserving low-income housing. Finally, development often meant that elected city officials had to provide incentives or giveaways to developers. In turn, these cities had to "tinker with the other part of the welfare state equation" and with "the conditions of redistribution" if they were to compete in the marketplace of urban renewal (Devine, 1988: 272). With respect to social control and self-regulatory theory, "one of the two indicators of social ideology, tax effort, was found to have a significant influence on welfare effort in the manner hypothesized giving support to the emphasis in social control and self-regulatory theory upon the role of ideology. However, party affiliation did not influence welfare effort in the manner predicted" (Devine, 1988: Abstract).

The attempts by Blau, Devine, and others to unravel the conjointing influences of various systemic conditions associated with homelessness is a welcome addition to the recent literature. These kinds of analyses lend themselves to explaining the characteristics of the economic and welfare systems rather than of individual homeless people. For example, as Blau has dialectically argued, the welfare state is both the cure and the cause of homelessness. Or in the words of Devine (1988: 143): "Just as fluctuations in the magnitude of poverty reflect on the level of welfare expenditures, place to place fluctuations in the kinds of numbers and persons found poor may reflect on the level of welfare effort as measured by the inclusiveness or exclusiveness of eligibility requirements."

These types of analyses need to be further developed by the inclusion of theories about the state and political economy within the context of the internationalization of global capital. When brought together, such analyses of homelessness are also capable of being put to empirical tests. This kind of political and economic analysis predicts that the growth and decline in homelessness should vary according to whether we are referring to areas in the rustbelt or the sunbelt. In other words, it would be expected, for example, that homelessness in the 1980s would have varied differentially, depending on whether or not a particular area was experiencing a depression, a recession, or an expansion in its particular economic and social relations. However, this is not to suggest that we should not be thinking about the local problem of homelessness as involving a national and international dimension, especially in terms of the developing ideologies and public policies.

THE POLITICAL ECONOMY OF THE NEW HOMELESSNESS

Since the term "political economy" was first introduced during the eighteenth century's Age of Enlightenment, it has had and continues to have different meanings. As used here, political economy refers to "the idea of human history going through stages of growth, with the key to each stage, as well as the transition from one stage to another, the mode of obtaining subsistence in any society" (Bottomore, 1983: 376). So as not to confuse or reduce political economy to "economic determinism," I am not referring simplistically to a monocausal explanation nor to a unilinear, unidirectional model of historical progress. On the contrary, as applied here the political economy of homelessness is dialectical in nature, involving class, racial, and sexual struggles; its analysis includes, among other things, such "noneconomic influences as social structures, political systems, and cultural values as well as such factors as technological change and the distribution of income and wealth" (Wilber, 1973: viii).

Following Marx, political economy refers to the study of history and society. It does not refer to any universal set of conditions, but rather to transitory developments relative to particular epochs. In the epoch of advanced capitalism, for example, Engels argues that political economy is the theoretical analysis of modern bourgeois society. More specifically, political economy incorporates the study of "the distribution and accumulation of economic surplus, and the attendant problems of determination of prices, wages, employment, and the efficacy or otherwise of political arrangements to promote accumulation" (Bottomore, 1983: 375).

The political economy of homelessness "recognizes that man is a social being whose arrangements for the production and distribution of economic goods must be, if society is to be livable, consistent with congruent institutions of family, political, and cultural life" (Wilber, 1973: viii). And as Anderson (1974) has argued, a viable Marxist theory of social order and social change explains that the way people relate to one another and the way they organize their productive forces gives shape to their social, cultural, and political institutions. The institution and institutionalization of homelessness are no exceptions to this rule. In other words, a political economy of homelessness can help explain why at least some 2 million Americans are homeless, why tens of millions of Americans are experiencing an economic squeeze, and why the number of millionaires continues to grow. All three of these economic groupings are interdependent on the developing political economy for their reproduction (or survival). With respect to the first group in particular, the homeless, their survival or reproduction as a class of people, regardless of any existing or nonexisting individual problems, depends specifically on the interacting capitalist forces of accumulation and legitimation as these impact on the welfare state.

As it was pointed out by Blau in the last section, the welfare state of advanced capitalism during the past decade and into the present one has been central to homelessness: "it is both the cause and cure of homelessness." Proximate cause and cure perhaps, but certainly not the ultimate cause and cure. The ultimate causes and cures of homelessness are related to the developing nature of the political economy and, in turn, to the developing character of the capitalist state. As viewed here the capitalist state is at present experiencing two counterdevelopments in relationship to the intensification of capitalist competition worldwide. On the one hand, authority under late capitalism has become state-centered, not simply a matter of the state serving as an instrument of the ruling class, but rather a matter of the state acting to secure the entire order of global capitalism. On the other hand, the role of the state to control and regulate capital has declined in the United States as the growth and expansion of multinational corporations has grown. As a result the capitalist state and the New Leviathan have become a complex apparatus full of global contradictions (Ross and Trachte, 1990).

Almost two decades ago, O'Connor (1973) identified the two fundamental contradictory functions of the capitalist state as involving accumulation and legitimation. The essence of the argument has been summarized by Marxist economists as follows:

The state attempts to support the accumulation of private capital while trying to maintain social peace and harmony. Since accumulation is crucial to the reproduction of the class structure, legitimation necessarily involves attempts to mystify the process and to repress or manage discontent. Both accumulation and legitimation are translated into demands for state activity. But while this implies an increase in state expenditure, the revenues for meeting those needs are not always forthcoming, since the fruits of accumulation (greater profits) are not socialized (Gold, Yo, and Wright, 1975: 41).

In the context of the interimperial rivalries and the decline of the United States, Petras (1990: 17) has argued that the "disjuncture between the power of the state and capital means, in effect, that all the costs of reproduction and defense of capital are borne by the state (and by the working taxpayers), while profits, interests and rents are accrued internationally." In short, the intensification of the capitalist state's socialization of the costs of production (and speculation) during advanced capitalism, and its acceleration of the privatization of profits in the United States over the past 20 years has not only decimated the old industrial working class, but it has also diminished the resources of the welfare state in general, which, in turn, along with certain demographic trends, have destabilized families and communities and created the basis for the massive growth in homelessness during the decade of the 1980s.

As Quinney (1980: 94) has written about the contradictions of the new capitalist (as opposed to liberal capitalist) state,

ultimately it cannot sustain private capital accumulation and at the same time legitimize the relations of advanced capitalism. On the economic level, the state cannot solve its own fiscal crisis that results from increasing state expenditures to assure private capital accumulation. On the level of legitimation, the state cannot continue to maintain its credibility as it fails to solve problems that it either creates or expands in the promotion of the capitalist economy.

Stated differently, unless the fundamental class nature of U.S. society and the underclass or marginal nature of homelessness are confronted, and unless the underlying contradictions of the capitalist state and political economy are tackled, then all of the tinkering with the welfare state and housing policies, at best, will provide only temporary relief (shelter) for the transitionally homeless as the numbers of homeless continue to grow. In other words, the production and reproduction of homelessness cannot be arrested without fundamental changes occurring in the political economy. In order to understand the political economy of homelessness, the rest of this chapter will review the recent developments in the class structure of the United States, in the global and domestic economies, and in the fiscal and housing crises that have accompanied these changes. In the process, the ultimate causes of the growing homelessness in the United States will be revealed.

THE DISTRIBUTION OF WEALTH AND POVERTY IN THE UNITED STATES

Hard work bears little relation to how much one earns, especially when investment income comes into the picture. As a consequence, most Americans are working too hard for too little, while living in a rich society which ought to be making it easier, not just to earn a living, but to raise a family, to care for children and elderly relatives, and to enhance the quality of our schools and communities (Brouwer, 1988: 24).

It used to be that the "rich got richer and the poor got poorer." Nowadays, the rich are still getting richer and the poor are still getting poorer, but there is a new axiom emerging; it seems that the so-called middle class is also getting poorer. This is not the work of God. Nor is it in the natural order of things. It is simply the contradictions of advanced capitalism doing its thing. Although the rest of this section will dwell on the material or economic differences of inequality and privilege in a class society, I am nevertheless implicitly referring to the "quality of life" of the average American that is undergoing a process of deterioration.

During the 1980s when government and corporate policies first began seriously to expand the wealth of the rich at the expense of everybody else, the rich as well as the Republicans in Washington, D.C. were celebrating their "postrecession high." In the meantime, the media pundits were engaged in discussions about "recovery" and the "new prosperity." The United States, however, in terms of the global political economy, was experiencing a period of decline. Slowly but increasingly, more people and more communities were experiencing a squeezing of their economies and a deteriorating of their quality of life as measured by all kinds of social indexes. Such are the contradictions of capitalist development, ideology, and legitimation. After all, as the economies of Japan and the Federal Republic of Germany surpassed the U.S. economy in many areas, and as other Asian and West European economies started gaining on the United States, the Republican-Democratic leadership and the capitalist state were busy creating huge debts, greater poverty, and arsenals of useless weapons, all for the rather unexpressed purposes of sustaining and improving the rate of profits for corporate America.

A consequence of these political and economic realities has been a widening of the divisions of class and inequality with the gap closer to that of Third World countries than other postindustrial nations. Hence, more and

Table 10
Changes in Family Incomes from 1978 to 1986 (figures adjusted for inflation)

1978		1986
18.0%	High Budget Americans (over $46,800)	21.2%
53.7%	Middle Income Americans (between $18,900-$46,800)	43.6%
28.3%	Low Budget and Poor Americans (under $18,900)	35.2%

Source: Brouwer, 1988: 5.

more Americans are having lives of austerity and poverty. As the poverty and privilege expand so do the numbers of homeless people.

While the vast majority of Americans either lost ground or barely stayed even, and probably worked harder during the 1980s as compared to the previous two decades, one out of five bettered their economic situation. By the end of the decade, .05 percent of the population owned 45 percent of the nation's financial assets, excluding the value of private homes.[1] On the other hand, 90 percent of the people owned a mere 17 percent. As for the other 9.5 percent, the affluent, they owned 38 percent of the remaining wealth of the nation.

For the average worker, real incomes (adjusted for inflation) between 1973 and 1986 fell. Average earnings were down 14.3 percent and median household income was down 6 percent. For the average wealthiest 1 percent, the superrich, income was up 50 percent between 1977 and 1988, averaging $452,000 per person per year. Thus the percentage of this group's pretax income grew from 9.2 to 12.5 percent of the total U.S. income. Table 10 shows the growing disparity in family income that occurred between 1978 and 1986.

The growth in the distribution of income inequality is actually understated in Table 11 because the figures were based on the Internal Revenue and Census reports that failed to account for much of the capital gains and underreported income of both the affluent and rich. Table 12 provides comparative data on income inequality of five nations—the United States, Japan, the Netherlands, India, and Mexico—and supports the argument that income inequality in the United States is more like developing than developed countries.

Changes in people's security and in wealth and poverty generally have been assisted by various pieces of tax legislation over the past 20 years. To say the least, this legislation has favored the rich over the nonrich and the poor. For example, Reagan's federal tax reform act of 1981, while cutting

Table 11
Income Distribution—Growing Inequality

	bottom fifth	2nd fifth	3rd fifth	4th fifth	top fifth
1969	5.6%	12.4%	17.7%	23.7%	40.6%
1980	5.1%	11.6%	17.5%	24.3%	41.5%
1986	4.6%	10.8%	16.8%	24.0%	43.8%

Source: Brouwer, 1988: 4.

Table 12
Comparative Data on Income Inequality

	% of Income Received	
	top fifth	bottom two fifths
Japan	37%	22%
Netherlands	37%	22%
U.S.A.	50%	14%
India	49%	16%
Mexico	58%	10%

Source: Brouwer, 1988: 4.

income taxes across-the-board, disproportionately favored the more affluent. Those families of four with incomes of $20,000, $50,000, and $100,000 in 1982 saved $224, $1,114, and $15,237, respectively. Between 1966 and 1985, taxes paid on labor or earned income rose from 17.6 to 20.6 percent while taxes paid on capital or unearned (investment) income fell dramatically from 33 to 17.5 percent. At the same time, between 1960 and 1986 the rate of taxation on corporate profits dropped from 46 to 21 percent, while the maximum rate for taxation of rich Americans fell from 70 to 28 percent. With respect to the average family living below the poverty line, between 1978 and 1985, its combined payments on income and social security taxes rose from 4 to 10 percent. The consequences of the Reagan "revolution from above" was the overthrow of the progressive system of taxation enjoyed by the average American during the 1950s, 1960s, and 1970s. In its place was substituted the currently regressive system of taxation where the corporate and rich sectors, including the affluent, pay less and everybody else (90 percent of Americans) pay more.

In terms of this book's focus, it is interesting to underscore the unequal tax benefits derived from the home owner's deduction for interest paid on home mortgages and property taxes. For example, in 1982 when a good mortgage interest rate was 12 percent, the effective rate of mortgage interest for rich families (incomes above $100,000) was near zero or 1.4 percent, for affluent families (incomes above $50,000) it was 3.7 percent, and for the average family (incomes of $20,000) it was 10.7 percent. As Brouwer (1988: 6) has pointed out, it was easy to

understand from these figures that home buying has been so heavily subsidized for the rich that they can afford two or three luxury homes. Somehow the conservative rich, who are often heard to complain about federal subsidies to the poor, never seem to mind the generous handout they receive from the government.

Consistent with the 1980s when the Reagan-Bush era of "well-to-do-fare" for the rich was taking off in all its guises, it was decided that there had to be cutbacks in the general welfare. When it came to Reaganomics, supply-side economics, voodoo economics, or whatever one preferred to call it, the outcome was the same: funding for the poor and working classes diminished. State governments also followed the lead of the federal government in the 1980s "either because they agreed ideologically with punishing the poor or because they were too strapped for money by the federal cut-offs in funds" (Brouwer, 1988: 8). The result was that many social programs like food stamps, subsidized housing for the poor, and Aid to Families with Dependent Children (AFDC) were cut significantly; contributing both to the feminization of poverty and to the impoverishment of children. For example, after adjusting for inflation and taking state averages, Brouwer discovered that monthly maximums for AFDC payments declined dramatically from a high of $572 in 1970 to a low of $322 in 1985.

Finally, with respect to the percentage of Americans living in poverty, the increases will have varied according to the poverty line or levels adopted. For example, in 1986 the U.S. government considered a family of four poor if it earned less than $11,200. However, in just about every location in the United States such a figure would have meant that such a family would have been living in "real" as opposed to "official" poverty. Brouwer has noted that when the income poverty line was $3,022 in 1960, 22 percent of Americans were classified as poor as compared to 13–15 percent in 1986 when the income poverty line was $11,200. But he went on to explain that the per capita shares of the respective GNPs for 1960 and 1986 were $2,877 and $17,797. In other words, "a more realistic poverty level for a family of four, and one proportionate to the 1960 figures, would [have been] $18,693" (Brouwer, 1988: 8). Using this figure, some 33 percent of American families would have been classified as living in poverty.

A SNAPSHOT OF THE CHANGING GLOBAL AND DOMESTIC
ECONOMIC PICTURE

The changing worldwide political economy of the 1970s and 1980s re-corded both the end of the postwar boom in the development of U.S. in-ternational capital and the decline of U.S. hegemony in international relations (Sherman, 1976; Mandel, 1980; Berberoglu, 1987). These changing global realities of advanced capitalism have not only established or set into motion a systemic response in the crisis of profitability and productivity resulting in the higher yielding speculative markets, but they also have had the effect of contributing to what now appears to be, at least according to some economic theorists, a permanent U.S. fiscal crisis, brought about by overproduction and the downward turns in the business cycle (Batra, 1987). At the same time, of course, this crisis has been fueled by the rise to world prominence of the West European and Asian economies, coupled with the effects of the transnational corporate expansion abroad on the domestic econ-omy. It was these structural transformations in the global and U.S. economy, for example, that accounted for the most severe recession since the 1930s in 1974–75. In 1979–80, the United States again fell into another recession and in 1982 it fell into an ever deeper recession.

The most recent recovery lasted from the beginning of 1984 to the end of 1990. Some theorists argue that the recession that began in late 1990 would last a year. Others believe that recent economic trends suggest the strong possibility of a coming crash by the early 1990s, which may prove to be much worse than any previously (Batra, 1987; Berberoglu, 1987). For example, the capacity utilization in manufacturing or the ups and downs of the business cycle during the past 20 years reveals that the general trend in business activity has been in a downward direction, as each peak in the cycle was lower than the one that preceded it (Economic Report, 1987). Data on unemployment rates told a similar story. In the 1971, 1975, and 1982 recessions the "official" government unemployment rates at their heights were 6.0, 8.5, and 9.7 percent, respectively. It is also worth noting that the unemployment rate was higher in the first two recoveries—5 percent in 1973 and 5.9 percent in 1979. By the end of 1989 the rate of unemployment had officially dipped to about 5.2 percent. It should be pointed out, however, that in addition to the traditionally hidden (or not counted) unemployed, there had been a very real growth in the number of underemployed persons during the 1980s. The changing social relations of postindustrial labor had lowered wages at the bottom end of the income scale. The combined effect of these trends had been that a greater number of both employed and unemployed persons were unable to afford the rising costs of housing in the United States. Homelessness followed.

As real wages declined for workers in the 1980s, the weakening U.S. domestic economy, as evidenced by the record number of bankruptcies among small businesses and family farmers, contributed further to the decline in workers' purchasing and consuming power. At the same time, the 1980s ushered in the highest recorded trade budget deficits in U.S. history. With respect to the former, trade deficits rose from $9.5 billion in 1976 to $124 billion in 1985. With respect to the latter, butressed by military expenditures that doubled between 1980 and 1986 and had tripled since the mid 1970s, the annual budget deficits had climbed from $54 billion in 1977 to $221 billion in 1986. By 1986 the total federal debt had reached $2.1 trillion, up from $709 billion in 1977 (Berberoglu, 1987). By the end of the decade, however, the debt had begun to decline a bit and appeared to some economists to have levelled off.

The rising debts were also a by-product of fictitious capital and the large tax cuts enjoyed by the rich and corporate America during the Reagan administration. Tax breaks such as those involving capital gains and other favorable governmental policies, like deregulation, not only allowed the profits of corporations to reach new heights—rising from $74.7 billion in 1970 to $117.6 billion in 1980 to $280.7 billion in 1985 (Berberoglu, 1987)—but had also accounted for the lost revenues and social expenditures to assist or subsidize the poor. Meanwhile, in an effort to manage the fiscal crisis, cutbacks in general welfare assistance and in housing assistance in particular for low-income people increased significantly in the 1980s when compared to the 1970s.

THE AFFORDABLE HOUSING CRISIS AND THE DECLINE IN SUBSIDIES

The primary [but not the ultimate] cause of homelessness in the '80's [was] the lack of low-income housing; all other causes of homelessness . . . have existed at other times in the past thirty years without bringing on a wave of mass homelessness [especially during a so-called recovery period]. A combination of two major forces [had] caused today's national housing crisis: (1) a massive federal withdrawal from public housing programs, and (2) urban "revitalization" projects that benefit only the rich and erode the stock of low-income housing (Coons, 1987: 5).

The argument developed so far has, explicitly and implicitly, maintained that the new vagrancy or new homelessness that emerged in the 1980s was due fundamentally to changes in the global and domestic economies, which produced a growing number of poor people who could not afford to pay enough in rents and mortgages, and the result was that many of them ended up homeless. As Appelbaum (1989: 6) has correctly concluded, "we are producing an economic underclass whose future growth will draw in part from what were once stable American working households"; thus contributing to shelter poverty or the inability to pay the rising nonsubsidized housing rates. Intertwined with the affordable housing crisis and the more general economic trends discussed above was the particular idea introduced at the beginning of this chapter and underscored by Harrington (1988): namely, that unequal control of investment or economic allocations of social (public) revenues causes some to reap all of the benefits and some to experience all of the costs. In other words, some of the rich and affluent become more wealthy while some of the poor and working people become homeless.

With respect to housing (and homelessness) during the past decade, there developed a condition where the production of low-income housing was no longer a profitable investment. For example, the Tax Reform Act of 1986 (H.R. 3838) "removed many of the incentives for investment in low-income housing (related to depreciation schedules, capital gains tax rates, tax credits, and so on) and placed a state-by-state limit on the volume of tax-exempt housing bonds that [could] be issued by state and local housing finance agencies" (Reamer, 1989: 6). Hence, developers could not raise the necessary capital for the production of low-income housing. Instead, capital, private and public, was being redirected upward. The outcome was that the social investments were producing condominiums, urban renewal, and gentrification—which benefitted the rich and affluent at the expense of and the detriment to the new poor, who found themselves in a position of paying more for less. More specifically, during the 1980s the existing number of publicly owned and assisted housing units was reduced significantly. Between 1981 and 1989, the number of new federally assisted housing units per year dropped from more than 200,000 to approximately 25,000. At the same time, the number of low-income housing units such as SROs dropped by more than a million as a result of abandonment, arson, demolition, and conversion to condominiums (Reamer, 1989). As a consequence of these developments, millions of poor Americans were displaced as there had been no concerted effort to replace the lost housing units for low-income people. The National Housing Law Project had estimated that during the first half of the 1980s some 2.5 million persons were displaced annually from their home (Coons, 1987).

Appelbaum (1989: 6) has argued that "this country has never had a coherent long-term federal commitment to housing" despite the goals of the 1949 Housing Act. In other words, demand for low-income housing has always been greater than market production. In the 1980s, whatever commitment may have previously existed was essentially gutted by the Reagan administration: "Between 1981 and 1989, federal expenditures for subsidized [low-income housing had] declined by four-fifths, from $32 billion to $6 billion. Total federal housing starts declined from 183,000 in 1980 to 20,000 in 1989" (Appelbaum, 1989: 7). By the end of the decade, the percentage of persons in poverty who could not obtain subsidized housing was one out of four, representing one of the smallest percentages in the industrialized world. At that time, there were at least 6–7 million low-income renting families who were receiving no housing assistance whatsoever.

During the 1980s the policies of the Reagan administration certainly exacerbated the homelessness situation by removing two supports that had historically "served to entice private investors into providing housing for poor people: subsidies which [brought] housing costs and poor peoples' income into line, and tax shelters which indirectly produc[d] the same result" (Appelbaum, 1989: 5). Without those former tax and investment incentives for the rich and the affluent, and with a reduction in direct subsidies for the poor, more and more low-income renting families were subjected to the unregulated housing markets, and more and more poor people found themselves homeless. By 1985 almost one out of four renters was paying more than half of their income on rent; by 1989 some 11 million families were paying more than one-third on rent and 5 million were paying more than half. Furthermore, by the end of the decade it was estimated that nationally there was a shortage of some 4.1 million affordable housing units for households earning under $700 per month (Appelbaum, 1989). For example, in 1989 there were about 200,000 people on the public housing waiting lists in New York City, 60,000 in Miami, 44,000 in Chicago, 23,000 in Philadelphia, and 13,000 in Washington, D.C. (Reamer, 1989).

In addition to the general trends that saw the average rents triple during the 1970s and 1980s while the average income only doubled, there were other demographic trends coupled with social spending cuts that contributed to an increase in homelessness during the 1980s. With respect to the demographic changes that emerged during the 1980s, there was the fact that the number of households was growing at a faster rate than the size of the population. In other words, as the size of living units became smaller because of an increase, for example, in the length of people's lives or in the increased frequency of divorces, the number of households had increased accordingly. Between 1980 and 1985 the number of single-person households increased dramatically from 11 to 24 percent. The outcome was that there were fewer affordable (available) rentals for low-income people. As for the impact of the federal cutbacks and related policies of the Reagan administration, close to $7 billion alone were cut from the food stamp program, and hundreds of thousands of elderly and disabled people were at least temporarily driven from the Social Security and disability rolls as a result of a combination of cuts in funding and tighter eligibility requirements. The net effect was that several million people found it more difficult to pay the rent as they had to choose between eating and shelter (Coons, 1987).

In sum, by the turn of the 1990s the policies and programs of the Department of Housing and Urban Development were reflective of an anemic national housing policy. They were also, at least, partially responsible for having decimated the stock of low-income housing as part of the orchestrated response of the capitalist state to the crises in profitability and productivity. Finally, as Appelbaum (1989: 7) has noted, "declining incomes at the bottom [had] converged with rising housing costs to produce a potentially explosive situation, which unwise short-term federal policies [had] served to worsen."

CONCLUSION

On February 19, 1990, some 500 people gathered at the northeast corner of Tompkins Square Park on Manhattan's Lower East Side to protest the practices of the "warehousers." This refers to landlords or owners of buildings who hold their apartments off the market so they can take advantage of tax breaks or big rent hikes brought about by capital improvements, or who simply demolish the old stock of low-income-generating rentals and substitute in their place new luxury structures. Eventually, the marchers made their way to South Street and the entrance to the *New York Post*, where they could be heard vigorously chanting, "Warehousing is a crime; Kalikow should be doing time." The next day, the *Post* ran a story on the homeless, but there was no mention of the homeless demonstration outside its offices the day before. In a city with some 75,000 homeless and some 75,000 warehoused apartments in the city, this seems rather odd until one learns that the *Post* "is owned by Peter Kalikow, who along with his brother has an intimate relationship to New York's housing crisis. They are among the biggest 'warehousers' in the city" (Cockburn, 1990: 334).

Warehousing has always played an important role in the political economy of capitalism. During the early emergence of capitalism, the warehousing of goods for market dominated. Those who owned the land or the buildings that stored products for market were in a position to make much money. With the rise of industrial capitalism came the warehousing of vagrants in jails and almshouses for the purposes of exploiting their free labor. In post-industrial capitalism, the warehousing of scarce space, property, and housing has joined the two traditional forms of warehousing for profit.

In 1990 as apartment buildings sit vacant, as tenants are harassed into vacating the premises, as services are cut in the areas where professionally torched buildings used to stand, and as low-profit housing is deliberately sabotaged in order to make a killing in the speculative marketplace of the cramped urban cities of the United States, the new vagrant classes of homelessness are born. Like the old vagrants who were warehoused for their cheap and hard labor, the new vagrants of today are warehoused in public and private shelters, and are busy providing similar kinds of inexpensive and hard labor as was discussed in some detail in Chapter 2. In Chapter 4 we will turn to an examination of the institutionalized forms of violence, crime, and victimization that surrounds the existence of the new homelessness.

NOTE

1. The information and data referred to in this section come from Brouwer (1988).

REFERENCES

Anderson, Charles. 1974. *The Political Economy of Social Class*. Englewood Cliffs, NJ: Prentice-Hall.

Appelbaum, Richard. 1989. "The Affordability Gap." *Social Science and Modern Society*, 26, no. 4 (May/June).

Batra, R. 1987. *The Great Depression of 1990*. New York: Simon and Schuster.

Berberoglu, B. 1987. "Labor, Capital, and the State: Economic Crisis and Class Struggle in the United States in the 1970s and the 1980s." Paper presented at the annual meetings of the American Sociological Association, Chicago.

Blau, Joel S. 1987. The Homeless of New York: A Case Study in Social Welfare Policy." Doctoral Dissertation. Ann Arbor, MI: University Microfilms International (1989).

Bottomore, Tom, Ed. 1983. *A Dictionary of Marxist Thought*. Cambridge, MA.: Harvard University Press.

Brouwer, Steve. 1988. *Sharing the Pie: A Disturbing Picture of the U.S. Economy in the 1980s*. Carlisle, PA.: Big Picture Books.

Cockburn, Alexander. 1990. "From 'Where House?' to Warehouse." *The Nation*, March 12.

Coons, Chris. 1987. "The Causes and History of Homelessness." In *Resources Guide: The National Teach-in on Homelessness*. New Haven, CT: Student Homeless Action Campaign.

Devine, Deborah Judith. 1988. "Homelessness and the Social Safety Net." Doctoral Dissertation. Ann Arbor: University Microfilms International (1989).

Economic Report. 1987. *Economic Report of the President, 1986*. Statistical Abstracts of the United States.

Gold, David, Clarence Y. H. Lo, and Erick Olin Wright. 1975. "Recent Development in Marxist Theories of the Capitalist State, Part 2." *Monthly Review*, 27 (November).

Harrington, Michael. 1988. "Socialists Help Shape the Best in Our Politics." *In These Times*, February 24–March 8.

Hopper, Kim James. 1987. "A Bed for the Night: Homeless Men in New York City, Past and Present." Doctoral Dissertation. Ann Arbor, MI: University Microfilms International (1989).

Janowitz, Morris. 1976. *Social Control of the Welfare State*. New York: Elsevier.

In These Times. 1988. Editorial, "Scientists' Homelessness Report is a Welcome Step," September 28–October 4.

Mandel, E. 1980. *The Second Slump*. London: Verse.

O'Conner, James. 1973. *The Fiscal Crisis of the State*. New York: St. Martin's Press.

Petras, James. 1990. "The Political Contradictions of Progress and Democracy." *In These Times*, February 21–27.

Piven, Frances Fox and Richard A. Cloward. 1971. *Regulating the Poor: The Functions of Public Welfare*. New York: Vintage Books.

Quinney, Richard. 1980. *Class, State, and Crime*, 2nd ed. New York: Longman.

Reamer, Frederic. 1989. "The Affordable Housing Crisis and Social Work." *Social Work*, January.

Redburn, F. Stevens and Terry F. Buss. 1986. *Responding to America's Homeless: Public Policy Alternatives*. New York: Praeger.

Sherman, H. 1976. *Stagflation*. New York: Harper and Row.

Spitzer, Steven. 1975. "Towards a Marxian Theory of Deviance." *Social Problems*, 22, no. 5.

Wilber, Charles, Ed. 1973. *The Political Economy of Development and Underdevelopment*. New York: Random House.

Wilensky, Harold L. 1975. *The Welfare State and Equality: Structural and Ideological Roots of Public Expenditures*. Berkeley: University of California Press.

4 The Crime of Homelessness Versus the Crimes of the Homeless

According to New York City transit authority police, on December 22, 1989, one homeless man stabbed another to death in a subway station, apparently to protect a turkey leg ("Man Killed," 1989: 2A). While hardly a frequent or even a typical event, such a homicide is, nevertheless, not an isolated act of violence associated with homeless living on the streets of urban America. More typical of the relatively few homicides, and of the kinds of violence and potential dangers facing those who survive at the margins of U.S. society, was the gruesome murder of the female prostitute briefly depicted at the beginning of the 1990 film, *Pretty Woman*. That tragic death, however, was mitigated, if not totally dismissed, in the movie by the fact that the victim was a crack head. This somehow implied that she got what she deserved. After all, she chose a life of drugs and prostitution on Hollywood's Sunset Strip.

Adolescent prostitutes, male and female, who number in the tens of thousands in this country, live with a constant fear of violence, as do other homeless people. This is especially true for women of all ages who either live on or work on the streets. For most homeless people, they are not volunteers who have elected to live a free and frightening life-style, subject to a variety of horrors that can be found on the urban (and to a lesser extent on the rural) landscapes of homelessness.

Yet, Michael Novak, a scholar at the American Enterprise Institute, a Washington, D.C.-based conservative think tank, could be heard claiming in early 1989 that homelessness was a misnomer because "a lot of these people have homes or a place to live," and they are simply looking for a free handout. In other words, he argued that homelessness should really refer "to people who are publicly dependent." He went on to explain that "stirring up compassion for the homeless" was wrong because it made "homelessness acceptable, thus it expands" (Corn and Morely, 1989: 296). This kind of reasoning and understanding of the conditions of destitution and homelessness are as old as capitalism itself, at least as far back as the time when the foreclosure movements first set the serfs free during the transition from an agriculturally based political economy to a commercially based political economy. The Michael Novaks of the world have been seriously deprived when it comes to appreciating the reality of what life is really like for people who are barely surviving at the margins, particularly those unfortunate folks living in the alleyways and subways of urban filth. As Gil (1989) has correctly argued, there has generally been a tendency to cover up the underlying dynamics of violence, the result of almost exclusively focusing attention on the counterviolence of violated individuals and groups. While such fragmented studies may serve the interests of the privileged and dominant social classes, Gil says that they also deny by implication the causal dynamics of societal violence. In the process, individuals and oppressed groups are used as scapegoats to help obscure the more fundamental need for structural changes toward nonviolent institutions. In short, homeless people of the early 1990s are vulnerable to all types of violence—physical, emotional, and psychological. These crimes of violence are far too numerous to count. Accordingly, Gil maintains that attention be focused on the developmental needs of these violated people.

The origins of today's crimes against the homeless, as well as the crime of homelessness itself, are rooted in the public policies and institutional orders of the developing political economy. Regarding the specific dangers of physical violence, for example, Chapter 3 has already implied that the roots of violence associated with homelessness, crack addiction, and crime in the streets are related. Each can be explained by its interrelated connectedness to the public and private policies of our country's own sociohistorically specific expression of welfare capitalism and the free-enterprise state.

THE VIOLENCE OF HOMELESSNESS IN AMERICA

Whether we are examining Los Angeles, Philadelphia, San Francisco, Chicago, Atlanta, Austin, Washington, D.C., New York City, Las Vegas, or most other metropolitan areas across the United States, there is coming into clearer and clearer focus a picture of the intensification of U.S. urban violence and decay. The growing abuse experienced by more and more people in this country, especially by women and children, homeless and homeful, reflects upon the multitude of separate and yet overlapping spheres of public and private behavior. This section attempts to provide a characterization, but by no means an exhaustive treatment, of the violence of homelessness in the United States. It is included, among other reasons, for two purposes: to underscore the seriousness of the crime of homelessness; and to begin establishing the framework for the discussion of the crime of homelessness versus the crimes of the homeless, which comes later in the chapter.

Only the brave, the desperate and the unwary use the public bathrooms at the Port Authority Bus Terminal in New York. For a commuter on his way home to New Jersey, a stop at the second-floor men's room in the main concourse can be an adventure only slightly less scary than a visit to the Tatooine bar in *Star Wars*. Around the urinals, unshaven men in overcoats linger over cigarettes, adding smoke to the pungent aroma of disinfectant and diesel fumes that permeates the building. In the stalls, voices argue over sex and drug transactions. By the exit doors, vials of crack are exchanged during prolonged handshakes. In the far corner, a teenager curses as he burns his finger heating up a piece of "rock" with a glass pipe. "I'll do you for a nickel, mister," whispers a Hispanic boy who looks about 12, offering himself for $5 (Hackett and McKillop, 1989: 22).

At the New York Port Authority bus station—where on any given day 6,800 buses carrying 200,000 passengers to and from the corners at 42nd Street and Eighth Avenue occur—these suburban commuters come face to face with New York City's unwanted homeless. While the homeless look for warmth, they become both victims and predators. For example, crime in the terminal reached unprecedented levels in 1988 when reported crime was up 44 percent compared to the year before: 5,663 to 3,935 cases. The number of arrests increased 115 percent, up to 5,081 from 2,366. Although most of these crimes were of a petty nature and most of the arrests were for minor offenses involving snatched bags, lifted wallets, and stolen luggage, both policing and living day-to-day beneath the streets of New York City has become more dangerous owing to the boom in crack and the heavily armed drug dealers smuggling cocaine on long-haul buses. In 1988 the terminal police reported 478 robberies, 45 rapes or sexual assaults, 214 weapons charges, and 479 car break-ins (Hackett and McKillop, 1989).

When it comes to violent felonies, most of those assaulted are, to quote the terminal police, victims of "garbage on garbage" crime. That is to say, lowlifes beating up and raping other lowlifes:

Last year a vagrant was discovered with his throat slashed from ear to ear. A man once doused someone with gasoline, lit a butane lighter and threatened to burn him unless he turned over his money. Officer Jim Guinto recalls encountering a man raping a one-legged woman, already in a coma from multiple assaults. She died soon after. Police say another homeless person, "Tammy," who is mentally retarded, has been raped at least 12 times (Hackett and McKillop, 1989: 24).

For the down and out homeless whose only crimes are those of destitution, they live in constant fear of periodic attacks on their personhood. These individuals receive little sympathy from either the Port Authority officials or the general public, especially when these homeless victims may, in fact, also be selling sex for drug money or shelter. As Ernesto Butcher, assistant director of operations for the Port Authority of New York and New Jersey, so bluntly phrased it, "when does failure to pay become rape?" (Hackett and McKillop, 1989: 24).

When the terminal closes at 1 A.M., some of the homeless head for the emergency stairwells where the potential for their victimization increases even further. Inside the stairwells, "the stench of feces and unclean bodies is overwhelming. Clusters of people hang out on the stair landings, grimy concrete slabs littered with crack vials, butane lighters, spoiled food, dirty matresses, old clothes and used condoms" (Hackett and McKillop, 1989: 24). Many of these "throwaways," as they have been referred to since the late 1970s, are mere children and adolescents escaping family situations where life on the streets may, in fact, be an improvement over their previous abuse or neglect.

It seems that even in San Francisco, where compassion for the down-trodden has a long history, the homeless have already begun to experience the city as a dangerous place to live. For example, in 1988 the homeless death toll in San Francisco reached an all-time yearly high of 116 people. These figures referred to those people who died in autos, trucks, alleyways, parks, hospitals, or emergency shelters. In addition, there were an esti-mated 75 unconfirmed homeless deaths that occurred through November of that year, bringing the total to close to 200 for the year (Safety Network, 1989a: 1).

The *Tenderloin Times*, which conducted a study of the situation in 1988, had also attempted to find the number of homeless deaths for 1987. The year before its count was 69 deaths. In terms of the violence toward or victimization of the homeless people dying in San Francisco, the 1988 home-less death rate was 58 percent higher than that for the city's general pop-ulation. With respect to 103 (of the 116) whose deaths had been reported to the coroner's office by the time of the study's release, the breakdown for the city's 6,000 homeless persons was:

- 47 percent (48 people) died outside on the streets, in alleyways, under freeway overpasses, or on park benches;
- 28 percent (25 people) died of substance abuse;
- 18 percent (16 people) were murdered;
- 10 percent (10 people) died in vehicles that they called home (Safety Network, 1989a: 1).

In Washington, D.C., where the contemporary War on Drugs formerly led by William Bennett, the first federally appointed "drug czar," had de-clared in 1989 that the nation's capital was to be the first "high-intensity drug trafficking area," the crime emergency and siege mentality went into effect. The City Council, not to be outdone, passed legislation that denied bail to drug dealers and put a curfew on youths under 18. Nevertheless, drug-related violence in Washington continued to increase and foreshadowed what will probably follow in most big U.S. cities should the government not abandon its law enforcement approach to what is first and foremost a social, political, and economic problem.

Take the situation on the 1300 block on Park Road N.W., not far from the White House, where a 24-hour, open-air drug market contributes significantly to a district homicide explosion that "as of April 4, [1989] stood at 129, compared with 83 a year earlier" (Tidwell, 1989: 16). A few blocks away on Park Road the D.C. Coalition for the Homeless runs a transitional house for some of the city's 10,000 homeless. Surrounded by crack houses, boarded-up apartment buildings, and the ramshackle tenements that still remain, this transitional house serves predominantly black men in their 20s and 30s, half of whom have been made homeless by addiction to crack cocaine. Counselor and manager of this transitional house for the homeless, Mike Tidwell (1989: 16), has described the violence plaguing one of many neighborhoods this way: "At night we lock the front door of our facility and listen to the police sirens outside, the angry drug disputes, the macabre screams, the crackle of gunfire."

During the day when these ex-addicts try to traverse the neighborhood to attend Narcotics Anonymous meetings or go to their new jobs, they are approached a half dozen times to buy crack before they reach the bus stop. As disturbing as the thought of the sale of cocaine at corner drugstores or hospitals might be, Tidwell rightly understands that the alternatives of declaring martial war in our inner cities or the permitting of the present drug-induced violence are not only more disturbing, but are highly counterproductive. To put it simply, the War on Drugs merely escalates the violence all around, engulfing the daily arrangements of this nation's homeless populations as they reside unprotected, whether they are sheltered or not, from the festering urban battlefields of the nation.

Another group of the homeless who have been particularly vulnerable, and who are likely in the not too distant future to become more susceptible to the violence of homelessness, are those with AIDS. Finding shelter for those persons afflicted with acquired immune deficiency syndrome has been very difficult because " 'no community wants to house these folks,' said Margaret Nichols, executive director of the Hyacinth Foundation, which offers AIDS support services in New Jersey" (Ryckman, 1987: 10B). Most AIDS sufferers are not so lucky and there are many advocates for the homeless, such as Robert Hayes, who have been predicting that by the early 1990s we will be witnessing the dumping of people with AIDS from hospitals onto the streets very much like in the 1970s when institutions for the mentally ill were doing the same. Homeless individuals with AIDS who try to reside in community shelters often find themselves subjected to various forms of harassment and violence by other homeless people who through ignorance are afraid of contracting the dreaded disease.

In the supplementary statement to the 1988 report of the Institute of Medicine's Committee on Health Care for Homeless, the essence of the violent nature of the homelessness situation was captured quite succinctly and serves as a fitting close for this section:

As we witnessed the suffering of America's poorest citizens, we came to understand that the individual health care problems of homeless people combine to form a major public health crisis. We can no longer sit as spectators to the elderly homeless dying of hypothermia, to the children with blighted futures poisoned by lead in rat-infested dilapidated welfare hotels, to women raped, to old men beaten and robbed of their few possessions, and to people dying on the streets with catastrophic illnesses such as AIDS. Without eliminating homelessness, the health risks and concomitant health problems, the desperate plight of homeless children, the suffering, and the needless deaths of homeless Americans will continue (Vladeck, 1988: 87).

CRIMINALIZING THE HOMELESS

Societies whose violent policies and practices give rise to counter-violence on the part of violated individuals and groups tend to respond by disregarding the actual causes, "blaming the victims," and steadily increasing repressive violence. The tragic, vicious circle of societal violence, counter-violence, and repressive violence will continue as long as its roots, systemic societal obstacles to human development as an aspect of the normal workings of everyday life, are not acknowledged and transcended within and among societies and nations (Gil, 1989: 41).

Although the U.S. Supreme Court threw out vagrancy laws years ago, loitering is still decided on a state-by-state basis. If the homeless are aggressively panhandling, committing a crime, or urinating in a doorway, then it is the feeling of a lot of people that the police should have the right to intervene. It also appears that in the not too distant future many homeless people will be viewed by more and more folks as some kind of "dreaded cultural entity" not unlike the inhabitants of yesteryears' penal colonies or madhouses (Hopper, 1987). This view, it can be argued, is consistent with those ideological justifications such as "you get what you deserve," which serves to undermine "justice for all," while it helps to legitimate injustice for a growing number of poor and homeless people in the United States. Already one can discern an emerging backlash in the struggle against homelessness and in the victimization of hundreds of thousands of men, women, and children daily in this country: "Although public sympathy has run high for the homeless, as indicated by polls, there have been signs of frustration and after years of work and billions spent, the homeless reappear everyday on corners" (Sullivan, 1990: 9B). In those cities across the country with significant homeless populations, for example, business owners can be heard complaining about the physical presence of the homeless vagrants panhandling on virtually every city block where commerce and services exist. In Atlanta, a group of business executives and civic leaders have proposed a "safeguard zone" to enforce "quality of life" crime ordinances in order to "provide significant control of the movement of street persons, transients, hangers-on, loiters and the street vendors" (Frazier, 1987). Opponents of the proposal had labeled such a legal idea as the "vagrant-free zone."

A number of cities such as Minneapolis and Tulsa have passed ordinances regulating panhandling. Other recently passed local laws against homelessness include those acts forbidding loitering and those that establish curfews in the cities and the parks. In Las Vegas, homeless men have even been arrested for the crime of "soliciting employment" (Safety Network, 1989a: 4). In Miami, where the police arrest their homeless residents for sleeping, eating, bathing, and congregating in public, the city successfully defended a lawsuit attempting to prevent the police from engaging in the annual, pre-Orange Bowl sweeps and mass arrests. The city maintained that it has a "legitimate interest in clearing the public streets of this 'small element of unfortunate persons' to 'protect the desires and needs of the greater mass of society who choose to attend public events in a lawful manner" (Safety Network: 1989b: 1). In Los Angeles in 1987, after bulldozers leveled a downtown tent city of the homeless known as the Dust Bowl Hilton, and the police began to enforce the city ordinances against sleeping on the sidewalks, Jennifer Wolch, an associate professor of urban planning at the University of Southern California and coauthor of a book about the mentally ill homeless, noted appropriately that "the homeless are increasingly being diverted to jails and to institutions. It's a very serious situation" (Gelman, 1987: 48).

Here is an example of the specific crimes or laws frequently used against the homeless in San Francisco:

CALIFORNIA PENAL CODE

Section

148	Resisting/DelayingPolice Officer	Misdemeanor
647 (c)	Begging—Disorderly Conduct	Misdemeanor
647 (f)	Drunk in Public—Disorderly Conduct	Misdemeanor
647 (c)	Obstructing Sidewalks/Streets	Misdemeanor

SAN FRANCISCO PARK CODE

Section

3.12	No camping	Misdemeanor/Infraction
3.13	No sleeping—10 to 6	Misdemeanor/Infraction
601(g)	No parking—10 to 6	Misdemeanor/Infraction

As Robert Hayes (1989:56), legal counsel for the National Coalition for the Homeless, has been quoted as saying: "You can outlaw panhandling and stop homeless people sleeping in public parks, but there aren't enough troops in the Western world to stop human beings from doing what they must do to survive." The points being, thus far in this chapter, that the condition of homelessness is not only fraught with all kinds of victimization and crimin- alization, but that the very condition itself is criminogenic or crime-pro- ducing. In other words, the "natural" expression of homelessness includes, but cannot be reduced to, a multitude of violent and victimizing acts, engaged in by both the homeful and the homeless. As for the future, who knows what that first generation of adults will be like who grew up from birth in a state of one homeless accommodation to the next?

President Bush may have called homelessness a "national tragedy" and Anna Kondratas, assistant secretary of HUD, may have stated that "the administration is committed to ending homelessness," even going as far as to promise that they were "prepared to do what it takes to get the homeless into permanent housing and to get them the kind of services they need to stay in that housing" (Sullivan, 1990: 9B). But the rhetoric of President Bush and his administration has far exceeded the actions of their proposed budgets for the homeless, for services, and for low-income housing. In fact, the proposed monies have fallen so short of the mark, that one news story headline that appeared in the *Montgomery Advertiser* on March 25, 1990, expressed it this way: "Help for the homeless 'a thousand points of hype.' "

As it has been pointed out elsewhere, "the notion of 'economies of make- shift,' developed by Olwen Hufton to describe subsistence strategies of the 18th century poor of France . . . , can be profitably applied to contemporary homeless practice" (Hopper et al., 1985: 213). The practices of the "economy of makeshifts" employed by the poor of France included:

an extra job, seasonal migration, turning the children out to beg, involvement in some seminefarious practice such as smuggling [or prostitution]. These makeshifts, or accumulations of innumerable forms of subsidiary income or means whereby the family did not have to support some of its members, were built up gradually . . . it took time and experience to learn to live in this way, and there were those for whom the expedients were far from adequate (quoted in Hopper et al., 1985: 213).

Sutherland and Locke (1936), in their study of 20,000 homeless men living in Chicago shelters during the Great Depression, found that there were five basic criminal and semicriminal activities or vices engaged in: petty larceny or stealing inside and outside of the shelter facilities, drinking, gambling, irregular sex practices, and begging. All of these activities helped to secure the necessary funds for survival, including the purchasing of alcohol, sex, and food. In 1985, Hopper et al. (p. 214) identified four essential charac- teristics of the modern-day economies of makeshift: "their strictly ad hoc character; mobility; resort to public relief, parochial charity or begging; and participation in the underground economy."

In their discussion of the homeless, Hopper et al. (p. 214) underscore the point that "what is distinctive about this homelessness is less the fact that it is resorted to under compulsion, or even the specific set of precipitating events that constitute the compelling forces, than it is the particular way homelessness meshes with other subsistence activities." Sutherland and Locke some 50 years earlier referred to "the process of shelterization" as a way of describing this phenomena. What these authors have all tried to represent was the way in which homelessness can become an institution-alized way of existence. In other words, "for those people for whom sub-sistence is a puzzle pieced together in highly irregular ways, periodic homelessness may be an expected part of a generally uncertain mode of livelihood" (Hopper et al., 1985: 214), and "shelterization" may be, in fact, an "adaptation not only to the shelters but to the total situation in which a man finds himself" (Sutherland and Locke, 1936: 144). Homelessness thus becomes an adopted life-style by the homeless, a way of managing under duress, reorganization of one's attitudes and values, and finally, a change of status or identity.

While the type of psychological, emotional, and physical victimization experienced by the homelessness condition is often accompanied by feelings of inadequacy and personal disgrace, leading to questions of self-worth and doubt, many homeless people still resist the shelterization process. In other words, not all homeless people, whether sheltered or not, will inevitably undergo a disintegration of their previous attitudes, modes of thought, and standards of conduct. Some personalities will become reorganized, some will not. But all homeless people dealing with the crisis of homelessness will to varying degrees engage in maneuvering their environments. As Hopper et al. (1985) have defined the situation, homelessness implies both need and response. For example, "displacement and the inability to find replacement housing may well be predicaments over which one has little control. But being homeless—and especially being homeless repeatedly—takes effort and work. It requires collaboration with circumstance" (Hopper et al., 1985: 215).

With the growing tendency to criminalize the homeless, even in an area like San Francisco where the Police Commission issued in November 1988 a "resolution that directed the department's officers to respect the legal and individual rights of the homeless, regardless of their appearance or of com-plaints by residents and merchants" (Evans, 1989: 3), a survey conducted earlier in the year by the Civil Rights Committee of the Coalition of Home-lessness revealed the extent to which police harassment of homeless people was a problem. Disregarding the fact that the questions responded to were not particularly "sound" and "free of bias," they still serve as a rough indicator of the criminalization process of the homeless that has occurred. Out of 284 informally surveyed homeless who were asked to "please mark whether the following has happened to you in San Francisco or you have personally seen it happen to someone else," the more "significant" findings are shown in Table 13.

In the end the products of homelessness and shelterization typically culminate either in defeatism or contentment. More rare are those homeless persons who do not accept their situation quietly, and who continue to rebel against the system in general and the shelter organizations in particular. This expression of defiance was captured nicely in one of the interviews quoted in Sutherland and Locke (1936: 162) and can still be heard in most shelters on any day of the week in the 1990s:

The shelters are like jails to us. If they gave the grub to the inmates of the penitentiaries what they give us here, they would burn the place down. And if we had any guts or organization we would burn these places down. Look at those damn bars. They're worse than a jail. In here they crowd us, and crush us, and boss us, and watch us, and make us stand in line for everything. They treat us as slaves and dogs, certainly not as men.

In the next section, the general description of criminalization and victimization becomes more specific as the relationship between domestic violence, homelessness, and adolescent prostitution is explored in some detail.

HOMELESSNESS AND VICTIMIZATION: THE CASE OF DOMESTIC VIOLENCE AND ADOLESCENT PROSTITUTION

The violent nature of homelessness and the victimization of the homeless are captured in the experiences of those persons who had previously endured lives of poverty, domestic abuse, or neglect, only eventually to escape into the world of homelessness. Women and children are the primary victims here. Abused first by their families, and second by the system's agents of social control (e.g., police, social workers), these homeless victims are typically regarded as "deviant (if not criminal) by virtue of their lack of economic and emotional dependence upon a male" (Cook, 1987: 28). Finally, for example, the proverbial "shopping bag ladies" or those women who are "vagrants," "urban transient females," or simply "homeless women," and who according to Webster's dictionary, at least temporarily, are without established residence, wander idly from place to place, and are without lawful or visible means of support, come to experience personal violence as a normative arrangement of their day-to-day existence. In one study, Coston (1988) interviewed 104 of New York City's shopping bag ladies in the main bag-lady territory (between 30th and 52nd streets) in Manhattan. She found that 94 percent of the women interviewed admitted to being criminally victimized; she also found that "eighty-two percent of these women suffered two or more of these types of victimization [e.g., rape, attempted rape, robbery, and theft] in one criminal incident" (Coston, 1988: 30).

Table 13
Police Harassment of Homeless in San Francisco

	YES
Order to "move along" when you were doing nothing wrong?	274, 96%
Told to produce identification when you were doing nothing wrong?	264, 93%
Treated with discourtesy by a police officer?	246, 87%
Had your body or clothes searched for no reason?	229, 81%
Had your belongings or possessions searched for no reasons?	225, 79%
Arrested/cited or threatened with arrest for "loitering"?	199, 70%
Had a police officer refuse to respond to or investigate a crime you reported?	176, 62%
Arrested/cited or threatened with arrest for "vagrancy"?	169, 60%
Had a police officer refuse to protect you from violence?	151, 53%
Falsely arrested/cited for "obstructing or blocking the sidewalks and streets" when you had not "blocked" anyone?	148, 52%
Physically beaten or brutalized by a police officer?	143, 50%
Falsely arrested/cited for "sleeping in a vehicle at night" or "camping in public"?	118, 42%
Falsely arrested/cited for "begging" or "panhandling" when you were not begging overly aggressively?	116, 41%
Arrested for "sleeping in public or in the park during the daytime"?	97, 34%

Bard (1988) found that marital victimization or the domestic abuse of women and female homelessness could be directly correlated. In effect, homeless women were often double victims—victims of criminal and psychological battering and victims of a system that functions to sustain and help reproduce patriarchy. In testing the relationship between domestic abuse and homelessness, Bard's analysis revealed that the prevailing guidelines connected to the prosecution of batterers had hampered appropriate attention to victims' immediate and future needs. In turn, she argued that the inadequacies of the system's response to domestic violence often resulted in increased domestic abuse or indigency and homelessness.

Of course, the type of violence that victims of domestic abuse or homelessness experience is not confined to physical pain, but also includes the psychological pain associated with constant denigration, humiliation, neglect, or social and economic isolation. Typically, those commonly identified victimization correlates that allow the battering to continue are: an escalation of the violence in cyclical fashion, often resulting in the death of the woman or in the woman killing her assailant; the immediate physical and emotional strain suffered by the children and the reproduction of their parents' behavioral patterns as adults; and an increase in the usage of alcohol, drugs, and pregnancy (Taub, 1983). As Bard (1988: 28–29) has noted, there were many other significant consequences of battering reported by the victims that she interviewed that are generally ignored or deemed irrelevant to the understanding of homelessness. She specifically cited posttrauma physical illness, supranormal experiences, food and sleep disorders, disorientation, phobias, victimization by particular individuals/systems/states, and recidivism. Moreover, battered women and homeless women alike often blame themselves for their victimization, incorporating the dominant norms and expectations of society, that one way or the other serve to provide scapegoats to explain the criminal behavior in the case of the battered victim and to explain the injustice in the case of the homeless person. In both scenarios, or syndrome-oriented pathological views, there emerge mitigating factors brought to bear even with respect to the most aggravating circumstances associated with battering or homelessness.

Hence, these homeless victims of the state in general and of the criminal justice and welfare systems in particular have recently been viewed by critical victimologists (Viano, 1976; 1983; Elias, 1986; Barak and Bohm, 1989; Barak, 1991b) as belonging to a larger group of human rights abuse victims that have been traditionally omitted from consideration as victims. These authors do not merely refer to the more obvious victims of commission, but to the less obvious victims of omission (Henry, 1991; Barak, 1991a). As Viano (1983: 25) has argued, the problem has been that both society at large and even victimologists "have preferred the most common, less controversial, more obvious, more easily explicable definitions of who the victims are and who may be a victim." The time, in other words, is past due for acknowledging that the homeless are in fact victims of the crime of homelessness, which mandates that more and more people must live according to "economies of makeshift" or marginality.

Finally, while it is far more common for the media, intellectuals, and the general public to focus attention on the real crimes by and against the homeless, an increasing number of victimologists can be heard talking about assaults or attacks on one's personhood. With respect to the victimization of personhood, Jonsen (1987: 3) has written:

It is of very little interest to me to be alive as an organism. In such a state, I have no interests literally. It is enormously interesting for me to be a person, with my history, with my place in life, doing the things I enjoy doing, loving those I love, causing the problems I like to cause. I live my life. It is the perpetuation of my personhood that interests me.

Although most homeless persons are preoccuppied with survival or the maintenance of life, the relationship between homelessness, victimization, and self-image, on the one hand, and the maintenance of personhood, on the other hand, is subject to normal variation. Bard (1988: 52), for example, has concluded that the victims of homelessness can be located on a continuum with respect to self-image and identification:

(1) there are individuals who identify themselves immediately as a "victim" . . . ; (2) there are individuals who tell a tale about circumstances which are clearly a process of victimization to an audience, but who do not identify as a "victim" . . . ; and (3) there are those who express prior victimization, but reject a current identity as "victim," considering the label negative to their self-image, and insist that they are "survivors."

Such a typology of victimization appears to have value when it comes to the examination of the reality of the victims of homelessness and adolescent prostitution.

One 15-year-old runaway told his story to Garbarino, Wilson, and Garbarino (1986: 41):

Yeah, I ran. I ran to get away from that house and the people in it. I wanted to be on my own without all the hassles. . . . Yeah, right so I ended up on the street. No job because I was too young; no place to stay because I didn't have any money. So when this dude approached me I went with him. . . . You know the rest of the story.

In her study of adolescent prostitution and its relationship to homelessness, Werfel (1985) concluded that these teenage prostitutes, female and male, did not like business sex, felt that prostitution had negatively affected their lives, and did not wish to remain prostitutes. These runaways or throwaways prostituted as a way of making money, whether they resided in shelters or had other living arrangements. However, like other victims of domestic abuse who have ended up homeless, these victims sell sexual services in return for money or drugs or both, and are often portrayed by scholars and the media as "amoral (slut), opportunistic (happy hooker), and underworld angel (the goldenhearted), social and sexual deviants, delinquents, mentally incompetent" (Werfel, 1985: 2).

Like homelessness, adolescent prostitution is widespread and can be found in most urban metropolitan cities in this country. In the United States it was not until the 1970s that adolescent prostitution was recognized as a serious social problem (Weisberg, 1985; Miller, 1986). By the 1980s there appears to have been a significant increase in the number of adolescent prostitutes nationwide, with estimates ranging from 90,000 to 900,000 (General Accounting Office, 1982). The parallels in the rising number of homeless and the rising number of teenage prostitutes, while not necessarily directly related, do suggest a common structural deterioration in the stability of a growing number of families. In particular, most of these homeless adolescents come from troubled families:

Houghten and Golembiewski concluded that more than 89% of all "serious" runaways flee serious family problems, particularly abuse and alcoholism. Gutierres and Reich indicated that a violent home life created stresses that led to runaway behavior. Farber and Kinast, in their study, found that three-fourths of those who ran reported having been subjected to severe maltreatment in the year prior to their runaway behavior. . . . An HEW report estimated that mistreatment figured in one-third to one-half the cases of running away served by agencies. Many "throwaways" report incestual or abuse problems as the major cause of leaving home. (Garbarino et al., 1986: 47).

Moreover, as Garbarino et al. (p. 47) have argued, when "we move from considering running away as an *effect* of adolescent troubles to running away as a *cause* of adolescent troubles, we encounter a pattern of developmentally disastrous victimization" in combination with "the deficits in social competence and self-esteem . . . as correlates of running will tend to make an adolescent particularly vulnerable to the psychological threats of life on the streets."

Without adequate financial resources to meet their basic needs, homeless youth become prime targets for recruitment into the illicit or underground economy of drug dealing, hustling, and prostituting/pornographing. Pimps are perhaps the most notorious exploiters of runaway youth, offering housing, food, cash, and even emotional support. Participation in the sex industry, of course, runs the added risks of being raped, assaulted, incarcerated, or merely harassed and subjected to a number of other denigrating experiences. Eventually, a lot of homeless prostitutes become assimilated into the life of prostitution and into identifying as a prostitute. While prostituting, these homeless victims "will typically encounter violence, substance abuse, physical and sexual abuse, and physical and mental health problems" (Werfel, 1985: 65). While both female and male adolescent prostitutes often become extremely dependent on their abusive pimps and sugar daddies, there are some significant gender-related differences. The male prostitutes tend to link into relationships where the dependency and abuse are generally mutual.

By contrast, the female prostitutes tend to be more isolated than the male prostitutes (who seem to have more of a esprit de corps or camaraderie). The females, especially those who work the streets, tend to be less supportive of one another and more competitive than the males. They also tend to experience greater victimization, abuse, and violence than their male counterparts (Werfel, 1985). With or without support, most adolescent, homeless prostitutes find themselves struggling with all of the typical problems of survival. During the course of their struggle, they usually become depressed, alienated, lonely, and frightened. As time wears on, adolescent prostitutes increasingly feel guilty and ashamed of their involvement in prostitution, find their customers to be revolting, and often hold intense feelings of anger and rage toward them (Werfel, 1985).

What Werfel (159) concluded about the adolescent prostitutes of her study is also true of homeless people in general; they are not "asocial, anti-social, sexually deviant" individuals, but are generally similar to other youths in "their morals, values, hopes, dreams and feelings." This is not to argue, as Werfel has pointed out, that self-destructive behavior and lack of self-confidence characteristic of homeless prostitutes does not lead to the usage of drugs and alcohol as a means of suppressing or denying feelings about oneself and others. Nor does such an analysis suggest that those individuals who may already be suffering from mental illness, alcoholism, or drug addiction are not particularly vulnerable to street victimization in all of its various forms. They most definitely are.

In summing up this section, it should be kept in mind that the homelessness associated with domestic violence and adolescent prostitution is not reflective of aberrant behavior per se. Instead this abusive behavior is normative to the extent that it has been both socially supported and institutionally reproduced. In short, these relationships should represent a devastating indictment against our prevailing political and economic arrangements because the opportunities to participate in such activities have been essentially rationalized by the predatory and exploitative aspects of "legitimate" society (Garbarino et al., 1986).

THE CRIMES OF THE HOMELESS: A COMPARATIVE ASSESSMENT

September 1988–Pittsburgh. "Robert W. T'Souvas died a bum, a homeless 39-year-old man shot in the head after arguing over a bottle of vodka under a downtown

bridge" (Associated Press, 1988: 1A). Arrested and charged with the criminal homicide was Kathleen T'Souvas, who was described by Robert's father as more of a
drinking buddy than a wife.

January 1989—New York City. "A homeless man [Steven Smith, 23] was arrested
Monday in the strangulation and rape of a pregnant pathologist in her city hospital
office" (Associated Press, 1989a: 9A). Prior to Smith's arrest, Mayor Koch had referred
to the murder of Dr. Kathryn Hinnant as "the No. 1 case to be solved" and the city
offered a $30,000 reward for any information about the slaying.

December 1989—San Fernando, CA. "Richard Froio, 50, launched his own campaign to uncover the truth about the death of his son, Rocco Froio, 32, an alcoholic
who lived on the streets" (Associated Press, 1989b: 3A). Because of the diligent work
of Rocco's father, police were able to obtain enough information to arrest John Bard,
37, a transient, for the murder.

While these types of murders involving the homeless may be captured in
print news stories, they are not particularly representative of the types of
criminality engaged in by homeless people. More typical of their petty types
of crime was a print news story from Montgomery, Alabama, in September
1989: "Police were called to the school at 2048 W. Fairview Avenue at 10:50
A.M. after officials reported a vagrant had entered the girl's bathroom. The
suspect was identified as Jimmy DeJarnette, 41, address unknown. "He was
charged with third-degree criminal mischief and placed in the city jail" (Staff
Reports, 1989: 2B). The arrest of DeJarnette or the majority of arrests of
other homeless people are for such minor offenses as public intoxication,
theft-shoplifting, violation of city ordinances, and burglary (Baumann et al.,
1985; Robertson et al., 1985; Aulette and Aulette, 1987; Snow et al., 1989).
From self-studies of the homeless we know that a high proportion (17 to 67
percent) of the homeless have been arrested and jailed (Redburn and Buss,
1986; Rossi et al., 1987; Lee, 1989).

The point is that any depiction of homeless men or women as serious
predatory criminals is far from accurate. Moreover, the fears often articulated
by citizens, especially those who are concerned about the possibility of a
homeless shelter being located in their neighborhoods, were captured in
one southwestern Texas city where opponents of a Salvation Army relocation
maintained that " 'thousands of womanless, homeless men' would inundate
their neighborhoods, 'rob their homes,' and 'rape the women' " (Snow et
al., 1989: 532).

Snow, Baker, and Anderson (1989) were the first to empirically investigate
the relationship between homelessness and crime. More specifically, they
compared the criminality of homeless and nonhomeless (homeful) men in
Austin, Texas, from January 1, 1983 to March 31, 1985. In terms of generalizing from their sample, while one should be cautious, their sample
demographically speaking was similar to homeless populations in other cities.
Analysis of their data yielded two significant sets of findings.

First, comparison of both actual arrests and age standardized arrest rates for the homeless and their domiciled counterparts revealed that while the homeless show a higher arrest rate, the majority of their arrests are non-violent, relatively minor, and victimless offenses. The second set of findings pertain to the distribution of crime among the homeless. They show that crimes, as measured by actual arrests, are committed more often by those who are under 35, have been on the streets longer, and have had contact with the mental health system (Snow et al., 1989: 546).

Their study also revealed some interesting findings with respect to the rates of victimization experienced by the homeless and the nonhomeless. For example, "the odds of being victimized by a homeless male [were] 12 times greater for another homeless individual than for a non-homeless person. Homeless individuals were victimized by other homeless men 32 times out of 1000 in comparison to 2.8 times for citizens at large" (p. 539).

In comparison, when attempting to assess the criminality versus the victimization of the homeless, I believe that it is safe to conclude that the homeless populations are much more representative of serious victims than serious criminals. For the most part, their arrests are typically for petty crimes such as "unpaid traffic violations, public intoxication, vagrancy, sleeping on private property, and shoplifting" (Snow et al., 1989: 539). There are essentially two kinds of criminality engaged in by the homeless: instrumental or adaptive and deviant or stigmatic. The former refers to crimes of survival or making ends meet. The latter refers to crimes of appearance or to the idiosyncratic behaviors of homeless marginality. Both of these kinds of criminal behaviors are derived, at least in part if not in total, from a state of destitution, and each increases the likelihood of the homeless having contact with the criminal justice and mental health systems. As for the victimization of the homeless, it takes many forms as we have already discussed at length in this chapter. Generally, we can lump the victimization of the homeless into three categories: (1) the actual extent of their criminal victimization by other homeless and nonhomeless offenders; (2) the criminalizing of their various survival techniques such as begging and scavenging; and (3) the exploitation of their forced immiseration and criminality.

Most fundamentally speaking, it is the contention here that the homeless are the victims of the crime of homelessness or of policies of state omission. As I have argued elsewhere, "crimes of state omission," such as the crime of homelessness, refer to acts of omission rather than acts of commission; to public and private policies that can be directly linked to both aggregate criminality and victimization (Barak, 1991a). For example, Henry (1991) has discussed in "The Informal Economy: A Crime of Omission by the State" the relationship between a free market economy and street criminality. He specifically argued that participation in the informal or underground economy could be traced to government policies. Accordingly, such state organized policies and activities could be held as coresponsible for crimes in the street. Henry (p. 253) concluded that "by excluding some people from a legitimate share of the wealth that they create, governments force marginalized sections of the population to participate in informal economies wherein some are introduced to opportunities for criminal activities, which harms both themselves and others." This is certainly true for the homeless populations, where perhaps 25 percent of the homeless one time or another participate in some form of the illegal or hidden economy.

U.S. POLICY AND THE VICTIMIZATION OF THE HOMELESS

In Chapter 3 I argued that it is crucially important that we focus our examinations of homelessness and the homeless on the forces underlying the dislocations occurring throughout our urban and rural environments. Moving beyond the individual disabilities or special needs of the homeless calls for an understanding of the distinctive relationships between the political economy and the capitalist state, on the one hand, and the welfare policies and the institutional arrangements, on the other hand. Once again I find the work of Devine (1988) and Blau (1987) to be of explanatory importance or value for any discussion on the victimization of the homeless.

After employing regression and path analysis to a number of hypotheses concerning homelessness and the social safety net, Devine (1988: 293–294) demonstrated that "a larger percentage of the unemployed or the mentally disabled in local populations has no commensurable effect on the rate of homelessness, whereas general [welfare] assistance, which is some times utilized by such individuals is associated with significant reduction in homelessness." Devine and others believe that because the official numbers on the unemployed and the homeless are always on the low side, it is also safe to assume that public housing policies (and, I would add, crime control and social justice policies as well) such as those in the United States based on the ideologies of laissez-faire and rugged individualism are powerful influences on the rate of people suffering from homelessness, criminality, and victimization. For example, in the United States, where an extreme variation of free enterprise has prevailed, the fundamental right to low-income housing has not become an entitlement. In fact, by the end of the 1980s the reality was that there were only some 1.4 million units of such housing available nationally. In Washington, D.C., with an estimated 35,000 homeless in 1987, there were only 9,200 units of public housing and 380 Section Eight units (housing for the very poor). In short, the available public housing, even in cities that have a large portion relative to the size of the poverty population, is so small that it hardly makes any difference in the numbers of homeless people.

Consequently, most poor or homeless people are forced to rely on the private housing market, which is increasingly out of reach for more and more people. The result has been that a scarce supply of privately affordable low-income housing has contributed to both overcrowding and homelessness. For example, Devine (1988) found that the extent of overcrowding in cities was significantly related to greater per capita homelessness. In those communities that have experienced gentrification, commercial redevelopment, housing abandonment, or the conversion of rental property into condominiums, low-income housing stock has virtually disappeared, owing to the escalation in both available rentals and the cost of building new housing. In these tight housing markets, the economically marginal with their meager housing resources already stretched beyond capacity have found it necessary to experience the phenomena of doubing or tripling up with other families on their path to homelessness.

In 1982 the Annual Survey of Housing conducted by the U.S. Bureau of the Census reported that "the number of households with two or more related families sharing space jumped from 1.2 million units to 1.9 million units—an increase of 58 percent, the first significant increase since 1950" (Devine, 1988: 298). It is also important to underscore that the present trends in public and private housing markets represent shifts not only in the value of urban residents, but in the governmental policies themselves (Kasinitz, 1984). For example, in 1990 it was well known that primary housing tenants made space in their units for "guests." In New York City the estimates go as high as 20,000 tenant/guest units. Efforts to evict the double tenants have proceeded slowly thanks to legal safeguards. So HUD, acting in cooperation with the War on Drugs, enacted the procedures of Operation Clean Sweep as a way of circumventing the legal technicalities, at least according to Chicago residents and activists who were opposed to the Chicago Housing Authority's (CHA) adoption of the policy of eviction without due process. Opponents of CHA's Operation Clean Sweep have claimed that thousands of "project-hoppers" have been evicted because they have no place to live, not because they are gang bangers and drug dealers (Greider, 1990). In any event, these eviction policies have the added effect of contributing to the homelessness problem.

More generally, as Blau (1987) concluded in his study of New York's homeless and its policies in social welfare, the driving forces behind the whole crisis management approach to homelessness has been the desire to save money. Two sets of policies were revealed in New York. First, there were those policies aimed at reducing the costs of maintaining the dependent population. Second, there were those policies intended to keep the potentially employable portion of the homeless population ready for work as a means for serving to further depress wages of marginal workers vis-à-vis the increased competition for low-paying jobs. Furthermore, the underlying assumptions about homelessness as a temporary phenomenon and the philosophy of individualism have combined to establish homeless policies that stress deterrence and hardship, complete with connotations of stigma and individual failure. The outcome has been that of extreme privilege for the most affluent, with everybody else slowly losing ground.

The spirit and encouragement of self-sufficiency, as it is usually called, cannot be separated from those policies of redistribution that emerged during the 1980s that so adversely affected public welfare programs and private housing stock to the detriment of poor and marginal Americans. As Devine (1988: 302) concluded in her dissertation, the result of urban renewal should be viewed "not only as an externality but as an extension of the public redistributive policies of cities, states and the federal government. Unlike cash transfer payments and the provision of public housing, policies leading to renovation and gentrification often involve redistribution to those who are better off." Accordingly, her analysis proved that crowding, which was the only tangible result of these redistributive policies, contributes substantially to homelessness. I too have been trying to argue that such policies also increase the criminality and victimization of the homeless and the marginal.

HOMELESSNESS AND THE MISSING SENSE OF INJUSTICE IN THE UNITED STATES

As individuals and as members of social groups, we use our sense of what is just to assess what we and others deserve both materially and psychologically. Thus, violation of our conceptions of justice presents a twofold threat: It challenges and weakens the moral base of our community and it brings into question the evaluative framework that provides a foundation for our individual and social action (Deutsch and Steil, 1988: 4).

Put most simply, my argument is that the United States is not yet willing to reexamine and redefine its notions of justice and equity as they relate to the homeless in particular and to the average person in general. Moreover, until we do so or until we discover our sense of injustice as it relates to homelessness, criminality, and victimization, these interacting phenomena will continue to exacerbate during the decade of the 1990s. In "Awakening the Sense of Injustice," Deutsch and Steil (1988: 4–5) maintained that "the sense of injustice may be directed toward the *nature, quality and quantity of the good or harm* being distributed; toward the *values* underlying the distribution; or toward the various *procedures* related to the determination and implementation of the distribution."

What I now want specifically to focus attention on is what Deutsch and Steil (p. 8) referred to as "the differential sensitivity to injustice in the victimizer." With respect to the sensitivity of the victim and the victimizer to injustice, Deutsch and Steil assume dialectically that asymmetry exists between the two. Nevertheless, they also assume that the asymmetry may be reversed with the victimizer identifying with the victim, and conversely with the victim identifying with the victimizer.

In general, the homeless (victims) are more sensitive and more aggrieved by homelessness than are the homeful (victimizers). As victims, the homeless are virtually powerless and possess a loss of control over their destinies or desired outcomes. They also suffer from threats to their self-esteem and from the derogations of their peers and society at large. In turn, they question their own self-worth as well as the value or justice of the world. Without a meaningful place to live, the homeless are less involved and certainly less committed than the homeful and the victimizers. Finally, the homeless victims are less likely to believe in official definitions of reality, in the indoctrination of the distribution of resources, and in the social institutions themselves.

On the other side, the homeful victimizers' perpetuation of homelessness and its concomitant victimization of the homeless, the marginally poor, and society in general is the product of unrestrained self-interest, social pressure, and ideology. By victimizers I am referring to those people, especially to the elite groups or classes of people who gain from the exploitive social relations associated with the ideologically justified definitions of bourgeois justice. Stated differently, most people whether victimized or victimizer attempt to maintain positive images of themselves, yet such relations can only produce contradictions in perceptions. As Deutsch and Steil (p. 9) note,

If I try to think well of myself, I shall minimize my responsibility for any injustice that is connected with me or minimize the amount of injustice that has occurred if I cannot minimize my responsibility. On the other hand, if I am the victim of pain or harm, to think well of myself, it is necessary for me to believe that it was not due: It is not a just desert for a person of my good character. Thus, the need to maintain positive self-esteem leads to opposite reactions in those who have caused an injustice and those who suffer from it.

Homeless victims, however, need not necessarily feel or experience the injustice of their situation, especially when the homeless people in order to express their outrage must challenge their victimizers or the very system itself. In fact, it might become downright dangerous for the homeless to "bite the hands" that feed and shelter them. Under such circumstances, the process of "identifying with the aggressor," as Anna Freud referred to it some 50 years ago, may actually be observed where the homeless learn to control their outrage by denying their more dangerous feelings and impulses. At the same time, by adopting the values of their homeful victimizers, the homeless internalize the derogatory attitudes of their oppressors toward themselves. Of course, the identification of the oppressed with the oppressor has always cut both ways. In other words, there have been those slaves, inmates, and other powerless people who have resisted the path of least resistance, and chosen to fight their oppressor rather than to become like their oppressor. Moreover, while the "training of blacks, women, and other subordinated groups for masochistic submission and for identification with the oppressor seems less prevalent than it was earlier in this century" (Deutsch and Steil, 1988: 9), the homeless as perhaps society's least powerful and most vulnerable members are still experiencing the legacy of this phenomenon.

For example, Harman (1989) has discussed the process of "reproducing domesticity" even within the context of a feminist-oriented emergency shelter for homeless women in Canada. Having examined both the hostel for homeless women and women working at this shelter, the latter possessing a high degree of consciousness and commitment to the struggle against gender inequality, she argued that in the final analysis "the lives of homeless women can only be understood in light of the larger context of patriarchy and social control within capitalist society" (Harman, 1989: 10). Harman (pp. 10–11) concluded her analysis of

when a hostel becomes a home [by explaining] how the relations between the lived experiences of homeless women and the dominant ideology of patriarchy and capitalism serve the explicit goals of providing shelter while at the same time implicitly serving to reproduce domesticity by making homeless women once again "homeful" within a context of dependency.

Instead of depending on husbands for money and resources, residents relied on shelter workers for various types of social support. The fact that these hostel workers might not provide the kind of ideal environment necessary to combat the socialization of dependency and the elimination of homelessness does not detract from a social reality where these feminist-oriented women are able to identify with their marginal sisters. All and all, Harman has sensitized the reader to the injustice of the wider political, cultural, and economic forms that perpetuate the problems of homelessness and gender inequality. She also has established the need for developing alternative modes of addressing homelessness in North America.

In summation, there is no comparison between the crime of homelessness and the crimes of the homeless. The former is far more threatening than the latter, both with respect to the homeless and the homeful. As Barak and Bohm (1989: 284) have concluded elsewhere,

Most of the homeless are not a serious or dangerous threat to society; they are more victims than perpetrators. The homeless are primarily victims of structural forces and governmental policies that subject them to all forms of abuse, neglect, and dehumanization. And while many homeless persons resign themselves to indignities and degradations, others struggle valiantly against the crime of homelessness, against their own criminalization, and against the crimes of others who prey on society's most vulnerable members.

REFERENCES

Associated Press. 1988. "Veteran Dies a Homeless Bum." *The Montgomery Advertiser*, September 14.

————. 1989a. "Arrest Made in Strangulation and Rape of Pregnant Doctor." *The Montgomery Advertiser*, January 10.

————. 1989b. "Son's Death No Accident, Father Finds Killer." *The Montgomery Advertiser*, December 30.

Aulette, Judy and Albert Aulette. 1987. "Police Harassment of the Homeless: The Political Purpose of the Criminalization of Homelessness." *Humanity and Society*, 11, no. 2.

Barak, Gregg, Ed. 1991a. *Crimes by the Capitalist State: An Introduction to State Criminality*. Albany: State University of New York Press.

Barak, Gregg. 1991b. "Homelessness and the Case for Community-Based Initiatives: The Emergence of a Model Shelter as a Short Term Response to the Deepening Crisis in Housing." In Richard Quinney and Harold E. Pepinsky, eds., *Criminology as Peacemaking*. Bloomington: Indiana University Press.

Barak, Gregg and Robert M. Bohm. 1989. "The Crimes of the Homeless or the Crime of Homelessness? On the Dialectics of Criminalization, Decriminalization, and Victimization." *Contemporary Crises: Law, Crime and Social Policy*, 13, no. 3 (September).

Bard, Marjorie Brooks. 1988. "Domestic Abuse and the Homeless Woman: Paradigms in Personal Narratives for Organizational Strategists and Community Planners." Doctoral Dissertation. Ann Arbor, MI: University Microfilms International (1989).

Baumann, Donald J., Cheryl Beauvals, Charles Grigsby, and D. Franklin Schultz. 1985. "The Austin Homeless: Final Report Provided to the Hogg Foundation for Mental Health." Austin, TX: Hogg Foundation for Mental Health.

Blau, Joel S. 1987. "The Homeless of New York: A Case Study in Social Welfare Policy." Doctoral Dissertation. Ann Arbor, MI: University Microfilms International (1989).

Cook, Dee. 1987. "Women on Welfare: In Crime or Injustice?" In Pat Carlen and Anne Worrall, eds., *Gender, Crime and Justice*. Philadelphia: Open University.

Corn, David and Jefferson Morley. 1989. "Beltway Bandits." *The Nation*, March 6.

Coston, Charisse Tia Maria. 1988. "The Original Designer Label: Prototypes of New York City's Shopping-bag Ladies." Paper presented at the annual meetings of the American Society of Criminology, Chicago.

Deutsch, Morton and Janice M. Steil. 1988. "Awakening the Sense of Injustice." *Social Justice Research*, 2, no. 1 (March)

Devine, Doborah Judith. 1988. "Homelessness and the Social Safety Net." Doctoral Dissertation. Ann Arbor, MI: University Microfilms International (1989).

Elias, Robert. 1986. *The Politics of Victimization: Victims, Victimology and Human Rights*. New York: Oxford University Press.

Evans, James. 1989. "No More Homeless Harassment." *San Francisco Chronicle*, February 1.

Frazier, Joseph B. 1987. "Atlanta's Homeless Face Ban from Business Districts." *Staten Island Advance*, March 17.

Garbarino, James, Janis Wilson, and Anne C. Garbarino. 1986. "The Adolescent Runaway." In James Garbarino, Cynthia J. Schellenback, Janet Sebes and Associates, eds., *Troubled Youth, Troubled Families: Understanding Families At-Risk for Adolescent Maltreatment*. New York: Aldine De Gruyter.

Gelman, David. 1987. "Forcing the Mentally Ill to Get Help." *Newsweek*, November 9.

General Accounting Office. 1982. *Sexual Exploitation of Children: A Problem of Unknown Magnitude*. Washington, DC: House Committee on Education and Labor.

Gil, David G. 1989. "Work, Violence, Injustice and War." *Journal of Sociology and Social Welfare*, 16, no. 1.

Greider, Katherine. 1990. "Sweeping Up Crime and Civil Rights. *In These Times*, March 21–27.

Hackett, George and Peter McKillop. 1989. "A Nightmare on 42nd Street." *Newsweek*, February 27.

Harman, Lesley D. 1989. *When a Hostel Becomes a Home: Experiences of Women*. Toronto: Garamond Press.

Hayes, Robert. 1989. "Interview." *Penthouse*, July.

Henry, Stuart. 1991. "The Informal Economy: A Crime of Omission by the State." In G. Barak, ed., *Crimes by the Capitalist State: An Introduction to State Criminality*. Albany: State University of New York Press.

Hopper, Kim James. 1987. "A Bed for the Night: Homeless Men in New York City, Past and Present." Doctoral Dissertation. Ann Arbor, MI: University Microfilms International (1989).

Hopper, Kim James, Erza Susser, and Sarah Conover. 1985. "Economies of Makeshift: Deindustrialization and Homelessness in New York City." *Urban Anthropology*, 14, nos. 1–3.

Jonsen, Albert. 1987. "Altering Nature: Ethics in the Bio-Revolution." *Humanities Network*, 9, no. 1.

Kasinitz, P. 1984. "Gentrification and Homelessness." *Urban and Social Change Review*, 17.

Lee, Barret A. 1989. "Homeless in Tennessee." In Jamshid A. Momeni, ed., *Homelessness in the United States*. Westport, CT: Greenwood Press.

"Man Killed Over Food." 1989. *The Montgomery Advertiser*, December 23.

Miller, Eleanor M. 1986. *Street Woman*. Philadelphia: Temple University.

Redburn, F. Stevens and Terry F. Buss. 1986. *Responding to America's Homeless: Public Policy Alternatives*. New York: Praeger.

Robertson, Majorie J., Richard Ropers, and Richard Boyer. 1985. *The Homeless of Los Angeles: An Empirical Evaluation* (Document No. 4). Los Angeles: Basic Shelter Research Project, School of Public Health, UCLA.

Rossi, Peter, James D. Wright, Gene A. Fischer, and Georgianne Willis. 1987. "The Urban Homeless: Estimating Composition and Size." *Science*, 235: 1336–1341.

Ryckman, Lisa Levitt. 1987. "AIDS Complicates Attempts to Help the Homeless." *The Montgomery Advertiser and Alabama Journal*, December 6.

Safety Network. 1989a. "Record Death Toll Among San Francisco Homeless in 1988" and "Homeless People Seeking Work Risk Arrest in Las Vegas." *The Newsletter of the National Coalition for the Homeless*, 8, no. 2 (February).

————. 1989b. Miami Advocates Challenge Anti-Homeless Policies." *The Newsletter of the National Coalition for the Homeless*, Vol. 8, no. 5 (May).

Snow, David A., Susan G. Baker, and Leon Anderson. 1989. "Criminality and Homeless Men: An Empirical Assessment." *Social Problems*, 36, no. 5 (December).

Staff Reports. 1989. "Vagrant Charged with Criminal Mischief." *The Montgomery Advertiser*, September 2.

Sullivan, Christopher. 1990. "Help for Homeless 'a Thousand Points of Hype.' " *The Montgomery Advertiser*, March 25.

Sutherland, Edwin H. and Harvey J. Locke. 1936. *Twenty Thousand Homeless Men: A Study of Unemployed Men in the Chicago Shelters*. Chicago: J. B. Lippincott.

Taub, Nadine. 1983. "Adult Domestic Violence: The Law's Response." *Victimology*, 8.

Tidwell, Mike. 1989. "D.C.: Death and Cocaine." *In These Times*, April 12–18.

Viano, Emilio. 1976. "Victimology: The Study of the Victim." *Victimology*, 1.

————. 1983. "Victimology: The Development of a New Perspective." *Victimology*, 8.

Vladeck, Bruce. 1988. "A National Scandal." *Health Care: Issues in Science and Technology*, Fall.

Weisberg, D. K. 1985. *Children of the Night*. Lexington, MA: Lexington Books.

Werferl, Pearl Bonnie. 1985. "Adolescent Prostitution and Its Relationship to Homelessness." Doctoral Dissertation. Ann Arbor, MI: University Microfilms International (1989).

PART II

Confronting the Problem

5 Responding to Short-Term Homeless Needs

I would be a bit surprised if the total number of programs and services available for the homeless did not triple across the United States during the 1980s. At the same time, the amount of labor expended and the number of dollars spent on homelessness, especially with respect to the private sector, increased significantly. Unfortunately, much of that money was not only wasteful of taxpayers' dollars, but ended up in the hands of private entrepreneurs. For example, in New York City, where total housing costs for giving shelter to homeless families was about $150 million in 1988, "almost half, $72 million, [was] spent to house over 3,000 families in hotels. Of this total, $14 million [went] to a business partnership, identified with a man named Morris Horn and several others, who own[ed] or operate[d] seven hotels (Washington Post Writer's Group, 1988: 2B).

It seems, at least in New York City, that the publicly and privately recognized need of the homeless in the 1980s could be channeled not only into the hands of private enterprise, but also into the campaign chests of locally elected officials. In other words, the politics of homelessness and the free-enterprise capitalist state may be quite symbiotic. In the New York illustration involving the business partnership,

one of their hotels, the Jamaica Arms, was selected by New York City to house 90 families with sick children. This building belonged to the city in 1982; it had been seized from former owners in default of taxes. Instead of keeping the site to operate a humane shelter, the city sold it to a private corporation for $75,000. It was then resold to its present owners for $200,000. 'The city,' writes the [Village] Voice, 'now pays about $1.2 million a year to house families in a building it owned four years [earlier]' (Washington Post Writer's Group, 1988: 2B).

It should also be underscored that the owners of the Jamaica Arms had contributed over $100,000 between 1980 and 1988 to elected city officials who had determined New York City housing policy for the homeless.

By the late 1980s, however, advocates for the homeless in New York and elsewhere were beginning to succeed in closing down many of the rat- and roach-infested hotels. Some of these were without hot water or heat and were located in areas of the city that sell drug paraphernalia and cater to the pornographic movie and bookstore crowd. Nevertheless, these hotels charged the city as much as $1,000 a month rent per room.

An unsuspecting public graciously footed the bill. As *The New York Times*-CBS News poll revealed in January 1989, the majority of "the 1,533 people interviewed by telephone . . . said they wanted the government to do more [for the homeless], and half said they would pay higher taxes to get it done" (Wire Reports from New York, 1989: 10A). People from coast to coast were becoming both increasingly conscious of the plight of the homeless and of the need to address the problem. By the end of the decade most citizens were in agreement with a comment made by Stuart Whitney, who has run a shelter for the homeless in Kansas City: "We have to move people out of homelessness into independent living" (Balz, 1989: 9C). Even Jack Kemp, the newly appointed secretary of HUD, was saying that if the savings and loan institutions could be bailed out by the federal government, then there should be some kind of commitment to finance innercity housing. Historically, the biggest theft ever could end up costing the American taxpayers between $500 billion and $1 trillion (Reeves, 1990). It is argued that the money lost will be expressed in many different ways, including a lowering of real estate values, if only temporarily. Who knows, maybe this will have a positive short-term effect on homelessness by lowering the costs of low-income housing. In any event, what I do know and what I can compare is the cost of this bailout with the estimated cost of bailing out the homeless. Most advocacy groups in the late 1980s were estimating the job of adequately housing the homeless in the United States to be around $40 billion annually. I would argue that with another direction in providing low-income housing or with an alternative development of U.S. domestic policy in general, in ten years' time the homelessness problem could be essentially removed as a social problem.

In fact, in the booklet *The McKinney Act: A Program Guide* (1989b: 2), published by the Interagency Council on the Homeless, Chairman Kemp was quoted as saying: "I intend to bring together all facets of the Federal Government in partnership with State and local government and the private and nonprofit sectors to help end the national tragedy of homelessness in America."

SHELTERIZATION AND THE SHELTER SERVICE COMPLEX

In the meanwhile, in the short term, however, many in the movement against homelessness and many more not involved in the movement have been content to believe that the necessary first step toward or perhaps the final step in solving the homelessness problem is simply getting people into affordable living quarters. "All of our residents get better instantly upon coming off the street and into housing," said the Rev. Chris Hall, director of Tender Mercies, a nonprofit agency housing mentally ill homeless people in Cincinnati (Johnson, 1988: 1A). The fact of the matter is that, oftentimes, such policies as providing temporary shelter or services for the homeless may actually prove to be inefficient, costly, and extremely short-sighted when it comes to addressing the long-term needs of homelessness. As for the quality of the programs and services for the homeless, they vary considerably. Most are humane but some of the crisis shelters, for example, are dangerous places to have to sleep.

Some of the worst conditions of crisis shelters in the 1980s could be found inside the larger ones located primarily in urban centers. These shelters are very reminiscent in a general way of the almshouses of the nineteenth century and to the worst of public mental institutions associated with the United States during this century. In at least one journalistic account, it was reported that crack was pervasive and associated with both fighting and theft at a municipal shelter for men in New York City (Caton, 1990). More typical, however, are the accommodations, which range from very inadequate to adequate—the former referring to those temporary shelters that were created from abandoned buildings or from armories, churches, and school gymnasiums. These facilities are often overcrowded, with as many as 100 or more homeless persons sleeping together in a single large area. Lavatories and cooking facilities are usually not able to handle the large numbers. During the evening, because of the actual or potential danger to residents, both lights and security are required at all times. On the other hand, the more permanent shelters that have been converted from former hospitals or other institutions "generally have more adequate sleeping, lavatory, and cooking facilities," and some of the "established shelters have a communal activities room for table games, music, or television watching" (Caton, 1990: 115). Finally, there are those smaller shelters that are more homelike and that resemble group homes or foster family settings.

In the long run, establishing more and more shelters and providing more and more services for the multiple homeless populations will prove to be as misguided as building more and more prisons and introducing more and more punishments for street criminals. In exactly the same way, both of these approaches address only the symptoms of the problem while ignoring the root causes. Furthermore, these responses are extremely costly in both human and economic terms. Such public policies as these have primarily helped to reproduce the very problems—homelessness and criminality— that they were supposed to ameliorate. Moreover, in all likelihood they will continue to do so. The fact, however, that these institutionalized policies for fighting homelessness and individual criminality have each contributed to the processes of shelterization and incarceration does not necessarily mean that one should abandon such policies overnight. With respect to the victimization and criminalization of the marginally poor and homeless, these policies are critical if the political will does not finally confront the underlying changes in global capitalism and in adopting public and private policies that are rational and consistent with those changes.

In other words, until such time as our domestic policies as a whole begin to rearrange the fundamental structural arrangements of inequality and privilege in our society, there will continue to be the need for sheltering the homeless. With the shelter phenomenon of the 1980s came also a burgeoning shelter industry. Once again, the situation in New York City is revealing. By 1988, at an average cost per family of $100 a day for shelter and services, it has been estimated that on the worst days of the year, as much as $500,000 a day was being spent (Moore, 1990). With welfare hotels virtually a thing of the past by the end of 1990, the new and expanding system of shelters figures will be even more expensive as intake facilities are upgraded, as the numbers of long-term transitional shelters are increased, as the average length of stay of a family in the 1980s was around nine months compared to less than two months in the 1970s, and as the apparently elastic demand continues to grow (Moore, 1990). In short, as the shelterization process becomes more institutionalized, professionalized, and bureaucratized, its costs will grow.

As Christopher Smith (1988: 233) has argued, during the 1980s there was a "building of arenas" around the powerful image of the homelessness problem: "Clearly homelessness has become an issue on which a number of individuals and groups have been able to strengthen their own claims-making activities." Arenas and constituencies here have included politicians, social service workers, and advocates for the homeless. Although there are many conflicting groups within and between these three groupings of electoral, professional, and coalition people, the evidence suggests that there have been benefits to derive for most of these people.

Continued publicity about homelessness had provided city officials with a weapon to use against the conservative trends of deregulation, Reaganomics, and read my lips, "no new taxes" Bush. Local governments despite the new federalism have been able to extract additional funds from higher levels of government:

Their argument is that homelessness, like other forms of dependency, has resulted from society-wide economic forces. They thus contend that though the cities themselves have not caused these problems, they are nevertheless responsible for dealing with them. In the 1960s this sort of argument was successful in winning federal funding through the Great Society categorical grant programs, but by the 1980s this type of funding had fallen very much out of favor. It would take an emotional issue like homelessness to help squeeze out scarce funds from such an unwilling source as the federal government (Smith, 1988: 233).

Moreover, the homelessness problem, in a related but also in a different kind of a way than the crime problem, provides the politician with an opportunity to be doing something, at least in the short term, about the problem. It allows him or her to take a highly visible stand in a compassionate way with a pressing community social issue.

Perhaps even more significant has been the concomitant growth of workers within the shelter industrial complex—that is, those social service providers who have become the operators and managers of shelters, not to mention all the other professionals, staff, and volunteers who see to the needs of sheltering the homeless. In effect, the homeless have provided social service workers with the opportunity to raise their status and to reverse the trend during the 1970s and beyond that saw "the more glamorous professions associated with medicine and psychiatry [take] over an increasing share of the treatment of mental illness, alcoholism, drug addiction, and even crime" (Smith, 1988: 234). Unfortunately, however, short-term solutions to homelessness, like their short-term counterparts of crime control, act only as stopgap measures that have to be reappropriated continuously in the omission of any long-term preventive solutions to the crisis in low-cost housing.

As I argued in Part I of this book, the new homelessness problem has been the result of a mix of political, economic, and social forces, and I will continue to argue in Part II that not until the fundamental problems underlying homelessness and the low-income housing crisis are dealt with will there be a resolution of the problem of the new vagrancy. I suspect until then the shelter phenomenon and the shelter complex will continue to expand slowly. To put it differently, while some still disagree on the structural nature or root causes of homelessness today, and while others are still trying to identify the key etiological processes, most of the various interests (and their constituencies) who are either in favor of or opposed to dealing constructively with the issue of homelessness, will have, at least for the short run, established as public policy the strategy of confronting homelessness not as a long-term permanent problem, but as a short-term temporary problem.

PROGRAMS AND SERVICES: AN OVERVIEW

The Stewart B. McKinney Homeless Assistance Act, signed into law on July 22, 1987, and subsequently reauthorized in November 1988, created The Interagency Council on the Homeless (ICH, or the Council) and established a number of new programs to address "the areas of emergency food and shelter, transitional and longer-term housing, primary and mental health care services, education, job training, alcohol and drug abuse programs and income assistance" (ICH, 1989b: 3). The McKinney Act mandated that the Council review all Federal activities and programs to assist homeless individuals; reduce duplication among programs and activities by Federal agencies; monitor, evaluate and recommend improvements in programs and activities conducted by Federal agencies, State and local governments and private voluntary organizations; provide professional and technical assistance to States, local governments and other public and private nonprofit organizations; collect and disseminate information; report annually to the President and Congress on the extent and nature of homelessness and evaluate the Federal response; [and] publish a bimonthly bulletin" (ICH, 1989b: 4).

Membership in the Council includes the various cabinet heads plus the heads of the following federal agencies: ACTION, Federal Emergency Management Agency, General Services Administration, Low Income Opportunity Advisory Board, Office of Management and Budget, and U.S. Postal Service.

McKinney Act Programs

The following is a listing of the programs with a brief description of the purpose of each as found in the Interagency Council (1989b: 5–16) booklet:

Adult Education for the Homeless Program "provides assistance to State education agencies so that they can provide a program of literacy training and basic skills remediation for adult homeless individuals."

Community Demonstration Projects for Alcohol and Drug Abuse Treatment "provides discretionary grants for demonstration projects that develop community-based alcohol and/or drug abuse treatment and rehabilitation services for individuals with alcohol or drug-related problems who are homeless or at imminent risk of becoming homeless."

Community Mental Health Services Block Grants "provides funds for outreach services, case management, mental health and substance abuse treatment, supportive housing for the homeless mentally ill and training for service providers."

Community Mental Health Services Demonstration Projects "awards discretionary grants to community-based demonstration projects for homeless adults with severe, long-term mental illness and severely emotionally disturbed homeless children and adolescents."

Emergency Community Services Homeless Assistance Grants "increasing existing programs and services for the homeless at the local level, assists the homeless in using these programs at the local level, assists the homeless in using these programs and services and promotes private-sector assistance."

Emergency Food and Shelter National Board Program "supplements and expands efforts to provide food, shelter and support services to homeless people; creates effective and innovative local programs; and makes basic repairs to existing shelters or mass feeding facilities."

Emergency Shelter Grants Programs "renovates, rehabilitates or converts buildings for use as emergency shelters for the homeless. Within certain limitations, funds can be spent on essential services for the homeless and some operating costs."

Food Stamp Program for the Homeless "allows the homeless increased access to food stamps by providing expedited service; precluding homeless people from monthly reporting of income changes; and excluding from countable income rent paid to house the homeless in hotels. Also permits families who are living with relatives to receive their own allotments."

Health Services for the Homeless "awards grants for health care delivery to the homeless, including primary care services, substance abuse treatment and mental health care services."

Homeless Children and Youth Education Grants "provides funds to state education agencies to develop and implement programs for the education of homeless children."

Homeless Chronically Mentally Ill Veterans Program "provides discretionary funds to VA Medical Centers to furnish treatment and rehabilitative services to eligible homeless veterans with a chronic mental illness.'

Homeless Veterans Reintegration Projects "expedites the reintegration into the work force by providing them with job training, remedial education, basic literary instruction, job counseling, referrals and other support services."

Job Training for the Homeless Demonstration Program "provides funds for job training activities for homeless individuals, including remedial education, job search, job counseling, job preparation training and basic literacy instruction."

Section 8 Moderate Rehabilitation Assistance for Single Room Occupancy (SRO) Dwellings "provides rental assistance for single-room occupancy by homeless individuals to Public Housing Agencies."

Supplemental Assistance for Facilities to Assist the Homeless "funds interest-free advance and grants to acquire, lease, convert or rehabilitate existing facilities to provide support services to meet the needs of the homeless."

Supportive Housing Demonstration Program—Permanent Housing Component "provides permanent housing assistance in developing community-based, long-term housing and support services for projects housing not more than eight handicapped people who are homeless or at risk of becoming homeless."

Supporting Housing Demonstration Program—Transitional Housing Demonstration Program "develops innovative approaches to short-term (24 months or less) housing and support services to persons who are capable of making the transition to independent living, especially homeless families with children and deinstitutionalized homeless individuals."

Veterans Domicilary Care Program "provides funds for converting surplus space in VA Medical Centers to domiciliary beds for homeless veterans."

Non-McKinney Federal Programs

In addition to the above programs, the Interagency Council (1989a) lists more than 60 federal programs and activities that can be of use in aiding the homeless. It is important for analyzing the question, "what is to be done about homelessness?" that we incorporate a listing and an appreciation for those programs that while not necessarily targeted to the homeless, have essentially been a part of the government's position and policy (or comprehensive" approach) as articulated by the ICH. In other words, the prevailing philosophy guiding the whole approach to the homelessness problem in particular and to all other domestic (social) problems in general, can be summed up nicely by the words "volunteerism, localism, and private-public partnerships." The role of the federal government or of state intervention into the homeless problem since the early 1980s has been that of reluctant cheerleaders, whispering on the sidelines about how they wish the problem (i.e., the other team, homelessness) would go away. Hence, the federal response rather than being all it could be has been the minimum it could be. In fact, our capitalist state's main objective seems to be getting everyone else from the private sector involved with the problem of the homeless.

Accordingly, here is a listing and brief profile of the government's commitment for developing a comprehensive homeless assistance program for the United States around the more direct efforts established in the McKinney Act (ICH, 1989a: 1–34).

ACTION Programs. These include Volunteers in Service to America (VISTA), Student Community Service Program (SCS), Foster Grandparent Program (FGP), Senior Companion Program (SCP), and Retired Senior Citizen Volunteer Program (RSVP). In addition, there are those Citizen Participation Programs administered under ACTION such as the Mini-Grant Program, the Volunteer Demonstration Program, the ACTION Drug Alliance, and the National Neighborhood-Based Drug Prevention Demonstration Project. Taken as a whole these programs constitute the federal domestic volunteer agency or ACTION, as it is called. The mission of ACTION has been to "advocate, promote, and support the voluntary efforts of citizens and public and private organizations in solving vital problems confronting the poor, the disabled, the elderly, and youth with special needs." During the 1980s major emphasis areas of these programs included drug prevention, illiteracy/unemployment, homelessness/housing, hunger and health, services to at-risk youth, community relations, teenage pregnancy, adolescent parenting, and families in crisis. The raison d'etre of these programs is as old as the Economic Opportunity Act of 1964, which created VISTA (ACTION's first volunteer program) to "mobilize community resources and to increase the capacity of the low-income community to solve its own problems." In serving the needs of the poor, programs such as SCS and the Volunteer Demonstration Program, in addition to VISTA, are aimed at securing resources to continue after federal support ends. By the end of the 1980s, approximately 15 percent of VISTA projects, for example, were devoted to helping the homeless.

Department of Agriculture. The USDA operates three programs that can be utilized to assist the homeless: Food Stamp Program, Food Distribution

Program, and Shelter Program. In general these programs have been designed to aid low-income people and are equipped to expedite processing of homeless people. The food programs distribute stamps or surplus food and purchase foodstuffs for the poor and for organizations serving the needy. The shelter program has been authorized through the Farmers Home Administration (FmHA). It leases single-family homes in FmHA-held inventory at the lowest possible cost to local housing authorities or to community nonprofit organizations for use as shelters for homeless persons. The single-family homes belonging to FmHA, not otherwise targeted for immediate disposition, have been made available and can be leased on a year-to-year basis for up to ten years. In 1989 a proposed regulation was issued by FmHA that would allow nonprofit organizations to purchase these homes.

Department of Defense. The DOD operates three programs that can assist the needs of the homeless: Shelter for the Homeless Program, Homeless Support Initiative Program: Donation of Bedding Articles, and DOD Commissary/Food Bank Program. Under the shelter program the military has made some of their facilities available on a temporary basis to be used either as homeless shelters or as warehouse space for food banks. While DOD can neither operate nor fund these shelters, it may provide utilities or security, which may be incidental to the establishment of a shelter on a military installation. (As of June 1989, there were a total of 15 shelters that had opened under this program.)

Department of Energy. The DOE operates two programs that may be of indirect benefit to homeless people: Weatherization Assistance Program (WAP) and State Energy Conservation Program (SECP). The first provides funds to low-income persons for weatherizing their dwellings. By definition, shelters for the homeless may qualify for assistance. The second program provides matching grant funds and technical assistance to states for the purposes of developing and implementing plans to achieve energy conservation. Some of the states' SECP programs include support to agencies that assist the homeless by increasing the energy efficiency and lowering the costs of homeless shelters.

General Services Administration. The GSA operates two programs that may assist homeless shelter providers or potential providers: the Surplus Federal Personal Property and the Use of Excess or Surplus Federal Real Property. The first administers the donation of surplus federal personal property to providers of assistance to the homeless. Such property typically consists of beds and bedding, sleeping bags, blankets, clothes, kitchen equipment, cleaning materials, and appliances. The second program provides HUD with a listing of excess properties, including land and buildings in urban and rural areas, that have been reported by the various federal agencies. Some of this real property may be used as shelters for housing the homeless.

Department of Health and Human Services. HHS probably has more programs to potentially assist the homeless than any federal department. To begin with, HHS has three programs aimed at different segments of the new homeless. First, there is the Community Support Program (CSP) to assist in the development of comprehensive community-based care for the homeless mentally ill. Second, there is the Runaway and Homeless Youth Program (or Runaway Youth: Title III, Part D, Section 341 of the Juvenile Justice and Delinquency Act of 1974 as amended), which provides assistance to establish or strengthen community-based centers serving runaway and homeless youth and their families. Third, there is the Homeless Youth Drug Education program (or the 1988 Anti-Drug Abuse Act) to help states, local governments, and private nonprofit entities develop demonstration projects for runaway and homeless youth, warning them about the dangers of substance abuse.

In addition there are 20 programs broken down between the following agencies within HHS: Family Support Administration (FSA); Office of Human Development Services (OHDS); Health Care Financing Administration (HCFA); Alcohol, Drug Abuse, and Mental Health Administration (ADAMHA); Health Resources and Services Administration (HRSA); and the Social Security Administration (SSA). These programs will be identified without comment because they were listed by ICH and because, for the most part, they do not really add to the welfare of the homeless. FSA includes Aid to Families with Dependent Children, AFSC Emergency Assistance Program, Community Services Block Grant Program, the Community Services Discretionary Grants, and the Child Support Enforcement Program. OHDS includes the Older Americans Act (or Title III, Section 303 as amended), Child Welfare Research and Demonstration (or Section 426 of Title IV of the Social Security Act as amended by P.L. 97–35), and the Independent Living program. HCFA consists of Medicaid and Medicare. ADAMHA includes the National Institute of Mental Health Program of the Homeless Mentally Ill, the National Institute on Alcohol Abuse and Alcoholism Program for the Homeless Alcoholic, and the Alcohol, Drug Abuse and Mental Health Services Block Grant. HRSA includes Maternal and Child Health Services and Primary Care Block Grant, Community and Migrant Health Centers, and the National Health Service Corps. Finally, SSA includes Social Security Retirement and Survivors Insurance Benefits, Supplemental Security Income, and Social Security Disability Insurance.

Department of Housing and Urban Development. HUD operates essentially four programs that are of little value to the homeless: Lease and Sale of HUD Acquired Single Family Poperties for Use by the Homeless, HUD Assisted Housing Programs, Housing for the Handicapped, and Community Development Block Grants (CDBG). Under the lease and sale programs, HUD Field Offices make certain properties in their inventory of foreclosed mortgages available for lease to units of local government or nonprofit organizations to use in their homeless programs. Rent is usually $1.00 per year with the possibility of renewal. All homeless costs for housing and services rendered must be funded from somewhere else. There are also foreclosed properties available for purchase by certain nonprofit organizations for direct use in homeless programs. Discounts of 10 percent off HUD's estimated fair market value are generally provided. A third lease and sale program involves lease with an option to purchase in connection with the Supportive Housing Demonstration Project.

The HUD Assisted Housing Programs involve rental housing for low-income families. Subsidized housing, or federal housing assistance as it is more typically known, makes up the difference between what a family can afford and the HUD-approved rent. Occupancy preferences are provided by statute for those families who have been displaced, living in substandard housing, or paying more than 50 percent of their income for rent. Of course, homeless people by virtue of their homelessness receive occupancy preference.

Housing for the Handicapped provides direct loans that may be used to finance the construction or rehabilitation of rental or cooperative detached, semidetached, row, walk-up, or elevator-type structures for both the non-elderly handicapped and the elderly handicapped, which may include the homeless.

Under the CDBG grant program, shelter acquisition, shelter rehabilitation, and shelter operations may be funded. HUD has also determined that CDBG funds may be used for the construction of temporary shelter and transitional housing, such as halfway homes for the chronically mentally ill, considering these as public facilities, not residences.

Department of the Interior. The Division of Housing of the Bureau of Indian Affairs administers a Housing Improvement Program that provides assistance to needy Indians who have no other source. For the most part, this program involves the repair or enlargement of existing housing and the construction of some new homes.

Department of Labor. Labor operates two programs that have any special relevance to the homeless: the Job Training Partnership Act—Disadvantaged Youths and Adults, and the Job Training Partnership Act (JTPA)—Job Corps. Since 1982 JTPA has been the nation's primary job training program for the economically disadvantaged. JTPA was amended by the McKinney Act to include the homeless in the definition of the term "economically disadvantaged." The amended JTPA also did away with the residency requirement for participation in the designed service area. While the Job Corps provides education, training, and support services for severely disadvantaged youth between the ages of 16 and 21, a special pilot program, "Shelter Corps," involving the Labor Department and the New York City Human Resources Administration, was announced in late 1988. The three-year contract called for 50 youths and young adults who were currently residing in homeless shelters to receive room and board, counseling, medical care, health care, driver education and other support services, in addition to the usual job training and educational instruction, as enrollees in Shelter Corps.

Postal Service. Alternative mail service delivery has become available to the homeless, including reduced rent for post office boxes, shared post office boxes, and the listing of shelters as their "home" address for the purposes of obtaining a box in the area of residence.

Veterans' Affairs. Those benefits (programs and services) that may be of value combating homelessness are: Home Retention Assistance (HRA), Community Residential Care Program (CRCP), Domiciliary Care Program (DCP), Mental Health Care (MHC), Readjustment Counseling (Vet Center) Program (RCP), and the State Veterans Homes Program (SVHP). HRA provides assistance to veterans who are in danger of losing their homes because of financial difficulties that are no fault of their own. Under CRCP, the largest of the VA's extended care programs, some homeless veterans receiving VA pension or compensation, Social Security, or other funds may qualify to participate in this program. It provides residential care—including room, board, personal care, and general health care supervision—to veterans who do not require hospital or nursing home care, but who, because of mental or physical health conditions, are not able to resume independent living and have no suitable family resources to provide the needed care. DCP initiated in 1987 the Domiciliary Care for Homeless Veterans Programs. MHC in the same year initiated the Homeless Chronically Mentally Ill Veterans Program, which through an outreach effort provides these persons with medical and psychiatric assessment and, when appropriate, places them in community-based psychiatric residential treatment facilities for continuing care and rehabilitation at VA expense. RCP administers a nationwide system of Vet Centers to address the needs of Vietnam-era veterans, providing readjustment counseling and networking with various VA and non-VA resources in meeting the shelter and other needs of homeless veterans. SVHP operated two grant programs—one provides federal funding to assist states in providing domiciliary, nursing and hospital care in state home facilities; one provides up to 65 percent federal funding "for the acquisition and construction of domiciliary and nursing home facilities, and expansion or alteration of existing facilities."

The 1988 National Survey of Shelters for the Homeless

In 1984 and again in 1988, HUD conducted national surveys of shelters for the homeless. In the introduction to the most recent survey, HUD (1989: 1) explains that the survey was taken for the purpose of obtaining "data on the number, occupancy, capacity, operational characteristics, funding, and available services of homeless shelters" throughout the United States. In 1988 it was estimated that the nation as a whole contained approximately 5,400 shelters. This calculation was made using two statistical samples—one based on homeless shelters in jurisdictions with populations of 25,000 or more and one based on homeless shelters in cities with populations more than 250,000. The first group accounted for about 5,000 and the second group for about 400. In 1988 it was estimated that the total shelter bed capacity for the United States was 275,000 beds. This estimate doubled the number estimated by HUD's 1984 survey. With respect to shelter utilization by the homeless, it was estimated that on any given night approximately 180,000 beds were being slept in. When comparing total bed capacity with average evening occupancy, it was apparent that about one out of every three beds was unoccupied on an average night. This ratio represented no difference from 1984. Evidently, homeless people's preferences for staying in shelters had no increases, regardless of the quality of the services provided. In other words, based on the most conservative population estimates of the homeless population, a sizable number prefer some kind of alternative sleeping arrangement.

When the numbers of shelters were compared with respect to population distribution, it was found that a disproportionately large number of shelter homeless persons were found to be in the largest metropolitan areas. For example, "while shelters in large jurisdictions (over 1,000,000 population) [were] 11 percent of the total, they account[ed] for 30 percent of all persons in homeless shelter on an average night" (HUD, 1989: 3). Accordingly, the nation's largest cities have tended to operate the biggest shelters. When it came to average bed capacity, it was found that larger jurisdictions' capacity was three to four times greater than the medium or small jurisdictions. More specifically, with respect to the average bed capacity by shelter size, the breakdown for 100 percent of the shelter sample was as follows: 44 percent of the small (less than 25 beds) shelters averaged 15 beds per shelter; 32 percent of the medium (26 to 50 beds) shelters averaged 36 beds per shelter; and 24 percent of the large (more than 50 beds) shelters averaged 133 beds per shelter.

Between 1984 and 1988, the HUD surveys revealed that the number of persons in homeless shelters on any given night had increased for all geographical regions of the country. The survey also revealed that one-half of all homeless shelters were in jurisdictions whose populations were between 25,000 and 250,000; about two out of five shelter facilities were in jurisdictions with between 250,000 and 1 million people; and one in ten shelter facilities were in the largest jurisdictions with 1 million or more people. This, of course, was consistent with the bed capacity space discussed above.

As examination of homeless shelters by population groups served, based on whether at least 75 percent of their clientele were primarily unaccompanied men or families with children, resulted in a breakdown which showed that about 25 percent of the shelters served single men, 36 percent served primarily families with children, and the remaining 39 percent were grouped as "other." In that group there was a real mixture with respect to the various homeless clientele served. For example, the total number of shelters for unaccompanied homeless women that met the 75 percent criteria was only 2 percent.

When it comes to the funding and costs of homeless shelters, the HUD surveys estimated that $300 million had been spent in 1984 and $1.5 billion had been budgeted for 1988. Concerning the sources of shelter expenditures, HUD found that most dollars came from the public sector (65 percent) and not the private sector (35 percent). Conversely, regarding the distribution of shelter dollars, most went to privately operated rather than publicly operated shelters, 62 percent to 38 percent. As for the operating costs of homeless shelters, as suspected the expenditures estimated for the public facilities were more than twice those estimated for the private facilities. At least, in part, this was because public shelters have a greater reliance on paid staff or professionals than do the private shelters, which tend to depend on volunteer workers. All in all, in 1988 the distribution of homeless workers nationwide was broken down as 30,000 full-time staff, 14,000 part-time paid personnel, and 80,000 volunteers estimated to have contributed some 30 million hours of free labor. In 1988 the estimated bottom line for the average per person per day cost was $22 for a privately run shelter, and for all shelters combined it was $28. This represented an increase of $9 per person per night since 1984 when the average for all shelters was $19.

ASSESSMENTS OF THE U.S. RESPONSE TO HOMELESSNESS

Assessments of the U.S. response to its homelessness problem will vary according to whom one listens to. In December 1988, Rep. Ted Weiss (D-NY) attacked Social Security Commissioner Dorcas Hardy for not acting on part of a 1987 budget act establishing grants for homeless outreach projects. The act authorized $1.25 million in 1987 and $2.5 million in 1988. Hardy maintained that Congress had failed to provide the money for the program, and argued that the outreach program would duplicate other services. Furthermore, she recommended that the Department of Health and Human Services repeal the program or find another agency to run the program. Weiss argued that "there are people out on the street who are clearly qualified for SSI benefits. The purpose of the legislation was to help states reach out and identify those people" (Washington [AP], 1988; 5A).

Accordingly, when it comes to assessing the federal response to the problem of homelessness, one should consult sources other than the government itself, especially with respect to those agencies responsible for carrying out the programs and services in question. I am not suggesting that students of homelessness should ignore the available governmental reports in making their evaluations. For example, in addition to those federal documents already referred to in this book, see the General Accounting Office's 1989 report, *Homelessness: HUD's and FEMA's Progress in Implementing the*

McKinney Act. More fundamentally, however, assessment requires that we turn to outside sources.

Since the programs and services outlined, discussed, identified, and summarized in the previous sections were those presented by governmental agencies responsible for administering and coordinating U.S. homelessness policy, I will now highlight the findings and evaluation of the federal response to homelessness from perspectives other than the government's—namely, those presented by the Low Income Housing Information Service (LIHIS) and the National Coalition for the Homeless (NCH or the Coalition). In brief, LIHIS concluded with regard to the Reagan administration's final or fiscal year 1989 budget proposal that low-income housing was treated less severely than previous Reagan budgets. "Nevertheless, a number of programs for the poor, in addition to low-income housing, [were to] be reduced significantly," thus, continuing the seven-year trend toward replacing all forms of low-income housing assistance with vouchers (LIHIS, 1988: 11). In another assessment of the federal response to homelessness, NCH (1989: 1) concluded the following about the Interagency Council on the Homeless:

Designed to oversee programs to aid the homeless nationwide, the Council should serve as the standard-bearer for the federal government's efforts on behalf of the homeless. Yet, far from playing a leadership role, in the year and-a-half of its existence, the Council has ignored its duties, mismanaged its funds, and violated its congressional mandate.

More specifically, LIHIS identified the proposed cuts and terminations for those programs serving both low-income housing and low-income people in general. Both types of programs in the president's proposed fiscal year (FY) 1989 budget were to suffer. All in all, the most extensive cuts or terminations in the budget were for low-income housing programs. For example, the Community Development Block Grants were to be slashed $.4 billion dollars "from their FY88 funding level off $2.8 billion to $2.4 billion in FY89 (LIHIS, 1988: 1). The budget also called for a reduction of $.7 billion in direct grant funding for public housing modernization, from a FY88 funding level of $1.7 billion to a proposed $1 billion in FY89. With respect to termination of existing programs, the budget proposed the following:

- Urban Development Action Grants
- Housing Development Grants
- Housing Counseling
- Congregate Services
- Section 108 Loan Guarantees
- Neighborhood Development Demonstration and Public Housing Child Care Grants

• Three of the special homeless assistance programs enacted as part of the Stewart B. McKinney Homeless Assistance Act in 1987: Emergency Shelter Grants, Supplemental Assistance for Facilities to Assist the Homeless, and Section 8 Moderate Rehabilitation for Single Room Occupancy (SRO) units (LIHIS, 1988: 1)

Less extensive proposed reductions than those pertaining directly to low-income housing were the associated reductions in other programs designed to serve the needs of low-income people. These included such programs as low-income energy assistance program, funding for emergency food and shelter programs, and community service block grants. Two programs of relevance to homelessness and to the potentially homeless that were proposed for termination were the low-income weatherization program and training for the homeless.

LIHIS took the time to explain in its memorandum the constraints that were established by the White House/congressional budget summit agreement negotiated in late 1987. In short, separate FY89 ceilings on defense and domestic discretionary spending were reached. This resulted in the two budgets not being played off against one another, which had become a tradition in Washington. Therefore, all domestic programs were forced to compete with each other for a limited amount of resources. We have already seen who the losers were. As for the winners, those who were to receive increased funding, they included a "number of Justice Department programs, the new supercollider project, and AIDS research and education" (LIHIS, 1988: 11). The biggest winner in the proposed appropriations was to be the space program, with an increase of $2.4 billion.

While acknowledging the fact that the Interagency Council on the Homeless had not been "completely idle" during the first 18 months of its existence, NCH proceeded to level a rather strong critique. In its assessment, ICH was given credit for expending its resources "to develop a sophisticated data base, to hire outside consultants, and to organize regional conferences for federal employees" (NCH, 1989: 1). Nevertheless, NCH's overall evaluation was that the Council had failed to perform the most basic and urgent tasks mandated by the McKinney Act. In the Coalition's summary of its findings, three excellent examples were provided to underscore the spirit or driving force of ICH. By statute, ICH was required, among other things, to "disseminate information on federal programs to aid the homeless to local groups around the country"; " 'monitor' federal agencies' implementation of programs to aid the homeless"; and "to report and make recommendations annually to Congress on the state of federal homeless assistance programs" (NCH, 1989: 1).

With respect to the first mandate, the Coalition reported that the ICH informational actions "were to publish three issues of a newsletter, send three notices to regional federal employees, and issue one 'program alert' " (NCH, 1989: 1). It was also noted that none of the documents provided any timely information on federal programs, deadlines, or application procedures. Regarding the second mandate, not only had the Council failed to monitor implementation, it also sought to conceal its members' noncompliance with the McKinney Act. In fact, at the time of the Coalition's assessment, ICH had already been successfully sued three times for having failed to implement programs for the homeless. As for the third mandate, ICH produced its first report on January 18, 1989. The only recommendations found in the report suggested "that primary responsibility for the homeless be shifted to the local government and non-profit sector and that the McKinney Act be abolished" (NCH, 1989: 2).

It appears that the near future in the federal response to homelessness will be pretty much as it has been in the recent past. Even the trends of the late 1980s are once again present in the latest proposed presidential budget for 1991: "President Bush's proposed budget for fiscal year 1991, sent to the Congress on January 28, 1990, will have little impact on the housing and supportive service needs of homeless Americans. The Bush budget proposals continue the major outlines of those submitted by the predecessor, Ronald Reagan" (Safety Network, 1990: 1). In short, after adjusting for inflation, low-income programs were cut by more than $2 billion, according to the Center on Budget and Policy Priorities. On closer inspection, it was found that

- all but four McKinney Act programs are cut in inflation-adjusted dollars (excluding the Interagency Council),
- all McKinney HUD programs and FEMA Emergency Food and Shelter program are cut below last year's appropriation level; the Interagency Council on the Homeless receives a 9.1% increase, however (Safety Network, 1990: 1).

Not only is it proposed that most McKinney programs in mental health, education, job training, and veterans' aid be reduced in FY91, but according to LIHIS the 1991 budget proposals "will expand housing assistance by only 82,049 additional households. This reflects an average increase similar to those achieved throughout the Reagan years, and it will have little impact on the nation's burgeoning homeless population" (Safety Network, 1990: 1). Moreover, a range of other programs that could be used to prevent homelessness face termination or serious cuts, according to the National Coalition for the Homeless. For example, excluding the McKinney homelessness portion, the Community Service Block Grant has been proposed for elimination. Also proposed for elimination was the Low Income Weatherization Program, which had been funded at $171 million in FY90. Also facing a drastic cut of 27.5 percent, from the 1990 funding level of $1.449 billion down to a proposed level of $1.05 billion, was the Low Income Housing Energy Assistance Program.

UP-CLOSE "SHORTS" ON HOMELESS ASSISTANCE

The attempt here is not to portray any kind of representative sample of the quality of assistance to homeless people. Nor am I even attempting to assess the value of these services and programs. Whether or not they are good or bad attempts at providing assistance to the short-term needs of the homeless, the majority of these efforts are carried out by people who are sincerely concerned. For the most part, these efforts, services, and programs are both compassionate and humane. The rest of this chapter focuses briefly on several examples of assistance to the homeless in order to convey to the reader a sense of what the world of homelessness aid is all about. At the same time, I try to place these efforts and programs into a very rough chronology with respect to their development and prevalence. Specifically provided is a sketch of both the profit-making and nonprofit-making services for the homeless.

In the early to mid–1980s, especially in the Eastern urban areas of the country like Washington, D.C. and New York City, welfare hotels for the homeless were a common means of providing shelter. By the late 1980s, these profit-making facilities offering shelter to the homeless had lost their legitimacy among both homeless activists and governmental offices. For example, on July 8, 1989, another baby, Comanta Reid, died in a fire at a welfare hotel. This time it was the Capitol City Inn in Washington, D.C. Months earlier, Mayor Marion Barry had promised to close the hotel down. According to one writer, if asked, the residents would talk about the burning death of the baby:

One woman holding her own tiny baby described the tragedy as "just another crazy Saturday." Her resignation and hopelessness contrasted with the apparently temporary indignation of the politicians speaking to television cameras. While they say these things should never happen, the residents know that they do happen—they happen all the time, only sometimes the babies don't die (Kaufman, 1989: 2).

What is life like living at the Capitol City Inn? At the time of the fire, all of the women residing there had been homeless for at least six months. Most of them had small children. They would spend a lot of time sitting around and discussing decent affordable apartments that do not exist. They would also talk about a voucher system that failed to reach enough people or that limited one's options. As one resident of the shelter stated, those "vouchers enabled recipients to shop on the 'free' market, which means they can only afford to spend their voucher for a lousy place, in a lousy area" (Kaufman, 1989: 2). Hence, the prospects of closing down this shelter for the homeless scared its residents.

Without any other place to go, these women and their children were living in the dirty and stark reality of a welfare hotel. As Kaufman explained, everywhere one looked, kids were to be found playing in the slimy and urine smelling hallways or on the treeless pavement covered with broken glass and other debris. What was missing, of course, were the obvious signs of childhood—bikes, balls, and dolls. The bodies of these children were undernourished, small for their age, and developmentally behind in their speech and reasoning. As Kaufman (1989: 2) wrote in her *Washington Post* article,

Comanta Reid's death should never have occurred, because people should not be living in inadequate shelters or substandard housing. But the truth is that this is how our nation shelters [some of] its homeless. In DC we guarantee people a place for the night—not a safe place, not a healthy place, not a place that says they are a priority, that we want the Comantas to have a future.

Welfare hotels/motels have not been exclusively confined to the urban metropolitan areas. They have also emerged in suburbia, even in places like Westchester County, New York, where the average house sells for $300,000. Take, for instance, the Elmsford Motor Lodge, formerly a Howard Johnson's, one of some 40 available motels for Westchester's 4,200 homeless people, including 1,700 children. In fact, Westchester in 1989 was leading the nation in homelessness per capita, followed by other affluent suburban communities. This has been simply the result of blue-collar workers being gradually displaced over the past couple of decades, no longer able to afford the rising rents owing to co-op conversion of former apartments and to gentrification more generally.

Located 40 miles north of New York City, the Elmsford Motor Lodge is right down the road from the corporate parks of the Platinum Mile and from the 3,000-acre Rockefeller estate. The displaced poorer residents for the new homeless of Westchester county, unlike their counterparts in the city, are highly diffuse or spread out. Adults and children may find themselves commuting from their designated welfare motels as far as 80 miles a day to work or school. The county picked up the daily cab fare for children attending school, paying as much as $220 daily in 1989. Monthly rentals for a one-bedroom motel unit were averaging $3,000 back then. The cost to the wealthy taxpayers came to about $64 million a year, but from their class perspective it was better than providing low-income permanent housing, depressing real estate values, and bringing "those people" out into the open. Instead these homeless people were to remain out of sight, "conveniently situated away from residential areas, along access routes or abandoned stretches of downtown" (Kessler, 1989: 309). In their isolated hideaways, these motel residents were living with as many as four to a room without a kitchen. Overcrowding was only one of their daily debilitating experiences. For in a typical motel like the Elmsford Motor Lodge, life without drugs or crime was highly unusual. At the Elmsford, residents claimed that more than 80 percent of the residents used crack. As one of the residents noted: "You get people coming in here that are so nice at the beginning. . . . But by the time they leave here, they're drug addicts or they're so bitter because this place just makes them crazy. And then nobody will rent you an apartment once they find out you've been living in a motel" (quoted in Kessler, 1989: 309).

Fortunately, motels and hotels for sheltering the homeless at the expense of the public and for the benefit of private profit were being phased out by the late 1980s and early 1990s. Since the mid–1980s, the more typical shelters for the homeless have been the residential facilities, supported, organized, and administered by not-for-profit entities. A large percentage of these have some kind of religious affiliation, philosophy, or orientation. Three examples of religiously founded efforts to assist the homeless are Meeting Ground, La Luz de Santa Fe, and Habitat for Humanity International.

Meeting Ground, Inc. is a religious community and partnership that follows the "ideals of the Gospels and the person and work of Jesus Christ and his followers" (Loaves and Fishes, 1989: 2). As a practical matter, Meeting Ground's "work is with and among the poor, homeless, the sick, and any who are outcast, living on the margins of society, or those who seek a refuge or a home" (Loaves and Fishes, 1989: 2). Like so many other church-based programs for the homeless, Meeting Ground (MG), and approved Mission Cause of New Castle Presbytery of the Presbyterian Church (U.S.A.), is interfaith in both its constitution and outlook. As a community and corporation, Meeting Ground operates some eight programs primarily in Maryland and Delaware.

In Maryland, MG runs Clairvaux Farm near Cecilton and Wayfarers' House in Elkton. Both are primarily shelters for homeless women, women with children, and families. In early 1990, MG opened Cecil County Men's Shelter, a refuge for homeless men in Elkton. Also operating in Elkton is MG's not-for-profit Carousel Corner Thrift Store. In addition to selling clothes and household items at a very low cost, job training and experience in cooperation with other community agencies is provided.

In Wilmington, Delaware, MG runs Friendship House and Epiphany House. The former is a day shelter and advocacy center for the homeless; the latter a homeless shelter for families. Also operating in Wilmington is the Stephen Swain Settlement House, a house of hospitality and assistance for persons with AIDS. Finally, in recognition of the worldwide problem of homelessness, Meeting Ground operates various projects to assist refugees from Central America. This program is called Casa, Borderlinks, and Refugees at Risk.

La Luz de Santa Fe is a nonthreatening, Christian facility providing temporary housing, meals, counseling, child care, playground equipment, privacy, clothing, child care, human services, fellowship, and a safe environment. La Luz de Santa Fe serves primarily homeless families during their sincere search for permanent solutions to their problems by offering them private quarters for as long as necessary. La Luz de Santa Fe's motto, "A safe haven for families in need of temporary housing," and its program are supported through the interdenominational funding of the church community in Santa Fe, New Mexico.

June 17–24, 1990, was Habitat for Humanity's House-Raising Week Worldwide. During that week more than 2,000 Habitat volunteers from the United States, Canada, and Mexico, including Jimmy and Rosalyn Carter, erected 100 homes in Tijuana, Mexico, and five homes in San Diego, California. This binational effort was just one building project, "underscoring Habitat's worldwide scope in working toward an active solution to the problem of inadequate shelter" (McMillan, 1990: 1). Habitat for Humanity International (HFH), founded in 1976 and based in Americus, Georgia, had in the spring of 1990 more than 300 U.S. city affiliates and more than 25 participating foreign countries. According to Tom Hall, director of affiliate education with HFH, Habitat is dedicated to the proposition that there should be "no more shacks!" in the world:

We begin by saying we have a ministry that we believe God has given to us, our work being to make sure that all of the people of the world are able to live in safe, healthful, simple, decent homes.

We will do it one family at a time, one house at a time. The house will be built in partnership with the family and priced so the family can afford it. To accomplish this, the house is sold at no profit and no interest using donated money. The family's house payments then go into a revolving fund which helps build more houses. There is no requirement that the family in need profess the Christian faith (Hall, 1990: 16).

Without going into any details, suffice it to say that Habitat is a large-scale national and international organization that continues to expand its mission yearly. In addition to the affiliates mentioned above, there are campus chapters nationwide as well as regional centers. A number of private building companies around the country have also joined in partnership with Habitat, not merely by donating money and materials, but by actually building not-for-profit housing for low-income people and by sponsoring other nonprofit initiatives. At its international headquarters in Americus, an elaborate volunteer program of serving three months or more (with or without housing and food stipends) is in place. Volunteer positions include, but are not limited to, the following: administrative assistant, data entry/secretary, receptionist, mail center clerk, construction foreman, homeowner educator, skilled construction worker, in-kind solicitor, internal auditor, trainer, archivist, editor/writer, graphic artist, developer, and media.

Three examples of private nonprofit secular agencies serving the homeless are: Atlanta Day Shelter for Women (ADSW), Birmingham's Partnership Assistance to the Homeless (PATH), and Cincinnati's Alcoholic Drop Inn Center Shelterhouse (ADICS). As the only day shelter in Atlanta, ADSW provides many services to homeless women, including medical and referral, identification acquisition (e.g., paying for birth certificates and I.D. photos), literacy program in conjunction with Volunteers of America, a weekly support group entitled "Women in Crisis," and job and housing location. The shelter exists primarily to provide an environment where women can engage in the rebuilding process of getting their lives together. The shelter allows these women to have a place where they can shower, use the phone, wash and dry their clothes, drink coffee, and share conversation in exchange for a small chore assigned to them when they sign in at the beginning of each day.

The Birmingham PATH Program was incorporated in July 1988 for the purposes of maintaining, developing, and expanding the existing shelter program (the PATH Center for Women & Children and the PATH Transitional Housing Program); addressing and responding "to the personal crises and housing needs of the homeless population in the Birmingham Metropolitan area"; cooperating "with other community agencies and merg[ing] resources to enhance our response to the needs of the homeless"; and doing "all things necessary to end homelessness" in the greater area of Birmingham, Alabama (PATH, 1988: 1). PATH's partnership, like so many other nonreligious, not-for-profit private efforts to assist the homeless, depends on financial and other types of contributions from hundreds of volunteers and religious, secular, and corporate organizations. In providing its assistance, PATH works in cooperation with an extensive network of social service programs, shelter providers, mental health agencies, and government support services. In addition, all of PATH's shelter sites are owned and leased by the Housing Authority of the Birmingham District.

PATH operates essentially four programs. The PATH Center for Women and Children provides a safe heaven during daytime hours, a hot midday meal served daily, social service referrals, and crisis and personal counseling. The PATH Transitional Housing program provides eight two-bedroom apartments. In addition, it offers life plan and employment counseling, and counseling for independent living and reentry into the mainstream. The employment program provides self-esteem and skills building, individualized assessment and training, in-house employment, employment placements, and on-going support services. The Cottage Industry program provides related job training, skills development, and in-house employment.

In the winter of 1989 the work force at Shelterhouse, a Cincinnati-based program serving alcoholic homeless people in the greater Cincinnati/northern Kentucky/Southern Indiana area, consisted of 11 paid staff, numerous volunteers, and the residents themselves. Half of the staff were recovering alcoholics, and there is a conscious effort to have a balance of blacks, whites, men, and women. The governing body of Shelterhouse provides for equal representation of one-third paid staff, one-third volunteers, and one-third elected representatives from the center's residents. While Shelterhouse, the only facility of its kind in the Tri-State area, has depended primarily on donations, it has also received a basic yearly grant from the Ohio Department of Health, channeled through the Southwestern Ohio Regional Council of Alcoholism.

The ideology and philosophy of Shelterhouse is rather straightforward: they believe that all people, including the alcoholic, have a basic right to shelter. Accordingly, its purpose is twofold: to provide shelter for homeless alcoholics as the first step in the development of an effective program of treatment; and to educate the general public about the fundamental right to shelter. In its third location, an abandoned Teamsters Union Hall, Shelterhouse has provided such services as individual and group counseling, weekly film seminars, and a close working relationship with detox programs, halfway houses, clinics, and hospitals in the greater Cincinnati area. Shelterhouse has also sponsored a Housing Co-op program, based on the belief that meaningful volunteer work to assist others can be an important step in regaining stability as well as one's sense of self-worth. On the weekends, a crew of the sober, recovering alcoholics in conjunction with volunteers have carried out ongoing construction. These have usually consisted of working to remodel abandoned buildings near the Shelterhouse facility for occupation by low-income people in the form of co-op housing. In 1988 Shelterhouse served more than 10,000 individuals.

By the mid- to late 1980s, a number of national and local foundations had been established to aid the homeless. Foundations such as the national Hope Foundation, the Homeward Bound Foundation of Hartford, and the Better Homes Foundation initiated by *Better Homes and Gardens* magazine have typically been the creation of successful people trying to do their part. While most of these foundations have essentially raised money for the homeless, for homeless shelters, and for other homeless projects such as the development of transitional and low-income housing stock or the provision of family support centers, some have also developed volunteer hotlines and even computerized data bases on shelter services for the homeless.

Perhaps the best-known charity and show on behalf of the homeless has been "Comic Relief" created by Bob Zmuda, a producer and comedy writer. In 1986 Zmuda brought the comedic talents of Billy Crystal, Whoopi Goldberg, and Robin Williams together and persuaded Michael Fuchs, the chairman of HBO, to underwrite all the expenses of putting together an annually televised national special for raising money on behalf of the homeless. After "Comic Relief" aired in May 1990, its total of money pledged since its debut four years earlier was in excess of $12 million. The money raised has gone directly to the National Health Care for the Homeless, a medical-aid program administered by the Robert Wood Johnson Foundation with centers around the country.

CONCLUSION

Despite the expanding networks of assistance and the increasing number of programs that emerged during the 1980s to meet the needs of the homeless, homelessness in the United States still continues to grow in the 1990s. The vast majority of programs, resources, and aid of the homeless have been aimed at meeting their short-term needs—namely, the provision of temporary shelter and crisis counseling. However, the long-term needs of providing permanent housing for low-income or no-income people, or for taking into account the changing political economy and its effects on wages, real estate, housing, and development as these intersect with trends in homelessness, have been virtually ignored by both the states and the federal administration. Excluding the exceptions found among some academicians, policy analysts, and homeless advocates, most persons concerned about homelessness have not been considering the larger macro forces at work or the structural changes underpinning the new homelessness. Accordingly, most social policy has responded to the surface symptoms and not the root causes of homelessness. Instead of adopting policies that would prevent future homelessness based on an assessment of economic and social trends, for example, the government and the private sector have focused their energies on the immediate satisfaction of the short-term shelter and developmental needs of existing homeless persons.

Whether one believes that the various public or private sectors are doing too much, too little, or the wrong thing altogether, a basic understanding of homelessness services and policies in America requires familiarity with the emergence and development of the movement on behalf of homeless persons. In order to further develop the case or the evidence for what should be done to prevent future tomorrows of homelessness, it is necessary for us to turn to an examination of this movement to resist the new homelessness. Understanding both the advocacy and the organization of the movement for the homeless as well as understanding those forces of the changing political economy of homelessness are prerequisites for developing the kind of long-term preventive strategies necessary to end homelessness in America.

REFERENCES

Balz, Dan. 1989. "For the Needy, 'A Decade of Neglect'." *The Montgomery Advertiser and Alabama Journal*, December 25. (*Washington Post* reporter).

Caton, Carol. 1990. *Homeless in America*. New York: Oxford University Press.

Hall, Tom. 1990. "Who and What is Habitat for Humanity." *Habitat World*, 7, no. 2 (April).

HUD 1989. *The 1988 National Survey of Shelters for the Homeless*. Office of Policy Development and Research. Washington, DC: U.S. Government Printing Office (March).

The Interagency Council on the Homeless. 1989a. *Non-McKinney Federal Programs*

Available to Help the Homeless. Washington, DC: U.S. Government Printing Office (July).

———. 1989b. *The McKinney Act: A Program Guide*. Washington, DC: U.S. Government Printing Office (September).

Johnson, Hayes. 1988. "Solutions take Public, Private Effort." *The Cincinnati Enquirer*, December 21.

Kaufman, Susan. 1989. "A Day at the Capitol Inn." *Safety Network: Newsletter of the National Coalition for the Homeless*, 8, no. 6 (November). (Originally published in the *Washington Post*).

Kessler, Brady. 1989. "Down and Out in Suburbia." *The Nation*, September 25.

Loaves and Fishes. 1989. *Newsletter of Meeting Ground*, 8, no. 3 (May-June).

Low Income Housing Information Service. 1988. "The 1989 Low Income Housing Budget." Washington, DC: LIHIS (April).

McMillan, Darryl. 1990. "Binational Project Focal Point for Building Global Awareness." *Habitat World*, 7, no. 2 (April).

Moore, Cassandra. 1990. "Housing Policy in New York: Myth and Reality." No. 132 in the Cato Institute's Policy Analysis Series. Washington, DC.

National Coalition for the Homeless. 1989. "The Interagency Council on the Homeless: An Assessment." Washington, DC: NCH (March).

PATH. 1988. *1988 Annual Report of Partnership Assistance to the Homeless*. Birmingham: PATH, Inc.

Reeves, Richard. 1990. "S & L Disaster Rips Off Taxpayers." *The Montgomery Advertiser*, April 23. (*Washington Post* reporter).

Safety Network. 1990. "Homelessness and the 1991 Federal Budget." *Newsletter of the National Coalition for the Homeless*, vol 9, No. 3 (March).

Smith, Christopher. 1988. *Public Problems: The Management of Urban Distress*. New York: The Guilford Press.

Washington [AP]. 1988. "Lawmaker Blasts Social Security Head Over Homeless Aid." *The Montgomery Advertiser and Alabama Journal*, December 4.

Washington Post Writer's Group. 1988. "A Homeless Shelter." The second in a three-part series excerpted from Jonathan Kozol's *Rachel and Her Children: Homeless Families in America*, carried in the *Tallahassee Democrat*, February 15.

Wire Reports from New York. 1989. "Many Get The Blame For Homeless." *The Montgomery Advertiser*, January 23.

6 Resisting Homelessness

By the closing months of the 1988 presidential race, according to the polls, most Americans had come to realize that the struggle of poverty's most victimized casualties—the homeless—was part of the larger struggle for a more fundamentally decent society. Even the soon-to-be-elected president, George Bush, could be heard promising a "kinder, gentler America" with a "thousand points of light" to lead the way. This type of rhetoric or social consciousness or both has been to some degree part of a slowly evolving backlash to austerity and to those cutbacks from the supply-side economics practiced during eight years of the so-called Reagan revolution. The policies of defederalism (or the new statism as it was referred to for a while), the deregulation of corporate America, and the intensification of repression against marginal and nonmarginal groups were clearly evident of a noninterventionist federal government, at least when it came to the laissez-faire monopolies of the marketplace. The concern, unfortunately, has remained primarily preoccupied with street crime and welfare fraud to the relative exclusion of suite crime and corporate greed. Meanwhile, the latter types of crime have literally robbed this country blind (the savings and loan rip-off), but neither the president nor the Congress wants to seriously confront white-collar crime. Just ask former Deputy Attorney General Donald Ayer, who resigned in May 1990 following the rebuff given by White House Counsel C. Boyden Gray to Ayer's recommendation on May 9 that the federal government go after corporate criminals with fines ranging up into the hundreds of millions of dollars (ETC., 1990).

By the end of the 1980s, most people, including those of the more conservative or ideological right-wing U.S. politics, had come to appreciate the direct relationship between Reaganomics, arrogant political indifference, and noncompassionate government as these had jointly helped to contribute to the increasing misery of the old and new poor, and to the swelling numbers of homeless Americans. Whether a person felt that she or he should become a volunteer in the war against homelessness, or whether one felt guilty or responsible, or whether one just wanted the embarrassing problem to go away, being "for" the homeless, especially when everyone knew that the fastest growing groups of homeless victims were children, families, and women, registered quite favorably with most social and political constituencies. Emotionally speaking, it has probably had the effect of lessening rich people's collective guilt or sense of responsibility for the problem. In any event, as homelessness continued to grow throughout the 1980s, so did the number of involved supporters, advocates, and activists.

In less than a decade, most politicians and businesspeople in general (i.e., the Chambers of Commerce across the country) had changed their tune, if not their practice, regarding the problem of homelessness. Most had reached the conclusion that something needed to be done about the homeless (Barak, 1991). In the early to middle 1980s, politicians, local government officials, and the downtown business communities had been rather hostile to both the idea and the reality of homelessness. Their initial position on the homelessness question was generally one of opposition. For the most part, they simply denied that the problem existed. At this time, the conservative thinking was that even if the problem did exist, acknowledging it and providing services like day shelters was a bad idea because this would only attract more homeless people from other places to make the matter worse.

Their next position evolved from the earlier one. Instead of denying that the problem existed, the business-oriented community denied having any responsibility for the homeless problem. They preferred to blame the homeless for their own troubles. In ideological terms, the homeless were still members of the undeserving poor. By the end of the 1980s, however, this had changed; all but the most right-wing ideologues had arrived at the position that many of the homeless were indeed members of the deserving poor. Most people by the decade's end had understood that "trickle down" never did. And most everybody had learned that all the money that was to be reaped from the capital gains tax reductions, the deregulation of the market, and the new prosperity had gone to the rich. The average person was worse off after eight years of Reaganomics, but the affluent were better off.

The homeless movement in the United States began to emerge in the late 1970s. By this time, all across the country, unprecedented numbers of people were sleeping on the streets and in their cars. Even before the homeless had become too visible, the earliest homeless advocacy groups were already forming in the mid–1970s:

Homelessness in the late 1970s spawned an entirely new network of soup kitchens and shelters. The number of Main Street drop-in centers grew exponentially with Ronald Reagan's budgetary imperatives. The shelters, the soup kitchens and the early advocacy groups were the first helpful response to the problem—a response that had more to do with crisis intervention and charity than with any demand for change (Kessler, 1988: 528).

The second wave of advocacy, involving the appearance of grass-roots or community groups, was not merely a charity-based affair to help the needy. These homeless advocacy groups represented a rather wide range of political purposes, and their constituencies included various foundations, housing campaigns, tenants' right organizations, block associations, legal advocacy groups, service providers, civil rights groups, homeless unions, and squatters. Collectively, as they say, they have been demanding housing now. These activists have been calling for the restoration of low-income housing federal funds to their pre–1981 levels. They have also been demanding that some 3 million housing units be built or renovated for the homeless in order to accommodate the deficit in affordable housing. No longer satisfied with temporary shelter and services, the second wave of advocacy was calling for change—namely, the provision of permanent housing for the homeless and potential homeless.

In 1990 the homeless movement is relatively mature, sophisticated, and national in scope. But by no means is the movement or are the various coalitions on behalf of the homeless without their share of both internal and external conflicts. And by no means is there anything approaching some kind of a monolithic structure or organization in the movement to resist homelessness and to advocate for the homeless. Like most other social movements, the one to abolish homelessness is full of the usual and not so usual contradictions involving political reform and legal change. Nevertheless, the struggle or the movement to eliminate homelessness in the United States is still expanding. I suspect that the movement will continue to grow so long as homelessness does, even though there is evidence that the interest of the media and the general public to a lesser extent has already begun to wane. At the same time, the homeless movement has recently been reaching out to join forces with other struggles for social justice, as activists have begun to realize that the homeless movement is not fundamentally about housing per se. These homeless advocates believe instead that the movement is about changing the whole domestic agenda, from economic development to political empowerment. In other words, today's progressive struggle to resist homelessness is basically a struggle about education, health care, day care, livable jobs, and equal rights for all.

CONFLICT, INJUSTICE, AND REDISTRIBUTION

Gil (1989) has argued that over 10,000 years of social-structure violence represents the tragic side of human history. He specifically refers to the history, ancient and contemporary, of inegalitarian work systems. Gil contends that such systems as slavery, feudal serfdom, agricultural and industrial wage labor could never have been established and reproduced without the various faces of societal violence—genocide, murder, torture, imprisonment, starvation, destitution, unemployment, and so on. Dialectically, Gil (1989: 44) recognizes that human history also has a brighter side.

a record of resistance and counter-violence by oppressed and exploited, social groups, and individuals against domination and injustice, and of struggles for human liberation and a renaissance of social orders based on egalitarian, nonexploitative modes of work and just and balanced terms of exchange and distribution of the products of human work.

The point is that in the contemporary United States, homelessness is at the cutting edge of the struggle to resist the prevailing order of societal violence and counterviolence. Today's new homeless or the new vagrancy exemplify the ultimate contradictions of advanced capitalism. Accordingly, class and social conflicts that revolve around the homeless can usually be understood when viewed within the historic context of societal violence and counter-violence, especially as these revolve around the organization of work and the exchange and distribution of the products of human labor.

I refer to those class and social conflicts captured by the printed media in the following article titles: "Watergate Residents Don't Welcome D.C.'s Homeless"; "Celebrities Rankled by 'Mayor' Sheen's Invitation To Homeless"; "Atlanta's Vagrant-Free Zone' "; and "Homeless People Protest the Closing of Plaza Park." The conflicts described in these news stories have reflected the various expressions and manifestations of the contradictions between individual and collective justice. In each of these dialectical cases, implicitly if not explicitly, the conflicts were between the rights of property on the one hand and the rights of human beings on the other hand.

In the first example, the story was about the "high and mighty" (e.g., Senator Bob Dole and Labor Secretary Elizabeth Dole, military officials, and Washington journalists) who were living in the pricey Watergate complex. The beef was not exactly with the homeless per se, but with the city which had decided to erect an aluminum village for the homeless across the street from the Watergate apartments. The object of their scorn was the proposed cluster of seven white trailers tucked into a triangle and in plain view of some of the loftiest apartments in the capital city. In their lawsuit to block this shelter for the homeless, "the 680 homeowners [didn't] come straight out and say 'we don't want to house the homeless.' [Instead, their] lawsuit claim[ed] that the city failed to run the idea past the Fine Arts Commission, which decides in certain areas if a structure is appropriate" (Rosenthal, 1990: 8A).

In the late spring of 1989, when Malibu's honorary Mayor Martin Sheen (who had portrayed homeless activist Snyder in the television movie, *Samaritan: The Mitch Snyder Story*) declared the California beach community "a nuclear-free zone, a sanctuary for all aliens, and the homeless, and a protected environment for all life, wild and tame," he had the local residents quite disturbed about the possibility of a wave of homeless people descending on the celebrity-soaked shores. After all, the thought does not easily come to mind of a tent city encampment exactly fitting into a town of 19,000 people with no coin-operated laundries, no mortuaries, and no car lots or washes, and when homes start at $500,000 and go up to $20 million (which was the price tag of Barbra Streisand's compound in 1989). Then again, in January of 1987 actor Sheen had joined Community for Creative Non-Violence activist Snyder and bedded down for the night on a steam gate in Washington, D.C. to call attention to the need for emergency aid for the homeless. The manager of the Malibu Inn and Restaurant, Tony Cassion, had this to say in reference to Sheen: "We should disassociate ourselves from him. There is no community that welcomes the homeless" (Wilson, 1989: 2A). Mary Lou Blackwood, the Malibu Chamber of Commerce's executive vice-president, who had received a number of telephone calls, put it simply: "The Community is pretty upset" (Wilson, 1989: 2A). On the other hand, the friends and defenders of Sheen, most of whom had been heavily involved in antinuclear weapons protests and the farm workers' grape boycott, had pledged to provide food and clothing if homeless people showed up: " 'We're not going to ask them to leave. We feel those people have suffered enough and they are being used,' said neighbor Maria Olk. Supporter Judith Israel said: 'Homeless people aren't meat' " (Wilson, 1989:2A).

A few years earlier in the hub of the New South a more serious conflict ensued between Atlanta's interests in development and the interests of its impoverished homeless residents. On Christmas Eve 1986, a demonstration took place when friends and advocates of Atlanta's homeless carried a black crucifix labeled "the vagrant Christ" along Peachtree Street to downtown Plaza Park. These homeless activists were protesting the proposed closing of the park. Ed Loring, a pastor at the Open Door community shelter at 910 Ponce de Leon Avenue, had this to say about the vagrant-free zone: "We're taking on the issue of Plaza Park to dramatize that everyone, not just the homeless, are losing space because of the revitalization. . . . We wanted to show that the rebirth of Underground Atlanta also represented a kind of death for the poor" (Beeber, 1987:1). As writer Joyce Hollyday (1987:11), observed in the *Sojourner*,

Plaza Park [had] become a symbolic and very real battleground in a conflict that [was] raging in Atlanta. For the city's business associates and developers, the park [was] a proposed entrance point to the "revitalized" future Atlanta. For several of the city's estimated 8,000 homeless people, it [was] home.

During the 1960s, Underground Atlanta had been an area of thriving shops and restaurants along the city's old railroad tracks. In the 1970s, the city's generally high crime rates earned Atlanta the title 'homicide capital of the nation." By the 1980s, buttressed by the media attention on the Atlanta Tragedy (the killings of 29 black youngsters between late spring 1980 and late winter 1982), crime and the fear of crime had driven people from downtown. Underground Atlanta was abandoned, not to be resurrected until spring 1989, with its grand reopening as a part of Atlanta's downtown revitalization and aggressive bid to secure the 1996 Olympics. In the meantime, it had been the homeless who for about five years had taken refuge below the streets of Atlanta. If the situation in downtown Atlanta was going to change, if people were going to come and spend their money on clothes, food, and entertainment, then the streets would have to be taken back from the homeless:

With the election of Andrew Young as mayor, "redevelopment" became the key to making Atlanta a preferred city for business, tourism, and conventions. A reborn Underground Atlanta has become a central component in the revitalization plan. If the plan is to work, according to its proponents, the city needs to shed its image of being plagued with crime. The nation needs to know that Atlanta is "safe" again (Hollyday, 1987:11).

Caught within this redevelopment conflict were, on the one side, the proposals by the city of Atlanta, Fulton County, and the Atlanta business community calling for "quality of life offenses" in order to arrest the panhandlers, the loiterers, the drunks, and the other aimlessly wandering homeless people. On the other side were the proposals of the homeless activists like Loring to block the closing down of Plaza Park to the homeless, to provide alternative parks and shelters, to see that free transportation enabling the homeless to reach decentralized shelters be made available, and that for every $100 spent on downtown redevelopment in Atlanta there be $10 set aside for the construction of low-income housing for the homeless (Hollyday, 1987).

Class and social conflicts involving the homeless are not always peaceful in nature, and some are downright violent. The latter conflicts between the homeless and the homeful in the United States have usually occurred when the issues have involved the middle and working classes rather than with the more affluent and corporate classes. A case in point was December 1989 when

police ejected 280 homeless from a park in Manhattan's Lower East Side . . . the latest action in a bitter conflict tearing this neighborhood apart. Fueled by New York's housing crisis, this conflict has included a police riot, a Hooverville, neofascist "anarchists" and the breakdown of local government. In addition, the crisis has hastened the decay of one of America's most progressive and historic communities (Vincent, 1990:18).

This was not the first time that violence had broken out in Tompkins Square Park. In fact, on August 6, 1988, when the police entered the park and were met by a group of punks, skinheads, and self-proclaimed anarchists, all hell broke loose:

The Tompkins Square Park Riot lasted until dawn. When it was over, 450 officers—many had taped over their badge numbers—had arrested and/or assaulted scores of people. One man, simply walking home, was hospitalized after cops attacked him with night sticks. Others were dragged out of restaurants and cafes and beaten. Civilians filed more than 100 complaints of police brutality. Six officers were eventually charged; none was convicted (Vincent, 1990:18).

Before the riot, there were about 125 homeless men and women living in Tompkins Square according to Neighborhood Community Board No. 3. Most people ignored these homeless people dispersed in the dilapidation of the park. After the riot, however, the anarchists could be heard contending that the imposed park curfew was tantamount to waging war on the poor and that with respect to displacing the homeless for the park, it was a matter of genocide. By the spring of 1990 things had quieted down in the park. No longer present were the tents and lean-tos. Instead there was a cyclone fence surrounding the park with park department signs announcing a $2 million renovation of the area. At the same time, however, these signs had the graffiti "Die, yuppie scum" and "Burn baby burn" scrawled across them. As Vincent (1990:19) concluded in his essay, "clearly, for community residents, grass-roots officials and anarchists—as well as the homeless caught in the middle—the battle for Tompkins Square Park is far from over."

THE CONTEMPORARY HOMELESS MOVEMENT: PAST AND PRESENT

Lee Grant's documentary film *Down and Out in America* and her made-for-television motion picture *No Place Like Home* established the director as a powerful advocate for homeless people. In 1987 her documentary received an Academy Award as well as cable television's Ace Award as Outstanding Documentary. By the time Grant's movie about a fictitious homeless family aired on December 3, 1989, on CBS prime-time, the Cultural Information Service (CIS) of CBS had provided complimentary Viewer Guides, resource material, and information on model programs for the homeless to secondary and postsecondary institutions of education throughout the United States. The cover letter that I received with my packet said, in part, that the Viewer's Guide was designed for "use in community awareness and outreach campaigns." The letter also said that "a detailed plot synopsis shows you how "No Place Like Home" might illustrate common situations and problems of homeless people in your community." Finally, it stated that "awareness building activities relate back to the film's story and to other issues identified by homeless advocates."

This degree of involvement and organization on the part of CBS and CIS, and its concerted effort to bring the homelessness story to the American people in general and to the educational community in particular, speaks to the fact that the movement to resist homelessness and to assist the homeless has become an institutionalized wide phenomenon in the United States. The degree of consciousness about homelessness that prevails in the early 1990s, and the little more than a decade in which it took for homeless advocates to win the ideological war on behalf of the deserving homeless, provide evidence that as a social movement, involving people without direct constituent interest, this movement compares favorably to both the civil rights and women's movements of the 1950s through 1970s, in terms of both the diversification of people involved and the celerity of the movement itself. Hopper (1990:164) reported at the close of the 1980s that one of the most striking things about contemporary advocacy was how rapidly its ranks had diversified: "Long-standing partisans for the poor (like the Catholic Worker movement) have found their efforts championed by members of the press, the pulpit, the academy, and by ordinary households."

Stated differently, homeless advocacy of the 1980s proved to be a powerful social force, a focal point for the convergence of a wide array of dissatisfaction with the contemporary social policy exemplified by the harshness and indifference of the Reagan administration. As Smith (1988:233) correctly observed, "statistics on unemployment and inflation, and even the staggering size of the budget deficit, have not been as effective in combatting the conservative trend as the continued publicity about the homeless." Blau (1987:57) made a similar observation about the movement to resist homelessness when he wrote, "mixing moral witness, education, and increasing political sophistication, it ha[d] helped the homeless become one of the few constituencies among the poor to gain program benefits in recent years." Moreover, as Chapter 5 demonstrated, the movement on behalf of the homeless in the 1980s resulted in a substantial accumulation of not only public and private resources, but in a volunteer army of more than 10,000 people committed to providing emergency food, clothing, and shelter. In a very real sense, by the mid–1980s, the level of interest in the plight of the homeless had captured

the imagination of the American public more strongly than any of the earlier epidemics such as mental illness, alcoholism, drug abuse, or crime. Disregarding the other problems experienced by the homeless, the simple fact of being without a home ha[d] resonated deeply within the consciousness of middle-class America, and this issue ha[d] been able to generate more awareness and a higher level of emotion than most other issues in recent memory" (Smith, 1988: 232).

During the 1980s, homelessness became a major media event at both national and local levels. At least one policy analyst has argued that the

pivotal year in homelessness coverage by the news media was 1982. Specifically, in March 1982 homeless stories were carried in *Newsweek*, *U.S.
News and World Report*, and the *Wall Street Journal*. In the same year,
however, there were

only a handful of stories about homelessness in the *New York Times*, but in 1983
there was an explosion of coverage, with an average of nearly two stories each week.
At the time the problem remained a seasonal one, in that there were only 14 stories
in the 5 summer months from May to the end of September. In 1984 and 1985 the
coverage in the *New York Times* increased to an average of more than three stories
a week, and the seasonal bias had almost disappeared. Homelessness had become a
fully fledged media event all the year round (Smith, 1988: 231–232).

The emergence of a mass movement on behalf of the homeless and excessive
media coverage during the mid–1980s did not occur without a struggle by
a small group of homeless activists, residing primarily in Washington, D.C.
and New York City. Without the actions of such people as Mary Ellen Hombs
and Mitch Snyder in Washington and Kim Hopper, Robert Hayes, and others
in New York, it would have taken both the media and the politicians a lot
longer, if ever, to acknowledge the serious condition of homelessness in
America.

Back in 1970, in Washington, D.C., the Community for Creative Non-
Violence was established as an organization to further peace education and
antiwar actions. By 1976 CCNV had become almost exclusively involved in
aiding the homeless and in bringing their plight to the attention of the
American people. It was, after all, CCNV's dramatic acts of protest that had
first gained the public's attention:

The dramatic confrontations. The illegal occupations of buildings. The pray-ins, eat-
ins, cage-ins, jump-ins and even laugh-ins. And most of all, Mitch Snyder's fasts.
The danger of his condition, the size of his risk ha[d] captured the nation's attention
and pricked our conscience about a group of people Americans didn't see, and didn't
want to see (Rader, 1986: ix).

Although local press and television initially ignored the problem of homelessness and ridiculed the protests by CCNV and others, eventually the
media adopted much of the activists' perspective as their own. As Rader
(1986:250) concluded in her excellent history and analysis of CCNV and its
struggle on behalf of the homeless, "the media never took back their earlier
criticism of CCNV claims as extreme and exaggerated. They never acknowledged that they had first ignored and then denied the serious suffering of
large numbers of Americans."

In other words, before homelessness was to receive its legitimization as
a serious problem as certified by its reality in the media, the issue's reality
had to be verified first by the actions of the advocates for the homeless. Two

books in particular placed homelessness on the public agenda. The first addressed the problem of homelessness in New York City. It was Kim Hopper and Ellen Baxter's *Private Lives/Public Spaces* (1981). The second addressed the problem of homelessness nationwide. It was Mary Ellen Hombs and Mitch Snyder's *Homeless in America: A Forced March to Nowhere* (1983).

The National Coalition for the Homeless claimed that the October 7, 1989, Housing Now! march in Washington, D.C. "marked the beginning of a national housing movement" as demonstrators had poured into the nation's capital from every region of the country (Safety Network, 1989: 1). Such a demonstration represented the culmination of the work and organizing efforts of hundreds of coalitions from virtually every state in the union who had come to join the movement against homelessness during the 1980s. Of course, it still remains to be seen if the movement can truly mount a concerted and nationwide campaign against homelessness that will succeed in establishing the institutionalized policies necessary to eliminate both homelessness and the fear of homelessness. Toward that end, the convening organization of Housing Now! (CCNV, NCH, and the National Low Income Housing Coalition) and some 200 sponsoring organizations—including such national endorsers as ACORN, AFL-CIO, Association of Federal, State, County, and Municipal Employees, American Friends Service Committee, Black Veterans for Social Justice, Church Conference on Shelter and Housing, Democratic Socialists of America, ELKS Grand Lodge, Gray Panthers, Habitat for Humanity International, National AIDS Network, National Alliance of Mental Patients, National Gay and Lesbian Taskforce, National Union of the Homeless, National Urban League, National Rainbow Coalition, SANE/FREEZE, U.S. Conference of Mayors, U.S. Student Association, War Resister's League, the YMCA, the YWCA—had "vowed to continue the struggle until every American is entitled to decent and affordable housing" (Safety Network, 1989:2)

The idea of a mass rally and demonstration in Washington D.C. for the fall of 1989 was adopted at the National Housing Policy Development Conference (January 14–15, 1989), as part of the strategy for developing a national agenda for aiding the homeless. Sponsored by CCNV and hosted by the Atlanta Task Force for the Homeless, the National Housing Summit held at the Crown Plaza Holiday Inn near Hartsfield International Airport drew some 250 people (including homeless and former homeless "representatives") from all over the United States. As a "participant-observer" at this conference, I can testify that without a prepackaged agenda (and with respect to what some had referred to as a summit meeting slightly "left of anarchy") there emerged an action agenda.

The Housing Summit resulted in a two-pronged strategy to push national "direct actions," including mass protests and illegal squatting in major cities across the country, and to help pass national and local legislation designed to fund housing for the homeless. This conference, more specifically, served to establish national unifying goals and objectives for resisting homelessness. For example, during the two-day summit, statements of unity and principle were adopted by those present. The statement of unity read, in part:

We came together here in Atlanta this weekend, over 250 people from across the United States: homeless people, shelter workers, housing advocates, activists, and religious leaders. We came together out of our sense of URGENCY and ANGER that people are homeless in the richest country in the history of the world; we are outraged that the numbers of homeless people are continually growing.

We are a network of people coming together for two purposes:

1. TO STATE CLEARLY AND LOUDLY:
   - Housing is a Basic Human Right: decent, affordable housing. It is a fundamental part of the American Dream for all our people.

2. TO UNITE BEHIND THE BIG PUSH:
   - A wave of national public political action;
   - Major legislation for necessary affordable housing funding to end homelessness in this land.

With respect to federal housing policy initiatives, the following seven principles were adopted by the Legislative Working Group:

1. The Federal government has the primary responsibility to provide resources that make housing opportunities available. Federal funding should give first priority to permanently affordable housing through public housing, nonprofit community-based development and other means.

2. People who are homeless or are in imminent danger of becoming homeless should be given priority for federal housing assistance.

3. Federal policies should support increased resident control and participation in all assisted housing. Federal funding should support state and local initiatives that meet these goals where such initiatives exist.

4. Federal housing policies should be cost effective. All available federal resources, including land, housing and other buildings should be used wherever possible to meet homeless and low income housing needs.

5. Current federal rules require many people to pay too much for their housing. We support reforms that would adjust payment levels to reflect the varying needs of poor people.

6. We oppose any actions which reduce the current supply of affordable housing for low income people. We call for all Federally assisted housing to be brought up to code by the Federal government. We oppose demolition or sale of federally assisted housing and we oppose any Federal preemption of state or local tenant regulations.

7. Housing opportunities cannot be realized without vigorous and uncompromised enforcement of Fair Housing laws.

Finally, the summit formed a national coordinating committee to mobilize for those national actions, to make affordable housing prominent on the agenda of the United States, to reverse the major U.S. government retreat from affordable housing, and to support ongoing initiatives of community-based groups who are creating/reclaiming their own housing.

Less than nine months later, the District of Columbia Police Department estimated that as many as 250,000 people descended onto the nation's capital on October 7 to protest the condition of homelessness in America. The crowd, which extended from the steps of the U.S. capitol to the Pentagon, was described by the *Los Angeles Times* as a "sea of humanity." On the mass demonstration, the National Coalition for the Homeless had this to say:

> People from every state in the nation and all walks of life came to Washington to show their support—with a particularly strong showing from churches and unions. Celebrities from the entertainment industry were also present to provide visibility and moral support. Among the well-known names were Jon Voight, Susan Dey, Valerie Harper, Dionne Warwick, and Linda Evans. The crowd was also treated to performances by leading musicians including Stevie Wonder, Jefferson Airplane, Los Lobos, and Tracy Chapman.
>
> At the front of the crowd were the New Exodous marchers—most of them home-less—who had earned honorary seating near the stage by marching hundreds of miles from New York City and Roanoke, Virginia. Braving hurricane weather and the lack of adequate supplies to sustain them, the New Exodous marchers came to demand that their government relieve their suffering.
>
> Children also took part. Earlier that morning, a brigade of children pulling little red wagons full of tens of thousands of letters written by children from all over the country delivered the mail to the Speaker of the House, Thomas Foley of Washington (Safety Network, 1989:1).

As a postscript, both political parties and the Bush administration could be viewed making public statements and pledging to implement policies favorable to the Housing Now! march on Washington, promises and com-mitments like the ones I have included here were circulating around the Capitol. For example, at a meeting on October 6, between the leadership of Housing Now! and the House of Representatives, Democrats (including Speaker Foley, Rep. Leon Panetta of California, Chairman of the Budget Committee William Gray [and a key member of the Appropriations Com-mittee]) had "promised to introduce legislation in 1991 that would restore budget cuts in housing made by the Reagan Administration" (Safety Net-work, 1989:1). In a separate meeting, HUD Secretary Jack Kemp committed to making 10 percent of HUD's single-family home inventory available for homeless people and made a number of other promises in response to the requests of Housing Now! activists. In a handwritten note, Kemp reiterated: "On this occasion of the 25th anniversary of the War on Poverty, be assured of my desire to work full time to win this war against poverty, homelessness, and despair" (Safety Network, 1989:2). More than a month later, on News-maker Sunday (November 26, 1989), Assistant Secretary of Housing and Community Development Anna Kondratas stated that the goal of the admin-istration is "to end homelessness in America and to confront the conditions that cause people to live in poverty."

Despite the Bush administration's rhetoric to the contrary, its policies, budget recommendations, and overall practice have continued in the Reagan tradition of federal retrenchment in the area of low-income housing. In short, the U.S. problem of homelessness is not being eradicated, and the number of homeless persons continues to grow.

THE RANK AND FILE OF THE STREETS

In the 1980s, when homeless people found themselves unable to earn wages that could support them and their families, unable to live in safety and dignity, and unable to find adequate shelter or nutrition, they organized a union—the Union of the Homeless:

It's not a conventional union, in that many of the members are not working and those who are do not share a common work place. But in its philosophy and goals— the drawing together of individuals to give them collective power to fight for a decent and humane living—it's pure union (McMullen 1988:3).

The forerunner to the Union of the Homeless was the Committee for Dignity and Fairness, founded in Philadelphia in October 1983 by a 48-year-old homeless man, Chris Sprowal, whose small business had failed in 1981 along with his marriage. In early 1984, Sprowal received a grant of $23,700 to run a shelter in a downtown Methodist church.

Sprowal's solution to homelessness, however, has not been based on the establishment of more and better shelters, because he knew from personal experience that shelters did nothing for human dignity. So, instead, he has been attempting to empower homeless people and he has been searching for power. To begin, Sprowal hooked up with some members of Hospital Workers 1199 in Philadelphia. They suggested the idea of a union structure and in 1985 gave Sprowal $5,000 in seed money to begin organizing the homeless around the country. Shortly thereafter, an organizing convention was held and the Philadelphia/Delaware Union of the Homeless was formed. A little later the union affiliated with Hospital Workers 1199 and has since gone national.

As of September 1988 membership in the union was 18,000 and it included only people who had been or were homeless at the time. Also, there were

14 cities with union chapters: Detroit, Chicago, Minneapolis, Los Angeles, San Francisco, Oakland, Tucson, Albuquerque, New Orleans, Washington, D.C., Boston, Baltimore, Philadelphia, and New York City. Organizing the homeless has been extremely difficult, as these people are already engaged in the everyday struggle for survival. And survival, of course, has come before organization.

Nevertheless, both organization and action have occurred. Generally the Union of the Homeless has focused its tactics on direct action and immediate change. The union has not advocated spending money on shelters. It has preferred that funding be spent for affordable housing, job training, and jobs. At the same time, the union has engaged in a variety of actions: it has successfully fought for the right of Chicago's homeless to vote; it has owned several houses in Philadelphia that have been leased affordably to the poor; and it has even renovated an abandoned warehouse in New Orleans that has sheltered 200 homeless persons.

Occupying, liberating, or squatting in publicly or privately owned and abandoned (boarded up) properties is one of the tactics employed by the union. On July 14, 1988, in 61 cities throughout the country, activists demonstrated for affordable housing. Protestors included those people who tore the boards off of abandoned housing and occupied the structures. Nationwide, nearly 100 individuals were arrested on that summer day. Although there are plenty of people who have questioned these illegal actions of the union for being too radical, Sprowal has questioned the use of the "radical" label to describe these political acts: "Do you think it's radical to want a job and a home for your family? We're as American as apple pie." Sprowal continued, "this is our country and we're not going to be content no more with the crumbs from the table. We intend to sit at the table and we intend to share in a full meal" (McMullen, 1988:3).

In summing up the purpose of a Union of the Homeless or of a rank and file of the streets, Sprowal said:

We want to mobilize and organize a whole generation of dependent people . . . Moving from dependency to independence and empowerment, means moving away from the shelter system. . . .

I don't give a damn how well run it is, shelters strip people of their dignity. They breed dependence and they cripple people. And when people wake up in shelters, they are still homeless (McMullen, 1988:3).

REFERENCES

Barak, Gregg. 1991. "Homelessness and the Case for Community-Based Initiatives: The Emergence of a Model Shelter as a Short Term Response to the Deepening Crisis in Housing." In Harold E. Pepinsky and Richard Quinney, eds., *Criminology as Peacemaking*. Bloomington: Indiana University Press.

Beeber, Steven. 1987. "Homeless people protest closing of Plaza Park." *Creative Loafing*, February 14.

Blau, Joel S. 1987. "The Homeless of New York: A Case Study in Social Welfare Policy." Doctoral Dissertation. Ann Arbor, MI: University Microfilms (1989).

ETC. 1990. *In These Times*, 14, no. 26 (May 23–June 5).

Gil, David. 1989. "Work, Violence, Injustice and War." *Journal of Sociology and Social Welfare*, 16, no. 1.

Hollyday, Joyce. 1987. "Atlanta's 'Vagrant-Free Zone.' " *Sojourner*, March.

Hombs, Mary Ellen and Mitch Snyder. 1982. *Homelessness in America: A Forced March to Nowhere*. Washington, D.C.: Community for Creative Non-Violence.

Hopper, Kim. 1990. "Advocacy for the Homeless in the 1980s." In Carol L. M. Caton, ed., *Homeless in America*. New York: Oxford University Press.

Hopper, Kim and Ellen Baxter. 1981. *Private Lives/Public Spaces*. New York: Community Service Society.

Kessler, Brad. 1988. "After Charity, Start Organizing." *The Nation*, April 16.

McMullen, Marrianne. 1988. "The Rank and File of the Streets." *Peace and Justice Journal* (American Friends Service Committee), 3, no. 1 (October/November).

Rader, Victoria. 1986. *Signal Through the Flames: Mitch Snyder and America's Homeless*. Kansas City, MO: Sheed and Ward.

Rosenthal, Harry F. 1990. "Watergate Residents Don't Welcome D.C.'s Homeless." *The Montgomery Advertiser and Alabama Journal*, February 11.

Safety Network. 1989. "Housing Now! The Birth of a Major Housing Movement." *The Newsletter of the National Coalition for the Homeless*, 8, no. 11 (November).

Smith, Christopher J. 1988. *Public Problems: The Management of Urban Distress*. New York: The Guilford Press.

Vincent, Steven. 1990. "On the Edge: The Lowdown on New York's Lower East Side." *In These Times*, 14, no. 18 (February 28–March 13).

Wilson, Jeff. 1989. "Celebrities Rankled by 'Mayor' Sheen's Invitation To Homeless." *The Montgomery Advertiser*, May 24.

7 The Rights of the Homeless

Getting a precise fix or handle on the rights of the homeless is extremely difficult to do because the issues involved cut across social, economic, and legal lines. When discussing the rights of the homeless one is subject not only to a variety of contexts—philosophical, political, and economic—but also to the complexities of the movement to resist homelessness in particular and to propagate the struggle on behalf of human justice in general. In this chapter, I will attempt to provide an overview and a sense of the dialectics of legal repression and liberation as the two interface with the needs of the homeless by exploring the recent trends in the judicial and legislative actions taken at both local and federal levels.

Even a nonexhaustive examination of judicial decisions and legislative acts affecting the expansion and contraction of the rights of the homeless reveals conflicts and contradictions in the nature of policy. development when it comes to low-income housing intervention. Accordingly, it is assumed, for example, that in recently enacted legislation (e.g., Homeless Person's Survival Act of 1987, Stewart B. McKinney Homeless Assistance Act of 1987 and as amended in 1989) the omission of a federal statutory right to shelter for the homeless renders that legislation inadequate. Moreover, concurring with the arguments of McKittrick (1988), this chapter underscores the need for the continued struggle on behalf of the homeless to further expand the rights of the homeless through judicial intervention and comprehensive legislation. In other words, both judicial and legislative initiatives on behalf of the homeless are still in their relative infancy, having only first emerged as recently as 1979.

When case law on the rights of the homeless is examined in some detail, the litigation and pending litigation surrounding particular cases could be separated into four categories:

litigation that attempts to draw attention to the plight of the homeless through public protest; litigation that attempts to obtain rights to short-term emergency shelter for the homeless; that attempts to obtain rights to short-term emergency shelter for the homeless; litigation that attempts to prevent specific placement of shelters and other facilities for the homeless; and litigation aimed at requiring states and the federal government to eliminate structural causes of homelessness (Dakin, 1987:112).

The point is that no single legal strategy can adequately begin to reach all the subpopulation groups of homeless people and the multiple levels of homelessness causation. With this in mind, litigation strategies have employed a series of actions in both state and federal courts; some attempting to meet the short-term needs of the homeless and some attempting to make long-term changes that would prevent homelessness in the first place.

In the next two sections, I will provide a review of the legal developments with respect first to the short-term emergency needs of the homeless, and second to their long-term structural and civil rights' needs.

THE STRUGGLE FOR LEGAL RECOGNITION OF THE HOMELESS

Although the conventional wisdom is that the judiciary lacks competence to decide "social" issues, this view is offset by the traditional protection courts provide to those lacking political power. Where a jurisdiction has a statute or constitutional provision concerning care of the needy, courts have a duty to interpret those statutes. In this situation, courts should not refrain from deciding "social" questions such as the right to shelter. (McKittrick, 1988:418).

As far back as *Marbury v. Madison* (1803), the U.S. Supreme Court stated that "the very essence of civil liberty certainly consists in the right of every individual to claim the protection of the laws, whenever he receives an injury." Moreover, the Court wrote that "one of the first duties of government is to afford that protection" [5 U.S. (1 Cranch) 162–163]. Not until the Great Depression of the 1930s did the Court begin to interpret these individual rights more broadly. During the past 50 years the Court has seen fit to expand these individual rights to include *classes* of politically powerless or vulnerable people (e.g., women, minorities, handicapped, etc.).

The judicial doctrine of political powerlessness was developed by the Supreme Court in *United States vs. Carolene Products Company* (1938) and *Frontiero v. Richardson* (1973). The belief that courts should protect the politically powerless has its roots in Justice Stone's famous *Carolene Products* footnote, where he suggested the possibility of heightened judicial scrutiny of legislative classifications that have an unfair impact on "discrete and insular minorities" or that curtail minorities' use of the political process altogether. Perhaps more directly, the Supreme Court held that gender was a suspect class in *Frontiero*. Justice Brennan's plurality opinion identified several factors that can be used to determine whether a group is a suspect class. Grounded in the theoretical basis of strict judicial scrutiny articulated by

Justice Stone's notion of "discrete and insular" minorities (certainly suggesting the possibility of a judicial responsibility to protect these people),
Frontiero [411 U.S. at 686] discussed the following relevant criteria: whether
or not a group's status or characteristic is immutable; whether or not a group's
history and continued experience is subject to discrimination; when the
statute at issue stereotypes a group without regard to the individual's ca-
pabilities; when the statutory trait bears no relation to the individual's ability
to perform or contribute to society; and when the group is politically powerless to alter their predicament.

Until recently, the historical legal meaning of "discrete and insular" had
referred primarily to racial and ethnic minorities. This restrictive interpretation eventually gave way to include such other classifications as women
and illegitimacy. As Professor Louis Lusky, Justice Stone's law clerk at the
time of the Court's decision in *Carolene Products*, suggested in 1982, "discrete and insular applies to groups that are not embraced within the bond
of community kinship but held at arm's length by the group or groups that
possess dominant political and economic power" (quoted in McKittrick,
1988:395). It follows that any group not represented in the political process
is unlikely to have its needs addressed. The powerlessness of the homeless,
therefore, suggests that the courts should closely scrutinize the treatment
the homeless receive in the administration of the law. Finally, extending
John Hart Ely's "representation-reinforcing" approach to judicial review that
calls for a political system of decision-making based on a fair process,
McKittrick (1988:395) concludes:

Where the decision-making process results in laws that infringe on the rights of
minorities, courts should intervene to protect minorities from the political process.
Although Ely's theory of judicial review applies to federal constitutional questions,
its underlying theme—protecting the politically powerless—can also justify judicial
interpretation of state law to aid the homeless.

In a case of the homeless mentally ill or the indigent chronically mentally
ill, for example, the 1981 class-action suit filed by the Arizona Center for
Law in the Public Interest alleging that 4,500 mentally ill homeless people
of Maricopa (Tucson) County "had been inappropriately and inadequately
served according to the standards mandated by the state law" was decided
for the plaintiffs in a nonjury trial that lasted one month, from October 22,
1984 to November 21, 1984 (Santiago et al., 1986:1575). On June 24, 1985,
the trial judge finally issued its findings of fact, conclusions of law, and order.
The judge ruled that the

Arizona Department of Health Services, the Arizona State Hospital, and the Maricopa
County Board of Supervisors have a joint legal responsibility to provide adequate
mental health services to the indigent chronically mentally ill patient. The judge
further rule[d] that the Arizona Department of Health Services has the primary

responsibility for coordinating and ensuring that services are provided to this population. Finally, the judge made the ruling that all of the defendants "failed to provide adequate mental health services to the plaintiff class" (Santiago et al., 1986:1577–1578).

As Santiago et al. (p. 1578) conclude in their discussion, this appears to have been the first case in the nation in which plaintiffs were able to establish a legal right "to receive community mental health services, unrelated to any institutionalization or deprivation of liberty." In other words, by avoiding constitutional issues and by emphasizing local statutes, this strategy of litigation succeeded in its claim that homeless mentally ill persons living in a community are entitled "to adequate care that consists of a full continuum of services in a cohesive and coordinated system."

More generally, what have the courts, federal and state, ruled in regard to the legal interpretation of the rights of the homeless? In *Clark v. Community for Creative Non-Violence*, Justice Marshall wrote in dissent that "the homeless are politically powerless inasmuch as they lack financial resources necessary to obtain access to many of the most effective means of persuasion" [468 U.S. 304 n.4 (1984)]. Justice Marshall also noted that the homeless were often physically and mentally vulnerable because of the hardships that accompanied their condition. As for the homeless being victims of discrimination and stereotyping, it has been revealed that many localities engage in discriminatory treatment of the homeless while other municipalities actually harass them.

In Arizona, for example, during the 1980s the homeless became objects of law enforcement and subjects for criminalization (Aulette and Aulette, 1987). In Tucson, the state's second largest city, where the unofficial policy of the city had been to run the homeless out of town, homeless people had been verbally harassed and physically abused by the police. The homeless there were subject to handcuffing, arresting, and charging for criminal trespass, squatting, and loitering. The police had gone so far as to harass individuals for trying to feed themselves and for constructing shelter by arresting them respectively for the "crimes" of possessing glass (i.e., a peanut butter jar in the park) and carrying a concealed weapon (i.e., cardboard cutters).

In Phoenix with more than 2 million people, Arizona's largest city adopted an "Anti-Skid Row" zoning ordinance to exclude shelters and food kitchens from the downtown area. The city also declared sleeping (or lying down) on public property illegal, and it declared garbage public property so that picking through trash cans became theft. The courts eventually struck these last two ordinances down. Nevertheless, Phoenix acted with extreme prejudice toward the homeless throughout the 1980s. In 1983, when there were an estimated 3,300 to 6,200 homeless people living in Phoenix, the city had not provided a single public shelter, and it had condemned its two private shelters in order to construct a public plaza. By 1988 the city was still harassing its homeless people. In the only publicly funded shelter in downtown Phoenix, the facility had adopted a policy that had "all the allure of a minimum security prison" and was, in effect, a deterrent to some homeless from seeking available shelter (*New York Times*, 1988: A10). In cooperation with law enforcement, the shelter was providing information on its homeless clients so the police could check to see if there were any outstanding arrest warrants. The policy was resulting in about 12 homeless arrests per week for such minor offenses as public drunkenness.

Arizona should not necessarily be singled out for its repressive policies toward the homeless. The same kind of hostility, or at least indifference, experienced by the homeless in Tucson and Phoenix during the 1980s could be found in cities coast to coast. Much of the harassment and hostile treatment (i.e., special zoning ordinances and other statutes) aimed at the homeless were based on stereotypes of these people as bums and drunks and crazies who would damage property or threaten neighborhood safety (McKittrick, 1988).

When it comes to the practical bases for judicial intervention, the Supreme Court held in *Lindsey v. Normet* (1972) that there is no constitutional right to adequate housing: "[we] do not denigrate the importance of decent, safe and sanitary housing. But the Constitution does not provide judicial remedies for every social and economic ill" [405 U.S. 56]. Nevertheless, some lower courts have based substantive rights to shelter on state law (as in the Arizona case mentioned above). Regarding the statutes on which homeless advocates rely, most of them do not expressly mention a right to shelter, but speak more generally of the government's duty to aid indigent persons. As McKittrick (1988) argues, because the homeless are destitute, courts should overcome this hurdle by concluding that the homeless qualify as "needy" individuals within the meanings of relevant statutes. Moreover, as the Supreme Court said in 1944 on the subject of equity jurisdiction, "the qualities of mercy and practicality have made equity the instrument for . . . adjustment and reconciliation between public interest and private needs as well as between competing private claims" [*Hecht Co. v. Bowles*, 321 U.S. 329–330].

At least eight states have constitutional provisions or statutes that courts have interpreted as imposing a mandatory duty to care for the needy. Again, McKittrick (1988) maintains that where case law suggests that such statutes establish a mandatory duty, the homeless should have a persuasive argument to secure a right to state-provided shelter. The seminal right-to-shelter case has been New York's *Callahan v. Carey* (1979).

In *Callahan*, six homeless men on behalf of all the homeless men in New York City sued the governor, claiming that the state and the city had violated their right to safe and adequate shelter under the state constitution, state statutes, and a city ordinance. Article XVII, Section 1 of the New York Constitution reads: "The aid, care and support of the needy are public concerns and shall be provided by the state and by such of its subdivisions, and in such manner and by such means, as the legislature may from time to time determine." Both the legislative history and case law indicate that this section has created an affirmative governmental duty (McKittrick, 1988). Moreover, the New York State Social Services Law explicitly requires that public welfare districts assist the indigent. Finally, the New York City Administrative Code of 1978 (and as amended in 1986) provides:

It shall be the duty of the commissioner or of the superintendent of any municipal lodging house acting under him, to provide for any applicants for shelter who, in his judgment, may properly be received, plain and wholesome food and lodging for a night, free of charge, and also to cause such applicants to be bathed on admission and their clothing to be steamed and disinfected [New York, N.Y. Administrative Code, ch. 24, sec. 604–1.0 (b) 1978].

A temporary injunction requiring that the state and city defendants provide shelter space for 750 men was granted by the New York Supreme Court in *Callahan*. Subsequently, the parties entered into a consent judgment under which the city agreed to supply shelter to any man who sought it. The consent decree also mandated that shelter facilities maintain specific minimum health and safety conditions.

As the problem of homelessness worsens, McKittrick (1988) believes that the courts are likely to interpret statutes broadly because of the belief that a judicial solution to the problem is necessary. For example, in *Seide v. Prevost* [1982], a federal district court did in fact recognize the powerlessness of the homeless and the mentally ill. The suit, which was brought on behalf of state psychiatric patients to enjoin the operation of a homeless shelter on the ground that it had deprived the patients of their rights to safety and treatment, did succeed. With respect to both the homeless and the mentally ill, the court noted that

each to a very large extent [is] the product of the swift, conflicting currents of our society, each without a political constituency to which they can refer their suffering, each driven to resort to the courts for enforcement of constitutional and state rights to achieve humane treatment at the hands of the society. While the impropriety of judges determining social policy is frequently sounded by those with loud trumpets, nonetheless, in the context of the needs of the homeless and mentally disturbed, it is the court that must decide the issues brought before it and seek to achieve a just result and do so promptly [536 F. Supp. 1121 (S.D.N.Y.)].

In another significant case, the West Virginia Supreme Court held, in *Hodge v. Ginsberg* (1983), that the state welfare department had a statutory duty to supply emergency shelter, food, and medical services to the homeless. The court reasoned that homelessness is a condition that threatens daily life functions and prevents the homeless from maintaining reasonable health [303 S.E.2d 245]. *Hodge* remains good law and has contributed to positive public discourse regarding homelessness because as McKittrick (1988:410) concludes,

once the court acted, the onus was on the legislature to reject the judicial solution if it disagreed with the statutory interpretation. Since the West Virginia Senate did not act to amend the statute, the majority of the house can be presumed to have acquiesced in the judicial interpretation.

Again, in 1987, the Superior Court of New Jersey, Appellate Division, ruled in *Maticka v. City of Atlantic City* [216 N.J. Super. 434] that regarding the conditions placed both by regulation and administration interpretation on availability of emergency assistance to homeless families with children, that the case be remanded to the New Jersey Department of Human Services for a rule-making hearing. In effect, the ruling held that prevention of homelessness is a necessary governmental function, at least when all private resources have proved unavailing. That was to say, the state was obligated not only to provide emergency or temporary shelter for those homeless families with children who requested assistance, but the state was also obliged to avoid emergent situations where appropriate under the principle of "opportunity to plan" (Hayes, 1987).

Finally, the legal recognition of the rights of the homeless has also prevailed in those cases where homeowners have brought legal action to stop the placement of homeless shelters or to enjoin the operation of shelters for the homeless. In *BAM Historic District Association v. Koch* [733 F.2d 233 (2d Cir. 1983)], for example, the association argued that by failing to give notice of the proposed opening of the shelter in the community, that the City of New York had deprived homeowners of both property and liberty interests. The Second Circuit held that

there was no taking of the plaintiff's property and that the community had no colorable liberty interest in preventing the establishment of a shelter. The circuit court affirmed the district court's denial of the injunction because the neighborhood produced no evidence demonstrating that the shelter would detract from the community. Moreover, the court reasoned that the closing of the facility would be detrimental to the public interest, given the need for shelters for the homeless (McKittrick, 1988:417).

Similarly, in one New Jersey community where the attempt was made to enforce a local zoning ordinance that restricted the use of a lot to those uses customarily incident to the principal use, the New Jersey Superior Court ruled against the ordinance. In *St. John's Evangelical Lutheran Church v. City of Hoboken* [195 N.J. Super. 414 A.2d 935 (Law Div. 1983)], the court decided that enforcement of the ordinance would conflict with the church's First Amendment exercise of religion and, therefore, the ordinance would have to yield. The court reasoned that because housing the homeless was a traditional church function, the First Amendment applied. The court also emphasized the harm that would result should the shelter be closed, especially since the local governments relied on the churches to shelter the homeless. In other words, public interest mandated that the churches be allowed to continue their practice of housing the homeless.

Although different rationales have been put forward by various legal cases, the point is that the magnitude of the homeless problem in America has become a legally recognized theme, if not principle, in the courts' opinions. And, although the above cases cited deal exclusively with the rights to temporary shelter, they suggest the legal possibility that some day the rights to permanent shelter will also be recognized. Thus far, however, as revealed by those cases discussed in the next section, the fundamental constitutional right to permanent housing has yet to become the official social reality or law of the land.

CONSTITUTIONAL QUESTIONS AND THE RIGHTS OF THE HOMELESS

Without permanent and appropriately supportive places to live, homeless people will remain at risk to their mental as well as their physical health. In just the last eight years the federal government has decreased its share of public housing funds by approximately 80%, and state programs have been cut as well. To change this deplorable situation, the federal government must recognize its historic obligation to help provide housing for all (Kanter, 1989:101).

When it comes to applying various constitutional issues to the civil rights of and the circumstances surrounding the homeless, or when it comes to the establishment of the right to permanent low-income housing, the U.S. Supreme Court has not seen fit to interpret the Constitution as recognizing the fundamental economic needs of all people residing in the United States. As I have argued throughout this book, there are even more basic questions than the right to shelter. Ultimately, we are talking about the right to human dignity:

American society will eventually answer the question of which the "right to shelter" is but a part: Do people have a right to life simply by reason of their humanity or citizenship? Put another way, shall we permit people to freeze to death in winter, to starve, to die from the effects of preventable disease, merely because they are poor, insane, or addicted to drugs? In the long run, the ways in which our society responds to that fundamental question will determine far more than the plight of the homeless. It will define our civilization (Blasi, 1987:175).

Although all of the constitutional and civil rights issues pertaining to homelessness and the homeless have not been heard yet, by the 1990 summer I think it was (and is) safe to conclude based on those relevant cases that have been decided (as well as on the trends in the development of local legislation) that the fundamental rights of liberty and property as expressed in the Bill of Rights are not going to be extended to homeless people in this century.

The disenfranchisement of the homeless first became the subject of litigation shortly before the November 1984 elections. In cases filed in New York City, Washington, D.C., Philadelphia, and Santa Barbara, plaintiffs were ultimately successful. Accommodations and procedures had to be worked out so homeless people without permanent addresses could register to vote. This is primarily the only constitutional right that has been expressly supported by the courts.

More typical have been those cases challenging the bans on sleeping in community parks or begging in public and private places where the courts have ultimately ruled that the First Amendment does not apply. In the first case of its kind, the U.S. Supreme Court (1983), in a 7–2 decision, reversed the Court of Appeals for the D.C. Circuit in Community for Creative Non-Violence v. Watt [Clark v. CCNV, *supra* note 60, 438 U.S. at 293–300, 104 S. Ct. at 3069–3073, 82 L. Ed. 2d at 226–31]. In 1982 after the CCNV received a National Park Service permit allowing a seven-day demonstration to educate the public about the problems of homelessness in America, but denying the participants (homeless people and advocates alike) from sleeping in tent cities on the grounds that such sleeping arrangements would violate the Park Service's anticamping regulations, a legal battle ensued over the usage of constitutionally protected "symbolic speech." Writing for the majority, Justice White held that the "National Park Service's regulation prohibiting camping in certain parks for the benefit of the public does not violate the First Amendment. The Park Service's regulations were held to be reasonable time, place, and manner restrictions on park usage, narrowly drawn to further a substantial government interest unrelated to the suppression of free speech" (Dakin, 1987:113–114).

Similarly, when it came to the constitutional questions of begging, a 1990 U.S. Court of Appeals for the Second Circuit in Manhattan, in a 2-to-1 decision, overturned two lower court's rulings that begging was a form of free speech protected by the First Amendment. At issue was whether or not the Metropolitan Transportation Authority (MTA) had the power to bar panhandlers from New York subways. The bottom line was that organizations, but not individuals, were protected by the First Amendment because in addition to soliciting money only the former were also engaged in trying to "convey any social or political message," wrote Judge Frank X. Altimari (quoted in Wolff, 1990:B16). Writing the majority opinion for the Second Circuit ruling, Altimari employed very strong language, such as "whether intended as so or not, begging in the subway often amounts to nothing less than assault, creating in the passengers the apprehension of imminent danger" (quoted in Wolff, 1990:A1). The same appeals court also upheld the right of the state to ban loitering for the purpose of begging. Not all folks celebrated the decision as hailed by MTA officials as a victory for a system beset by crime and homelessness.

Certainly Doug Lasdon, executive director of the Legal Action Center for the Homeless (LACH) in Manhattan who filed the original suits and who believes that LACH will likely appeal this ruling to the U.S. Supreme Court, and Federal District Judge Leonard B. Sand, whose two decisions were reversed by the Second Circuit, were not pleased by the May 1990 decisions. Judge Sand in early 1990 had ruled that the New York City ban on panhandling in subway stations was in violation of the First Amendment because begging is "informative and persuasive speech" (quoted in Will, 1990:8A). As Sand maintained, "a true test of one's commitment to constitutional principles . . . is the extent to which recognition is given to the rights of those in our midst who are the least affluent, least powerful and least welcome" (quoted in Will, 1990:8). Sand further argues that what turns beggars' conduct into constitutionally protected expression is the unsettling nature of beggars and their message.

Litigation to secure the legal right to short-term or emergency shelter for the homeless has thus far had mixed results. A number of legal claims have recently been brought to both state and federal courts. As indicated above, most of these claims have not succeeded unless there has been an *express statutory authority* for the provision of services to the homeless in the state law (Dakin, 1987). For example, in 1988 a unanimous decision by the New Jersey Supreme Court held that the state of New Jersey could evict thousands of homeless men, women, and children from emergency shelters after five months. In other words, the N.J. Supreme Court sided with the state in its claim that there is no permanent right to shelter, especially since the Department of Human Services for New Jersey had already established a "safety net" to meet the plaintiffs' needs through alternative programs to emergency assistance and shelter (Safety Network, 1988).

On the other hand, like Judge Sand's ruling on begging, there have been rulings "around the nation to suggest that a roof over one's head is as essential to life, liberty and the pursuit of happiness as voting" (Shapiro, 1990:12). In January 1990, Connecticut Judge Anthony DeMayo wrote in his final ruling on a series of housing cases brought by the New Haven Legal Assistance Association, "there are times 'when the political system fails' in its social responsibilities, and 'this is one of those times' " (Shapiro, 1990:13). Accordingly, DeMayo issued injunctions against eviction of homeless people receiving emergency shelter after 100 days, he reinstated state emergency-housing funds for families, and he ordered the creation of two additional shelters, threatening officials with contempt if they did not act fast enough. In declaring housing to be a civil right, DeMayo stopped just shy of declaring housing a constitutional right. Acting in good faith with state law, which requires that judges decide cases on the narrowest of grounds possible,

DeMayo found state law and historical precedents aplenty to support the argument that impoverished residents "shall be provided for."

There are other constitutional questions surrounding homelessness, such as the right to counsel for those facing eviction, or whether or not a property interest requiring due process exists, and the issue over the claim of a protected privacy interest under the Fourth Amendment. Since the latter two questions involve structural issues that raise fundamental challenges to capitalist notions of liberty and property, I will briefly discuss two unsuccessful types of legal cases that if ever adopted by the Supreme Court could radicalize U.S. responses to homelessness overnight. Driven by a developing global capitalism, the types of legal precedents envisioned here include a fundamental transformation in our values and in our property and equity relations. Specifically, I am referring to the foundation-shaking import of the direct extension of civil rights from the political to the economic realm. I am talking about, for example, the decommodification of a portion of all available housing and construction or the creation of socially rather than privately owned housing.

Both of the unsuccessful cause-aimed litigation efforts share the potential for contributing to the formulations of permanent solutions to homelessness. Both of these cases challenge the prevailing and existing domestic arrangements of both the state and the culture; and each of these legal struggles represents an attempt to implement structural changes in the areas of social services and housing policy, and ultimately in the areas of community development. The first case involved the failed attempt to establish a due process entitlement with respect to "housed" or sheltered residents [Caton v. Barry, 500 F. Supp. 45 (D.D.C. 1980)]. The second case involved the failed attempt to establish due process rights stemming from various privacy, property, and liberty claims in accord with the Fourth and Fourteenth Amendments [Amezquita v. Hernandez-Colon, 518 F. 2d 8 (1st Cir. 1975), cert. denied, 424 U.S. 916, 96 S. Ct. 1117, 47 L. Ed. 2d 321 (1976)].

Caton v. Barry in 1980 was an attempt by housing policy analyst and attorney Florence W. Roisman, of the National Housing Law Project in Washington, D.C., to establish a due process entitlement to her "foreclosure avoidance" principle with respect to "housed" residents in a family shelter scheduled for closure. In Caton, Roisman argued against the transfer of a group of plaintiffs from one shelter to another when the plaintiffs had reservations and complaints about the proposed move. The district court, however, did not accept Roisman's foreclosure avoidance arguments. It held that

the plaintiffs had no constitutionally cognizable claim of an *entitlement to remain in the particular shelter where they were housed* rather than to be housed in some other shelter operated under the same program. The existence of some adverse impact arising from a governmental decision was not sufficient basis for finding a constitutional property interest requiring due process (Dakin, 1987:120).

Amezquita v. Hernandez-Colon in 1975 was an attempt by a group of squatters, who had set up a shelter community on land owned by the Commonwealth of Puerto Rico, to claim a constitutionally protected privacy interest in their "homes" as well as a property and liberty interest in the shelter community. Failing to leave voluntarily, commonwealth officials ordered the forced evacuation of squatters. A clean-up operation was put into motion using bulldozers to destroy structures with the assistance of the police. In response to the squatters' Fourth Amendment argument, the First Circuit held that the squatters had no privacy interest in the structures:

The community was not the squatters' "home" since they had constructed and occupied it in bad faith with no legal right to do so. The court also held that the due process clause of the Fourteenth Amendment was not implicated when the squatters had no "liberty" or "property" interest in the land since process is only due when a citizen has a protected liberty or property interest (Dakin, 1987:115).

Litigation like *Amezquita* and *Caton* raise the political and economic stakes considerably. These types of legal cases represent efforts to make changes in the substantive rights of poor people to housing. Changing these legal rights of the homeless could have a significant impact on the homeless crisis in the United States. However, as Dakin (1987:121) has pondered, "housing policy may be more suited to change through legislative action than through the judiciary." As revealed in the next section, neither is particularly receptive to the ideas of eliminating homelessness.

PENDING LEGISLATION

Much legislation, at both the federal and local levels, needs to be passed into law to properly address the multifaceted problem of homelessness. With regard to the most recently analyzed federal housing/homelessness bills (1988–89), a case can certainly be made that the necessary legislative changes for confronting the long-term nature of the "reproduction of homelessness" is conspicuously absent as pointed out by the inclusion, in this section, of the Low Income Housing Information Service's "Side-by-Side Comparison of Pending Legislation on Low Income Housing and Homelessness." Before turning to LIHIS and its analyses of low-income housing and community control legislation, an overview and summary of the National Coalition for the Homeless' Model State Legislation is presented for the purpose of underscoring what a comprehensive approach to homelessness would look like.

The narrative statement of the National Coalition for the Homeless (NCH, 1989:1) begins:

The State Homeless Persons' Assistance Act of 1989 is a comprehensive effort to alleviate the distress of homelessness by providing long-term housing assistance measures, preventing future homelessness, and providing for emergency relief and services to meet the immediate needs of the homeless. The Act seeks to address permanent housing solutions through initiation of new state programs, to strengthen coordination with existing state programs to aid homeless and low-income Americans, and to assure adequate emergency assistance is available.

The act contains three titles, which will be briefly summarized. Title I (Low-Income Housing for Homeless Individuals) contains long-range programs designed to increase the availability of low-cost housing. This part of the act assumes that "rehabilitation of existing housing and construction of housing are both critically needed. The purpose of Title I is to provide decent, safe, sanitary housing to low-income and very low-income persons through funding assistance for construction and rehabilitation of affordable housing" (NCH, 1989:2). Title I establishes the Affordable Housing Trust Fund as a "nonlapsing, revolving fund to provide grants or loans to public or private *nonprofit* entities to develop affordable housing" (emphasis added) (NCH, 1989:2). Funds may be used for the development of new public housing units and for the conversion of existing stock. The act gives a preference to applicants using existing publicly and privately owned housing stock. A preference is also given to applications by those local government units that have enacted controls to preserve single-room occupancy units. Finally, the priority of Title I is to be given to "projects creating, acquiring or rehabilitating affordable housing for the homeless in allocating funds raised by the issuance of mortgage revenue or tax exempt bonds and tax credits under the Federal Low Income Housing Tax Credit Program" (NCH, 1989:3).

Title II (Prevention of Homelessness) takes affirmative action to prevent needless evictions and the loss of affordable housing. Title II has two primary objectives. One is to establish emergency rent and mortgage relief programs to not only avoid needless eviction, but to prevent the continued loss of affordable housing units for low-income families. The other is to improve the quality and adequacy of public assistance and minimum wage benefits in order to prevent homelessness.

With respect to the prevention of evictions, this title would establish a revolving fund, administered by a local government agency, to assist low-income tenants and homeowners who face homelessness as a result of eviction from or imminent foreclosure on their primary residence. Once an applicant applies for relief, neither the private landlord nor the mortgage holder may proceed with the eviction or the foreclosure, unless or until the application is denied or benefits are terminated. When an applicant is financially able, he or she is expected to make repayment of the monies received. With respect to the preservation of low-income housing, this part of Title II "seeks to preserve remaining low-income housing units, including SROs, through the enactment of inclusionary zoning, anti-warehousing ordinances, and demolition and conversion controls" (NCH, 1989:5–6).

Title III (Emergency Relief for the Homeless) assumes that the emergency needs of the homeless are wide and broad-gauged, including food, shelter, clothing, medical and mental health services, job-training, and work placement. In addition, it assumes that vigorous outreach efforts are necessary to inform the homeless of available assistance from these as well as other entitlement programs. This part of the act establishes

accessibility by the homeless to ongoing income, food and medical assistance programs by removing residency barriers and requiring the delivery of benefits despite the lack of a permanent address. This Part also provides state funding for education and job training assistance to homeless adults and guarantees access of public education for the children of the homeless (NCH, 1989:9).

When one compares the model state legislation proposed by the National Coalition for the Homeless with the LIHIS comparative analysis of pending federal legislation, grounded in and assessed from the perspective of the principles adopted by the National Low Income Housing Coalition (NLIHC), the inadequacy of all but one of the proposed federal bills—Dellums Bill, H.R. 4727—becomes apparent. Below is a summary of Rep. Ronald Dellums' (D-Oakland, CA) bill introduced into Congress June 2, 1988, as summarized by the Boston chapter of Jobs With Peace Campaign (1988). Following that is Table 1A, the LIHIS (1988) comparison of pending bills for 1989.

HR 4727 National Comprehensive Affordable Housing Legislation

- Fund $53 billion in affordable housing by significant reductions in the military budget.
- Fund acquisition and construction of housing by community development corporations and other nonprofit groups. Reduce interest costs and dependence on borrowing by using one-time capital grants, thereby greatly lowering costs in the long run.
- Encourage and fund the transfer of ownership of privately owned housing to nonprofit organizations to ensure permanent affordability.
- Call for local housing plans to meet local situations.
- Stop the demolition and sale of public housing. Fund full operating subsidies and capital grants for complete modernization and rehabilitation of all public housing. Include funding for child-care centers in housing developments.
- Provide employment and job training opportunities, especially for women and minorities.
- Prevent the displacement of low-income tenants of Farmers Home Administration housing, HUD Section 221 (d) (3), Section 8, and in Section 236 housing.

Table 14

Side-by-Side Comparison of Pending Legislative Proposals and NLIHC Policy Positions

Oct. 20, 1988

NLIHC Position	Dellums Bill H.R. 4727	Kennedy Bill H.R. 3891	Frank Bill H.R. 1990	Conyers (Jesse Gray) H.R. 918	Cranston D'Amato (Concept Papers)	Vento-Saiki Bill H.R. 5016
Make Housing an Entitlement for All Who Need It-- provide an adequately funded entitlement to income-based housing assistance to all who need it	Declares that "the attainment of the national housing goal is a priority of the highest order...The basic principle(s) of this Act (is) to allocate housing resources on an equitable basis and provide adequate resources to meeting housing needs" Bill provides $8 billion for operating assistance only for units placed in social sector; does not make provisions for income-based subsidy programs outside of social sector	No--provides only develop-ment subsidies, does not address income subsidy questions	No--emphasis entirely on production and rehabil-itation	No--provides only for public housing development and modern-ization	No--would maintain a modified version of current Section 8 program, with 5-year terms and greater degree of flexibility in local program administra-tion than under current law	Provides $2 billion over FY89-90 for permanent housing for homeless people through ex-isting sub-sidy programs

Table 14 (Continued)

NLIHC Position	Dellums Bill H.R. 4727	Kennedy Bill H.R. 3891	Frank Bill H.R. 1990	Conyers (Jesse Gray) H.R. 918	Cranston D'Amato (Concept Papers)	Vento-Saiki Bill H.R. 5016
Provide an adequate and affordable supply of housing—at least 750,000 units per year for 10 year	Authorizes $24 billion per year for construction and rehabilitation	No—would provide $500 million in development grants, with three-to-one federal-local match required	Yes—would provide for production and rehabilitation of 7.5 million permanently affordable rental units with priority for homeless persons	No—provides for 5 million new public housing units over 10 years	No—no specific commitments for production or rehabilitation levels	Would finance rehabilitation or Section 8 Certificates for 141,050 households
Retain and improve the present housing stock to provide decent housing for lower income people—maintain currently HUD-subsidized and all public housing for affordable low-income housing	Yes—the Act seeks to improve the affordability and livability of the subsidized housing stock, assure security of tenure, and increase resident control for existing and future low and moderate income tenants ...to assure the permanent retention of existing public and non-profit ownership, and facilitate	No—does not address the preservation issue	No—does not address the preservation issue	Partly—would provide for total modernization of existing public housing stock	Would establish new Office of Assisted Housing Preservation to offer technical and legal services to preserve privately owned housing; unspecified new resources to preserve public housing and and privately owned subsidized housing	$500 million in Public Housing modernization funds (estimated 31,250 units); 30,000 in rem properties to be rehabilitated at cost of $300 million

Provide resident control of housing through a strong role for tenant organizations, limited equity cooperatives, community-based housing groups, and homeownership--emphasize community-based housing supply solutions; community-based nonprofit organizations and limited equity cooperatives should have a major role in the provision of housing	Yes--emphasizes nonspeculative ownership models including co-ops and community-based development	Provides funds to state and local governments for use in local programs to acquire, rehabilitate or develop affordable housing for low- and moderate- income people using community-based and other nonprofit forms of ownership	Provides funds for public housing and community-based nonprofit housing development models	Provides funds for public housing development, through public housing authorities	Proposes new Housing Opportunities Program (HOP) to provide state and local governments federal funds to use in locally developed programs; at least 10 percent of localities' money would have to be spent on projects sponsored by nonprofits	No provisions

conversion of privately-owned subsidized units to forms of non-speculative social ownership

Table 14 (continued)

NLIHC Position	Dellums Bill H.R. 4727	Kennedy Bill H.R. 3891	Frank Bill H.R. 1990	Conyers (Jesse Gray) H.R. 918	Cranston D'Amato (Concept Papers)	Vento-Saiki Bill H.R. 5016
End displacement of low-income people--national policy should focus on the prevention of displacement by private as well as public actions; housing and community and economic development programs should be designed and carried out so as to benefit low-income people and their neighborhoods	Would require a Federally Mandated Local Housing Program which would have to include tenant protections such as warranty of habitability, eviction controls, rent and conversion controls, and prohibit demolition where a local housing emergency exists. Would require local governments to set performance standards for private rental housing management firms; establish collective bargaining rights and procedures for	Requires that housing produced using subsidies remain permanently affordable to low-income residents. Fund recipients would have to insure that each nonprofit sponsor receiving assistance develops and follows an affirmative action program designed to maximize the participation of minorities in construction, management, and maintenance activities; discrimination prohibited in housing assisted under the act	Includes mandated federal minimum protections for tenants in housing assisted under the act; priority given to recipients who would employ homeless persons in construction and rehabilitation work; requires that grantees will not involuntarily displace lower income families either directly or indirectly	Would require employment of eligible residents in development and rehabilitation work	No specific provisions; would establish new Office of Affordable Housing to work with owners, state and local governments to prevent loss of privately owned assisted housing supply	No provisions

Strengthen and enforce fair housing laws and equal opportunity requirements-- expansion of Fair Housing Act to cover families with children and the disabled; vigorous enforcement; expanded housing opportunities	All localities would be required by local ordinance to insure residents' maximum freedom of choice in the selection of housing; it would be unlawful to discrimination against any person in the sale or lease of residential property on the basis of race, national orgin, and other protected classes in Fair Housing Act	No specific provisions; discrimination prohibited in units assisted under the act	No specific provisions; discrimination prohibited in housing assisted under the act	No specific provisions
democratically organized tenant associations; and require management firms to develop project-specific management plans that comply with localities' housing objectives	Discrimination would be prohibited in any housing assisted under the act			No specific provisions; current law would apply

Table 14 (continued)

NLIHC Position	Dellums Bill H.R. 4727	Kennedy Bill H.R. 3891	Frank Bill H.R. 1990	Conyers (Jesse Gray) H.R. 918	Cranston D'Amato (Concept Papers)	Vento-Saiki Bill H.R. 5016
Reform federal tax laws to reflect priority for aiding people with the greatest housing needs--mortgage interest and property tax deductions should be converted to credits; amount of these should be capped at a level which will protect low- and middle-income owners while curtailing subsidies to people who do not need them	Would overhaul current tax treatment to eliminate favorable depreciation schedules for rental housing; eliminate home-owner mortgage interest deduction over long term as part of overall tax reform to "close off loopholes and a wide range of inequities." Would impose windfall profits taxes on speculative real estate gain; impose antispeculation or deed transfer tax; permit tax-exempt financing only for housing in the social sector	Would exempt housing produced under the act from restriction under low-income housing tax credit	Does not address	Does not address	Would extend Mortgage Revenue Bonds; otherwise does not address	Does not address

Provide the financing needed to preserve, build, and rehabilitate housing	Would adopt a variety of techniques to steer private credit toward social housing objectives--CRA concept would be strengthened and expanded; differential taxes imposed on private credit institutions; loan set-aside requirements for designated social housing objectives; differential reserve requirements; impose require-ment for below market interest rates on lenders	Does not address	Provides capital grants for housing assisted under the act; does not address overall financing issues	Provides direct grants for public hous-construction, renovation; does not address overall financing issues	Proposes allowing home buyers to invest IRA and other retirement account capital in housing down pay-ments; would lib-eralize FHA lending requirements to decrease down payments and raise maximum purchase price limits; would estab-lish new secondary market to increase capital available through HOPs	$1.55 billion in Section 8 and public housing modernization subsidies for rehabilitation
FUNDING LEVELS	$5.5 billion to convert private rental housing	$500 million in direct grants for development,	$15 billion per year, to be raised through tax	$15 billion	No commit-ment of funding levels	$450 million for Sec. 8 Certif. $250 million for

Table 14 (continued)

NLIHC Position	Dellums Bill H.R. 4727	Kennedy Bill H.R. 3891	Frank Bill H.R. 1990	Conyers (Jesse Gray) H.R. 918	Cranston D'Amato (Concept Papers)	Vento-Saiki Bill H.R. 5016
	to social ownership; $8 billion to protect existing home owners and convert private homes to social ownership; $3 billion to expand home ownership opportunities through social ownership models $5 billion to convert privately owned subsidized housing to social ownership; $32 billion for new construction, rehab, and operating assistance through production of housing for social ownership Total: $53.5 billion per year	acquisition, and rehab $10 million in grants for for capacity building among nonprofit housing providers	changes		included in Concept Papers	Sec. 8 Mod Rehab; $500 million for public housing modernization; $500 million for Rental Rehab Grants; $300 million for rehab on in rem properties

- Expand housing for the elderly (HUD Section 202) under the ownership of nonprofit organizations.
- Expand funding of elderly congregate housing.
- Increase funding for the HUD homesteading program.
- Include housing units for handicapped people.

The policy positions adopted by the NLIHC and applied by LIHIS reveal the strengths of the Dellums Bill compared to the Kennedy Bill (H.R. 3891), the Frank Bill (H.R. 4990), the Conyers [Jesse Gray] Bill (H.R. 918), the Cranston-D'Amato (Concept Papers), and the Vento-Saiki Bill (H.R. 5046).

Two of the more significant bills pending before Congress in early summer 1990 were S.B. 566 and H.R. 4621. A highlighting and an evaluation of each of these bills by the National Coalition for the Homeless rounds out the rest of this section.

National Affordable Housing Act S. 566 (Cranston-D'Amato Bill)

On May 2, 1990, S.B. 566 emerged out of committee to reauthorize the McKinney homeless programs, to raise the 1989–90 housing authorization from $14.6 billion to $17.7 billion, and to incorporate modified versions of the Bush-Kemp proposals, including Home Ownership and Opportunities for People Everywhere (HOPE), Shelter Plus Care, and the voluntary Operation Bootstrap demonstration. The centerpiece of this legislation was the Housing Opportunity Partnership (HOP). HOP proposed to provide

funding to States (40%) and localities (60%) on a needs- and population-based formula for provision of low and moderate income housing by private nonprofit and for-profit developers and public agencies. Each state or locality would have to provide a 25% match of HOP monies.

Each state or local government receiving HOP or Community Development Block Grant funds would have to develop a five-year comprehensive housing affordability strategy, updated annually. This strategy would have to assess local housing needs, including the extent and nature of homelessness, and set out a strategy for avoiding homelessness and helping homeless people find decent housing (Safety Network, 1990a:1).

Although the NCH was very supportive of this bill, arguing in a legislative memorandum (dated June 15, 1990) mailed to its phone-tree members that "passing this bill is vital to the struggle against homelessness," the Coalition was still critical of parts of the bill, and was supportive of some debated changes in the act (NCH, 1990:1). The memorandum pointed out that historically no omnibus housing bill had ever been without serious flaws. And unless the passage of this bill was to occur, the memorandum continued, then "we won't see housing legislation this year and maybe not for years to come" (NCH, 1990:1).

More specifically, the NCH opposed any amendments to delete or undermine HOP, possibilities raised by the administration and Secretary of HUD Jack Kemp, who were looking for ways to transfer funds instead to Community Development Block Grants (CDBG). NCH maintained that with or without the additional funds, CDBG was not equipped to meet the homeless demands. The Coalition also supported the amendment to add the provisions from the Homelessness Prevention and Community Revitalization Act (S. 2600) to S. 566. S. 2600 was sponsored by Senator Edward Kennedy and 24 other senators, and would provide $265 million in grants giving "to community-based organizations to establish on- or off-site 'support-centers' which would provide an array of health, nutrition, education, and employment services to low income families who reside in subsidized housing who are formerly homeless or are at risk of being homeless" (NCH, 1990:2). Finally, the Coalition supported an amendment to keep public housing alive by authorizing additional capital for the purposes of providing affordable housing for people at the bottom of the income scale. Concerted efforts to kill public housing date as far back as the Nixon administration.

Mickey Leland Peace Dividend Housing Assistance Act of 1990, H.R. 4621 (Flake Bill)

With 48 cosponsors, H.R. 4621 was introduced by Rep. Floyd Flake (D–NY) and a group of other members of the Housing Subcommittee on April 19, 1990. The Leland bill proposed new spending authority totaling $125 billion over the next five years, and an array of programs designed to provide 4 million additional subsidized housing units. In response to the Washington, D.C. Housing Now! march in October 1989, which brought out about 250,000 supporters for the homeless, NCH argued that this bill represented an important milestone in that it provided the first and only comprehensive housing program for the nation's homeless and for those at risk of becoming homeless. The potential consequences of such a law is a reflection of the very broad-based and diverse coalition of more than 200 national organizations, and an equal number of local and regional groups, having come together. NCH maintained that the addition of newly subsidized units would get the U.S. housing policy back on track:

First, it would make up for the two million subsidized low income units lost during the 1980s due to Reagan budget cuts. Second, it would provide another two million units, making a substantial downpayment on meeting the total estimated low income housing need of at least 8 million additional subsidized units. Finally, it would require an assessment of the progress made by 1994 and development of a program to meet all low income housing needs by the end of the century (Safety Network, 1990b:1).

However, NCH did not believe that this bill had even a remote chance of passing the U.S. Congress. Nevertheless, it was the hope of the Coalition that massive and sustained grassroots efforts would help to ensure that the bill was at least seriously discussed.

THE DIALECTICS OF THE RIGHTS OF THE HOMELESS

The rights of the homeless in legal, political, and economic terms have certainly been codified in the minds of many Americans, if not necessarily in the laws of the land. In relationship to homelessness these rights have been established in both discourse and custom, but more specific recognition of a right to permanent shelter as part and parcel of the inalienable rights to civil and social justice has yet to be legally sanctioned. These contradictions in the rights of the homeless exemplify the dialectics in how far we have come and in how far we have to go. The following illustrations, in addition to the foregoing analyses of homeless legal developments, should provide the reader with a sense of the conflicts and dilemmas confronting the response to homelessness in America today.

In July 1990 the City Council of Washington, D.C. voted to set limits on the right to shelter, which Washington was the first to establish nationwide in 1984, by passing Initiative #17 (Right to Overnight Shelter Act). Two months earlier, "Philadelphia cut $2 million from a program for the homeless, a reduction that officials said would mean the loss of 500 beds" (DeParle, 1990:6A). In 1989 the California legislative session came to an end with the following statistics on homelessness and housing bills: 28 of 36 bills introduced by homeless advocates were passed and sent to Republican Governor George Deukmejian; the governor signed 17 and vetoed 11 (Safety Network, 1989:2). Moreover, the results of the California elections held in November 1988 and June 1990 revealed a divided picture as well: Housing and Homeless Bond Act (Prop. 84) passed and Hunger and Homeless Act (Prop. 95) failed in 1988; in 1990, Homeless and Housing Act (Prop. 107) passed (Sacramento Elections Division, Secretary of State's Office, California).

Meanwhile, the federal record looks about the same as the local and state one—mixed reviews at best, inadequate at worst. Strapped by enormous deficits, there has certainly been a profound absence by the federal government to assume the full burden of the homeless (Mathews, 1988). In 1987, Congress made its first moves in the area of housing since 1981, by passing the McKinney Homeless Assistance Act and by authorizing HUD to extend federal subsidies to 152,000 families and to renovate 10,000 dilapidated public-housing apartments. However, Congress came up with only $700 million for two years out of the $1 billion provided by McKinney for emergency and transitional shelters. With respect to the subsidies and renovations, early 1990 estimates place the need of low-income housing at more than 10 million persons.

In the relatively small area of Union Square, in downtown San Francisco, where the homeless had been congregating since the early 1980s, the mayor ordered the park area cleared of homeless tents and people in July 1990. Two years earlier, in November 1988, the Police Commission had adopted the "Rights of the Homeless" resolution, which states that "when a person is disheveled, dressed in bizarre clothing or just looks impoverished, police cannot detain him—even briefly—or engage in an identification check (Viets, 1988: 2A). Police Chief Frank Jordon, who led the nonviolent evacuation mission, could be heard two years before espousing such progressive lines as these:

It is not a crime to be homeless. So everyone has to understand there's only so much police officers can do.

If the homeless are aggressively panhandling, committing a crime or urinating in a doorway, then we can do something (Viets, 1988:2A).

In concluding this chapter two comments are presented, one from some representatives of the medical-legal community concerned with the treatment conditions for psychiatric patients, and the other from the Community for Creative Non-Violence, which was addressing the state of the homeless movement and the question of a backlash toward the homeless, following the October 7 Housing Now! march and rally in Washington, D.C.:

It is now clear that the initial efforts to change mental health systems through litigation at the federal level have failed. The method of ultimately relying on the federal courts to reform systems of care may not be effective. More recently, lawyers have begun using state laws and state constitutional provisions to achieve change without relying on federal constitutional claims (Santiago et al., 1986:1575).

As we inch our way toward real solutions, and an honest acknowledgement of the magnitude and urgency of homelessness and the shortage of affordable housing, the powers and principalities intensify their resistance to any significant change in the status quo (CCNV, 1989:2).

REFERENCES

Aulette, Judy and Albert Aulette. 1987. "Police Harassment of the Homeless: The Political Purpose of the Criminalization of Homelessness." *Humanity and Society*, 11, no. 2 (May):244–256.

Blasi, Gary L. 1987. "Litigation on Behalf of the Homeless: Systematic Approaches." *Journal of Urban and Contemporary Law*, reprinted in Robert Hayes, ed., *The Rights of the Homeless*. New York: Practicing Law Institute.

Community for Creative Non-Violence. 1989. "Dear Friend" letter. December 4.

Dakin, Linda S. 1987. "Homelessness: The Role of the Legal Profession in Finding Solutions Through Litigation." *Family Law Quarterly*, 31, no. 1 (Spring) 93–126.

DeParle, Jason. 1990. "Advocates for Homeless Debate How to Continue Cause." *Sunday Montgomery Advertiser*, July 8.

Hayes, Robert M., Ed. 1987. *The Rights of the Homeless*. New York: Practicing Law Institute.

Jobs With Peace Campaign. 1988. "Summary of H.R. 4727." Boston: JWPC.

Kanter, Arlene S. 1989. "Homeless but not Helpless: Legal Issues in the Care of Homeless People with Mental Illness." *Journal of Social Issues*, 45, no. 3: 91–104.

Low Income Housing Information Service. 1988. "Side-by-Side Comparison of Pending Legislation on Low Income Housing and Homelessness." Washington, DC: LIHIS.

Mathews, Tom. 1988. "Homeless in America: What Can Be Done?" *Newsweek*, March 21.

McKittrick, Neil V. 1988. "The Homeless: Judicial Intervention on Behalf of a Politically Powerless Group." *Fordham Urban Law Journal*, 16: 389–440.

National Coalition for the Homeless. 1989. "State Homeless Persons' Assistance Act of 1989: Model State Legislation." Washington, DC: NCH

———. 1990. Memorandum. "Urgent Action Needed On Senate Housing Bill," June 15.

New York Times. 1988. "At Shelter, Homeless Monitored by Police," February 22.

Safety Network. 1988. "N.J. Supreme Court Ruling Threatens Homeless Families." *The Newsletter of the National Coalition for the Homeless*, 7 no. 5 (July/August).

———. 1989. "California Governor Slashes Homeless and Housing Bills." *The Newsletter of the National Coalition for the Homeless*, 8, no. 12 (December).

———. 1990a. "Housing Bills Begin to Move." *The Newsletter of the National Coalition of Homelessness*, 9, no. 6 (June).

———. 1990b. "Mickey Leland Housing Act Introduced." *The Newsletter of the National Coalition for the Homeless*, 9, no. 6 (June).

Santiago, Jose M., Amy Gittler, Allan Beigel, Leonard Stein, and Patricia J. Brown. 1986. "Changing a State Mental Health System Through Litigation: The Arizona Experiment." *American Journal of Psychiatry*, 143, no. 12 (December) 1575–1579.

Shapiro, Bruce. 1990. "Life, Liberty and a Clean Well-lighted Place." *In These Times*, January 31–February 6.

Viets, Jack. 1988. "Street People's Rights: Top Cop Visits the Homeless." *San Francisco Chronicle*, November 8.

Will, George F. 1990. "Judicial Activism Now Dangerous." *Montgomery Advertiser*, February 1.

Wolff, Craig. 1990. "U.S. Appeals Court Upholds Ban on Begging in New York Subways," *New York Times*, May 11.

8 Social Change and Homelessness: Past and Future

Without the creation of a new social order or without an alternative framework for making sense out of the trends in homelessness and housing, there is simply no reason to believe that the U.S. government by itself or in cooperation with the private sector will ever effectively address the sources and changes taking place in this society that have been responsible for the recent and projected growth of homelessness in America. The decade of the 1980s has sufficiently demonstrated that without a federal mandate to alleviate homelessness in the United States, the significant efforts of volunteerism and privatization acting in concert with each other are not enough to conquer this societal problem. The decade of the 1990s will determine whether or not the U.S. government is sincere about fulfilling its commitment (obligation) to provide secure and decent housing for all Americans. Such a pledge was first articulated nearly a half century ago in the 1949 Housing Act. It should be clear to the reader by now that social problems such as homelessness do not just occur in some kind of vacuum. Ultimately they are the products of public policy and can never fully be separated from their social, political, cultural, economic, and legal context.

The social history of contemporary homelessness presented in this book has included a comprehensive analysis of the problem and its context. At the same time, it has described the private and public responses to this social problem. The book has also concerned itself with the emergence and development of the movement to resist homelessness in the United States. Throughout my discussion I have portrayed not only the changing nature of homelessness during the transitional period from monopoly capitalism to global capitalism, but I have attempted to demonstrate the violent nature of U.S. homelessness. Finally, I have explained that the recent growth of homelessness during the emerging period of the information age has been the product of a changing political economy and its influence over domestic policy. The logic of such an analysis recognizes, therefore, that to alter the present trends of homelessness—that is, to adapt or respond effectively to

a changing world—the United States must be prepared psychically, cultur-
ally, and materially to reassess and reevaluate some of its core values and
assumptions concerning "free" enterprise and "liberty" for all. In other
words, the United States must come to grips with the new order and social
reality of global capitalism.

As a country, we can no longer simply stay the course that once upon a
time made us a strong nation and world leader. That course of action—call
it Keynesian democracy or demand-side liberalism—made sense during the
previous epoch of monopoly capital. It worked fairly well for about 75 years.
The conservative alternative of the past decade, commonly referred to as
the Reagan revolution, was a feeble attempt to accommodate the changing
world order. Trickle-down or supply-side economics, as it is more accurately
known, has worked terribly for all but the rich, especially the very rich. It
has never made any sense and the proof has been in the fiscal and trade
deficits. As the twentieth century comes to a close, such policies have been
more than partially responsible for the current domestic mess in which the
United States finds itself.

I am referring not only to the crisis in housing and homelessness, but also
to the crises in public health, education, and family policy. The entire domestic agenda is in a state of serious disarray. The consequences of this state
of affairs is self-evident, not only in the escalating violence among the poorest
of our society, but in the increasing violence toward women, gays and les-
bians, and other minority victims. Adding fuel to the civic terrorism that
especially haunts our urban areas is the racial and ethnic polarization as well
as the slowly decomposing families, schools, neighborhoods, and communities. These problems are made worse by our decaying infrastructure, and
they will not disappear on their own accord nor will they respond to the old
liberal and conservative paradigms. In short, the new social realities of global
capitalism necessitate a whole new approach.

GLOBAL CAPITALISM AND THE NEW SOCIAL REALITY

As we prepare for the twenty-first century, "the hegemony of capitalist
culture and the perceived realities of political choice are such that the given
structure of choice appears to be rational, inevitable, 'natural' " (Ross and
Trachte, 1990:9). Hence, there is often no debate, no discussion, or no issues
as the 1988 presidential election demonstrated all too well. This state of
apolitical affairs, that is to argue, "no large scale conflict or explicit contention
about this structure of choice," exists "because it has been accepted by
potentially contending parties before public agendas are constructed. There
is a "prepolitical' process which constructs the public agenda and thus pre-
disposes 'politics' to a narrowed set of choices" (Ross and Trachte, 1990:9).

To put it simply, the answers to our contemporary societal problems are
located outside the confines of the prevailing political consensus. This is

precisely why our national politicians in particular are impotent when it comes to addressing any of the numerous domestic problems that confront us. When it comes to choices surrounding the domestic agenda of housing and homelessness, alternatives to the current policies are both inconceivable and absolutely necessary. Unless these contradictory political and social relations are changed sometime in the near future, then the nightmare associated with the conditions of homelessness will exacerbate well into the next century. By the end of the 1990s, if we stay the present course, the homeless population is estimated to grow as high as 20 million.

What has accounted for the recent emergence and development of a deregulated, free market consensus among Republicans and Democrats, and for the sorry state of political affairs in the United States? Ross and Trachte (1990) argue that in the developing period of postnationalist monopoly capitalism, the capitalist consensus is no longer achieved through the political state processes of the old social contract or the Hobbesian notion of what they term the Old Leviathan. Instead, they claim that the New Leviathan or a newly invigorated system of global capitalism—its agents, global firms, and financial institutions—symbolized crudely by multinational conglomerates, has been in the process for nearly two decades of decreasing the relative autonomy of the state. The most obvious domestic consequence of these changes in the global political economy has been the atrophy in any kind of debate between the traditional liberal Democratic party and the traditional conservative Republican party. In short, when it comes to the basic structure and fundamental values of the system, there is for all practical purposes not a dime's worth of difference between the two establishment parties. More astonishingly perhaps is the historical fact that there is not an established party of opposition—left, right, or otherwise.

More specifically, Ross and Trachte (1990:10) contend that

global capitalism *does* enlist a kind of consent to its new regime, but this "consent" is not a positive political or social accord; it is more like the resignation with which humans accept the "natural" force of the weather. This resignation is based on acceptance of the parameters of capital investment in a "competitive" world in which the poor of South Korea, and tariff-protected workers of peripheral Europe and Latin America, and the middle-income workers of the industrial "core," are all part of the same global labor force, all accessible to the global firms, acutely conscious of the stakes of the games in international trade, but hardly ever conscious of their common fate.

While fundamental global relations are changing before our very own mass-mediated eyes, it seems that we are, nevertheless, living in "a time when the American government seems simultaneously to be vacating its role as the principal power-broker in world affairs and abandoning any serious effort to lead useful debate here at home on the shape of the new world" that is emerging (Broder, 1990:8A). Like other declining empires from the past, it seems that the United States is desperately trying to hold on to a time gone by. The flexing of U.S. military muscle in the Persian Gulf crisis of 1990 seems to demonstrate this point.

Regarding the global ruling classes or capitalist powers, they have agreed in the post-Cold War period, as evidenced by the 1990 NATO meeting in London on July 6 and the Houston summit a few days later, that the First and Second Worlds are no longer adversaries. However, there still remains some disagreement over how much credit to extend the Soviet Union, and over the seriousness of the U.S. deficit that had underwritten the 1980s boom. As for the multinational firms, as Cockburn (1990:118) has put it, "under the sheltering sky of a world market and the open vista of free trade, the task is simply to roam the planet for cheaper labor." For the global work forces, the consequences of an expanded free trade and the free movement of capital are only just beginning to appear:

Fortune's U.S. 500 is already, to a large extent, the World 500. Mergers involving Europe's thousand largest firms quadrupled over the past five years, with major U.S. participation. At present U.S. workers have declining wages, relatively low unemployment, low social services and declining unionization (heading toward 5 percent in the private sector). Workers in Europe, still highly unionized, have relatively stable wages, better social services and high unemployment. How long before the disciplines of the world market and the world firm compel the most attractive combination of all these traits in the form of low wages, low social services, no unionization and high unemployment, in Europe as elsewhere? (Cockburn, 1990:118).

For the purposes of my discussion of the social reality of the origins of contemporary homelessness and the struggle against it, there are at least two significant characteristics to grasp about the changing nature of global capitalism. First, as Ross and Trachte have predicted, in the global cities of the United States such as New York and Los Angeles, where there has been a decline in the competitive industries of monopoly capitalism, there has also been the emergence or the creation of substandard conditions of life in the "core of the core," which had traditionally been associated with the Third World periphery. In other words, here in the First World we are now experiencing the widespread poverty and homelessness, the high rates of illiteracy and infant mortality, and an increasing concentration of wealth, heretofore characteristic of the developing nations of the Third World. In addition, the last decade witnessed the creation of a permanent underclass, an explosion in both street and suite crime, an erosion of the middle class, and an acceleration in the decline of education and productivity, not to mention the upward spiraling deficits of supply-side economics.

Second, the changing relations of global economic development have altered in part the old tensions of the dialectic of capitalist accumulation and legitimization. In other words, the imperatives and opportunities available to local and national politicians have changed. Just as the forces of monopoly capitalism remade the tasks of government and the alignment of class interests during the transition away from laissez-faire capitalism, so too are the forces of global capitalism today: "the constellation of function and power that characterized the monopoly era is giving way under the geologic pressures of a new variant of capitalism" (Ross and Trachte, 1990:16).

Hence, the recent increased power of business interests in state policy, locally and nationally, and the conservative regimes of the 1980s in Western Europe and North America were reflective of a fundamental change in the relation of the capitalist class to the state. This change has resulted not only in an intensification of the immiseration of the impoverished, but it has already introduced policies of austerity for the working and middle classes in the form of lost wages and benefits. In the previous era of monopoly capitalism, the greater autonomy of state policy was partially supported by labor's political influence and partially by divisions among the various fractions of capital. With labor's power continuing to wane today and with new bases of unity among the fractions of capital appearing worldwide, "state policy is more responsive to the transient will of capital" and to the New Leviathan of global capitalism, which "confronts the schemes of local and national actors with a stern and rigorous discipline" (Ross and Trachte, 1990:16).

Translated into domestic public policy, this means that within the prevailing hegemonic capitalist consensus the likelihood of developing rational, humane, and just programs for eradicating homelessness in the United States is doubtful even in the best scenarios. Thus, in terms of the struggle against homelessness, it becomes imperative that some alternative consensus be formed with a new social vision and a new set of priorities and values. To say the least, this is a very tall order because it calls for reforms that are capable of transcending the myopic tinkerings of the status quo that have already proven themselves bankrupt in practical, if not, unfortunately, in ideological terms. In short, this analysis requires the creation of a new paradigm, a new language, and a new ideology for dealing with U.S. societal problems.

VISIONARY GRADUALISM AND FREE-MARKET SOCIALISM

In his last book, *Socialism: Past and Future*, Michael Harrington (1989) was grappling with a number of questions concerning the forces of global capitalism. He recognized the fundamental need for democratic socialization to unseat corporate socialization. Since the Left is so organizationally weak in the United States, however, he did not foresee this happening for at least 50 years. Nevertheless, by employing the notion of "visionary gradualism," Harrington called for a new culture and a new civilization, grounded in the global principles of feminist, antiracist, and ecologist communitarianism. The cultural radicalism that Harrington envisioned was not mere fantasy nor utopian idealism as evidenced by this acceptance of the capitalist structure of accumulation or economic growth. His desire, however, was for this accumulation to be redirected toward qualitative living for all and away from quantitative consuming for a much smaller minority.

Harrington's basic argument was that "the hope for human freedom and justice in the future rests upon the capacity of people to choose and implement democratic forms of socialization in the face of 'irresponsible,' 'unthinking' and 'unsocial' versions of corporate socialization" (West, 1990:59). According to Harrington, the fundamental choice was not between the rigid "command" economies and bureaucratic collectivist regimes versus the "free-market" economies and capitalist democracies. He understood that this old paradigmatic distinction was no longer, if ever, valid. On the one hand, the capitalization and democratization of Eastern Europe was already under way when Harrington died. On the other hand, and more importantly in terms of the West, despite the conservative and corporate rhetoric of Thatcherism and Reaganism regarding laissez-faire capitalism, no such economic relations exist. In other words, corporate or top-down socialization, as opposed to democratic or bottom-up socialization, has been deeply *statist*, with its military-industrial complexes, socially authoritarian regimentation of the work forces, mass-mediated restrictions on individual choices, and debt-financed public and private spheres.

The transformation of the political economy from monopoly capitalism to global capitalism, as Harrington knew all too well, simultaneously requires and enables nations working together to finally bring forth a common and human existence for all the earth's peoples. Of course, to accomplish this globalization of community or radicalization of culture, it will demand not only the establishment of postnational values, but the creation of a whole new paradigm reflective of the emerging global order. Historically, free-market socialism as the paradigm of the future seems to best exemplify this new vision of a hybridization of both capitalism and socialism—a political economy, in short, that would socialize both the costs and benefits of private accumulation for the general well-being of all people, beginning with the worst off.

In the East, the necessary radical (or structural) changes are already under way. Classical socialism is giving way to free-market socialism. In the West, however, the necessary radical (or structural) changes are still slumbering fast asleep. Nevertheless, the bankruptcy of classical liberalism and conservatism as exemplified by the current state of political and social affairs in the United States foreshadows that the days of ennui, cynicism, and complacency among the masses are numbered. Sooner or later, the U.S. citizenry will wake up and come to the realization that the classical period of capitalism, like the classical period of socialism, is over. Like the calm before the storm, this relatively unproductive and dormant period in U.S. economic, social, and political development will eventually give way to a new and dynamic period; a period that will involve a fundamental break with some of the dominant bourgeois ideology such as the belief in the sanctity of free enterprise, on the one side, and in the vilification of socialism, on the other side. As syndicated columnist Jim Fain (1990:8A) has written,

if you believe in the human experiment—and God help you if you don't—you know a new group of prophets will crop up soon. History shows we'll scorn them as long as we can. Then some . . . crisis will erupt, we'll embrace them as saviors and a fascinating new era will start to unfold.

Today the former communist nations of the East are experimenting economically with marketization and politically with democratization. Classical socialism—the centrally planned economy and the centrally supplied human services—as practiced by fragmented societies rather than by a global world order has met its demise. Under the universalism of global capitalism, no individual country can sustain a closed, self-sufficient economy. In order to be competitive in world markets and part of the emerging global economy, nations find that they must become less protective of their people and ultimately more abusive of their environments.

The rise of global capitalism has made both privately controlled monopoly capital and socially controlled state capital obsolete. During the transition from classical socialism to free-market socialism, "virtually all centrally planned economies are experimenting with a wide range of market mechanisms: privatizing the means of production and distribution; creating stock markets; decentralizing; allowing bankruptcy; letting markets set prices; deregulating" (Naisbitt and Aburdene, 1990:95). Meanwhile, in the West, the historically capitalist and social democratic nations such as France, Australia, and Spain are referring to their respective societies as "free-market socialist," "market-driven socialist," and "supply-side socialist." In other words, other countries are also experimenting and groping with global change (i.e., the establishment of a European common currency and market).

The kinds of reforms demanded by global capitalism call for fundamental changes in the political, economic, and social spheres of society. In the USSR, for example, Gorbachev's reconceptualization of socialism has recognized that the reform and restructuring of the economy of *perestroika* would be impossible without an openness and criticism of the old way or *glasnost*. In the United States, we also need to open up our discussion and to seriously start debating our future domestic and international policies. Thus far, the U.S. response to the rise of global capitalism has been the repudiation of liberalism and the retrogression into the policy preferences of nineteenth-century laissez-faire capitalism. The consequences of this "back to the future" approach have been devastating to marginal people everywhere. The significant rise of homelessness in the United States over the past decade has been only one manifestation of how such policies have contributed to the growing subjugation of more and more people living here.

In an *In These Times* (ITT, 1990) editorial, "If Moscow can do it, why can't we?" the similarities of the problems suffered by those living in state-owned and -operated housing in the USSR and those living in public housing in the United States were noted. It was also noted how mainstream media such as the *Wall Street Journal* can celebrate the privatization of housing in Moscow, yet remain conspicuously silent about the continuing deterioration of low-income housing in urban areas throughout the United States. What the newly elected Moscow City Council did in July 1990, acting under a new federal law on land, was proclaim the city to be landlord of all of Moscow, and then it voted to give all the city's apartments to their tenants. Regarding new construction of apartments, it appears that tenants will have to buy, or rent if they cannot afford to buy. In general, these approaches will give tenants "more control over their living conditions and, therefore, greater independence from the state . . . all of this is consistent with socialist principles, which to us means social, or democratic, control, not state ownership of individual private property' (ITT, 1990:14).

The ITT editorial went on to recognize what has been obvious to anybody who is remotely familiar with homelessness and the low-income housing crisis in America—namely, that the free-market system is incapable of providing affordable housing for a small yet growing percentage of the U.S. population. We are currently referring to more than 10 million people who reside in substandard housing. "Clearly there is a critical need for a massive program in federally subsidized or federally constructed housing. And there is an equally pressing need for greater tenant control or tenant ownership of apartments in existing public-housing developments" (ITT, 1990:14). The editorial (p. 14) concluded that

if private ownership of apartments will encourage Moscow's tenants to take pride in their property and to maintain it in good condition, the same would be true of the tenants now living in the miserably maintained and partially abandoned public housing that plagues our big-city ghettos. Title to these apartments should be given to the people now living in them. Local governments should help tenants organize cooperative management of their new property, with all rents going toward maintaining and improving the buildings and immediate environs. That would be a good first step toward improving housing for low-income Americans, one that could reduce the cost of government by eliminating most of the existing public-housing bureaucracies, while dramatically improving housing conditions.

This is no pipe dream, it has already been successfully accomplished in public housing projects in Washington, D.C., Philadelphia, and Chicago.

Can the heretofore historically opposing or contradictory economic systems of capitalism and socialism integrate? More specifically, as states, East and West, succumb to the political and economic forces of global capitalism, can market-driven systems socialize their distribution of goods and services so that the worst-off persons can have a just and humane existence? I believe not only that they can, but that they must if the marginal people living in the United States and around the world are ever to become truly free and independent members of the global community.

SOCIAL SUBJUGATION OR SOCIAL JUSTICE?

Free-market socialism does not attempt to do away with all privilege and inequality, yet it does believe in the eradication of the social subjugation of people, and in the establishment of social justice for all. Because we live in a world without physical and technological shortages, free-market socialism believes that crimes of exploitation such as homelessness and poverty or the creation of dependent classes of people should be eliminated no differently than smallpox or hunger. Put a different way, free-market socialism believes that individuals should be limited by government to accumulating wealth only to the extent that accumulation does not deprive another coproducer or coconsumer of a minimal and humane share of the created wealth, based on what is commonly regarded as "fair" were their positions reversed. Institutionally speaking, as Gil (1989:44–45) has argued,

since societal violence has been used throughout history to establish and maintain different types of unjust social orders, the establishment of just social orders depends on the eradication of societal violence [homelessness] and the vicious circle of counter- [street crime] and repressive [criminal justice] violence. Institutional justice means therefore transcendence of societal violence and attainment of nonviolent social orders free of coercive practices and conditions.

In *Justice and Modern Moral Philosophy*, on his way to making sense out of such concepts as natural and social justice, Jeffrey Reiman (1990:211) contended that "real community exists among people in some interpersonal relationship, when each desires not only his own satisfaction but that of the others as well; the satisfaction of the others must be desired as good in itself, not only as a means to one's own satisfaction. . . . " Accordingly, one of the dominant assumptions underlying this book has been the belief that the U.S. public policy-making apparatus is not a truly democratic and just one. Therefore, as has been shown from the demonstrated arguments throughout the book, the United States does not adhere to the fundamental principle of mutual well being. If we did in reality practice the principles of fairness and mutual well being today, then there would currently be no homelessness problem in America to speak of.

More specifically, Reiman (1990:206) argues that justice is the precondition of true community: "the theory of justice as reason's *answer to subjugation* maintains that justice has primacy over all other ideals . . . because justice

guards the boundaries between people." His theory of justice further maintains that the principle of compatible liberty is the first principle of justice:

The theory is deontological because it is not aimed at maximizing aggregate liberty
(considered, say, as the total number of effective free choices) across people, but
rather at maximizing liberty for every single person, even if this requires a lower
aggregate liberty or aggregate anything else than might be obtainable otherwise.
Accordingly, it holds the appropriate relations of non-subjugation to be prior in
authority to any other conception of good (Reiman, 1990:207–208).

In other words, an unjust social order is one where people are subjugated
and where people do not freely share justice. Conversely, a just social order
or structure is one where people are not subjugated and where all people
can call the society their own. The just society is

one whose terms all people can openly affirm, a society in which members can look
one another in the eyes and speak honestly about the conditions under which they
share their fates. Seeing in the social structure a system of cooperation aimed at
enabling each to realize his aims, they can feel from one another respect and toward
one another affection, a kind of civic friendship out of which all can take deep pleasure
in the flourishing of their fellows, even those whose names they do not know (Reiman,
1990:309).

Reiman's moral vision of justice as a prerequisite for community need not
remain simply a part of abstract discourse. His conceptions are easily located
in an understanding of both the concrete realities of global capitalism as well
as the possibilities of free-market socialism. Building on the power and
limitations of John Rawls' theory of justice, Reiman articulates a new social
contract capable of achieving social justice for all. Utilizing Rawls' "principles
of difference"—the requirement that inequalities work to the greatest benefit
of the worst off—Reiman examines how human beings and social orders alike
can be acquitted from the charge of subjugation. For example, regarding
social and economic inequality worldwide or the distribution schemes that
are principally responsible for the subjugation of, say, homeless people,
Reiman would argue that such relations are only justifiable if the shares of
goods and services to the worst off cannot be improved by decreasing those
inequalities.

Take the distribution schemes of countries at a similar level of development
such as Sweden, Germany, Japan, and the United States. It can be shown
unequivocally and comparatively speaking that the worst-off inhabitants of
these four countries live in the United States. Thus, the existences of other
alternative distribution schemes charge, indict, and find the United States
guilty of unnecessarily subjugating its poor people. In the case of the homeless, we can argue that we have the crime and violence of homelessness.
We can also argue that the public policies that reproduce the conditions of

homelessness are not rational, inevitable, or natural. On the contrary, they are politically irresponsible. A politically responsible response to the social problems associated with the low-income housing crisis and the homeless would include, but would not be limited to, the following changes in domestic policy: the establishment of a maximum wage (or absolute limits on income) and a minimum guaranteed income for all; requirements that contingent or part-time workers receive full benefits and equal hourly wages with full-time workers; comprehensive child care and national health care; urban renewal of buildings and infrastructures and a general ecological cleanup; and the creation of noncapitalist spheres of economic and social activity or the decommodification of certain goods and services for the needy such as housing and education.

I would go even further and argue that not to implement such policies should not only be held in contempt by the citizenry, but it should in the area of housing in particular be regarded as criminal because the United States could simply rearrange its distribution system and homelessness would be history in this country. As Henry (1991) has suggested, if an intoxicated driver can be found guilty of negligent homicide, then an ideologically misguided (and "intoxicated") government whose public policies directly or indirectly result in loss, injury, or death should also be accountable. In fact, as Chapter 7 revealed, some of the nation's local litigation has resulted in municipalities and counties being held liable and in contempt for not providing housing to the indigent. The point, however, is not to litigate all public and private officials into submission or into providing the necessary policies to solve our social ills, but *merely* to alter our national and international priorities.

It should be underscored, especially for those capitalist diehards and ideologues, that the principles of difference do not call for the elimination, or even a significant reduction, of the gross inequality in the United States. In fact, these principles do not call for a redistribution of the wealth per se. That is to say, the principles do not require that those who are better off in a just society give some of what they have to those who are worse off. The principles of difference refer to the social order as a whole and apply to the organization of the distribution schemes. Schemes of distribution may allow inequalities, but in order for these inequalities to be just, they must be part of a scheme that works to the greatest advantage of the worst off. In other words, how the principles of difference operate is a matter of the design of the scheme, not of the better off giving things to the worst off.

For example, the distributive schemes of Sweden's social democratic order, by no means a utopian model and not without flaws when it comes to its housing policy, have figured out in Harrington's terms how to overcome the worst inegalitarian abuses of corporate socialization. Hence, as part of the project of visionary gradualism, "collective capital formation" as practiced by Sweden makes sense. Collective capital formation represents a positive step taken toward the creation of social justice because it not only links growth to efficiency and democratic management, but it establishes a system where solidaristic wage demands are first distributed to those at the bottom of the labor force. Consequently, with a population of about 3.4 million in Sweden, the number of homeless there was estimated to be around a hundred at the end of 1987 (Karyd, 1988).

On the other hand, while the principles of difference do not require the distribution of equal shares, neither do they allow unlimited benefits to those at the top. In the scheme of things, the principles of difference would support, for example, a progressive as opposed to a regressive tax system. The decade of the 1980s should have demonstrated the negative effects of the U.S. regressive taxing scheme, which was put into place during Reagan's first term in office. Such policies as capital gains tax reductions and other supply-side economic sleights of hand have benefitted primarily the rich, as the middle class has struggled to barely keep up with the cost of living and the working and marginal classes have fallen further behind than they were two decades ago. Such highly irresponsible and socially unjust distribution schemes as those associated with the policies of free market capitalism during the 1980s not only reduced the shares of wealth of all but the rich, but they contributed significantly to the subjugation of more and more people, including, of course, the worst-off homeless populations.

In discussing the governing principles of social justice and the articles of the social contract, Reiman (1990:302) "does not speak only of maximizing the worst-off person, but of maximizing each position from the worst-off up, subject to the constraint of not reducing the shares of anyone below." He further argues that "economic systems are to be judged by their overall contribution to people's ability to pursue their sovereign interests, of which goods are only a part" (p. 302). In other words, in a just society such as the one envisioned under free-market socialism, mass communication would consist of communication among the masses, not merely communication to the masses. Although to different degrees and in different ways, under both classical socialism and classical capitalism, mass communication has been primarily unidirectional, from the top-down. Similarly free-market socialism requires mass political participation among the masses, not just among their supposed representatives, appointed or elected. Again, classical forms of both socialism and capitalism have subjugated various groupings of people, especially marginal people, to differing degrees of mass control. Accordingly, the lesson for the United States is to realize that the freedom to accept work or to refuse work, or to receive food, clothes, and shelter or not to receive these essential human necessities, as dictated by the allegedly free market, is anything but liberty and justice for all.

In a country as wealthy as the United States, we have the luxury to decide if we will continue to unnecessarily subjugate people such as the homeless. In other words, with alternative distributive schemes in general and in relationship to low-income housing policies in particular, we could virtually eliminate homelessness in America overnight. The question simply becomes: is our federal government ready to adopt the values of social and community justice characteristic of the new global potential, or will the prevailing capitalist state apparatus cling to the values of repressive justice characteristic of the old nationalistic divisions of race, class, and gender? In the next to the last section of this book, I will review general policy alternatives for combatting the crisis in U.S. low-income housing and homelessness. The housing policy proposal plans shared below are consistent with the progressive vision of an integrative and cooperative global capitalism capable of providing a decent standard of living for all people in the world. These policy proposals on housing and homelessness, if adopted, would indeed represent a reversal in the housing policy trends of the past decade. They would also constitute a legitimate program aimed at serving the long-term permanent housing needs of low-income persons and their dependents. Whether or not these policy proposals are adopted in the United States or not will depend, in part, on whether or not the values of social justice or free-market socialism are subscribed to by the electoral masses, and, in part, on whether or not middle-income voters stage a populist revolt any time soon against the legacies of Reagan's policies of reverse Robin Hoodism.

A NEW HOUSING POLICY FOR THE UNITED STATES

A quarter of a century of imperial wars, neoliberal retreats and Reaganite counterrevolution have eroded the country's economic base to the crumbling point. The social agenda, once deferred, is now permanently abandoned. Speculation has replaced production, imports overrun exports, and gross inequality has supplanted even the modest moves toward economic justice that were made in mid-century (*The Nation*, 1990:259).

The poverty of political will that characterizes both the Republican and Democratic parties is rationalized by the budget deficit paralysis, a statistical fiction if there ever was one. Not that the deficits are not real. But the statistical reality is that despite the deficits, money in this wealthiest of all nations can be found when Congress and the president have the will to do so. There have been funds enough for Operation Desert Shield and for the Contras, death squads, defense forces, anticommunist and antidrug crusades. There have been trillions spent on murderous weapons and the military-industrial complexes. In 1989 there was enough money for Congress to recommend itself a 50 percent pay raise. Currently, there is going to be between $500 billion and $1 trillion to bail out the savings and loan institutions. But when it comes to the welfare and the health of ordinary citizens, and when it comes to the needs of the homeless or the poor, including some 30–40 million children, then we hear all about the need to balance budgets and to meet the supposed goals of Gramm-Rudman. The refrain is always the same, it makes no difference nowadays which of the two great American parties is singing:

Money for housing? The word is No. National health plan? Uh-uh. Social investment, public enterprise, child care, support for the elderly, research and development, progressive taxation, antitrust enforcement, environmental action, job security, reindustrialization, economic justice—a thousand times No (*The Nation*, 1990:260).

The decade of the 1980s, if public policies do not change, has revealed what the future will look like. What first emerged with the Reagan revolution and has continued unabated into the early 1990s does not forecast a bright future. The immediate and not so immediate consequences of failing to achieve a new housing policy for the United States has been described by Schwartz, Ferlauto, and Hoffman (1988:283):

If our national government is unable to adopt a new, more expansive housing policy soon, profoundly negative consequences are likely to be visited upon millions of American families, on the American economy, and on many American communities. Acceptance of lowered homeownership levels, inattention to the needs of the frail elderly, continued failure to prevent homelessness, malign neglect of both urban and rural housing requirements, cuts in needed housing construction programs for the poor, weak anti-discrimination laws weakly enforced—these characteristics of our present policies just don't hurt individuals and families. They hurt our economy; they truncate our middle class; they reduce equality of opportunity; they sap the vibrancy of our efforts to revitalize cities or to restore farm communities; they create new ghettos (mostly for the aged) while reinforcing a culture of poverty in the too many older ghettos and slums. A national governmental decision to continue these policies, or a non-decision (which has the same effect), will accelerate these hurtful trends and diminish the quality of life, the moral stature, and perhaps the social peace of the nation.

When it comes to the policies that address housing and homelessness, there are certainly more than a few good ideas. One such idea is the growing number of "linkage" laws that require developers to fund public works, including anything from improved streets and sewage facilities to affordable housing or job training and employment. It comes as little or no surprise that linkage works best in those communities where land is scarce and valuable. Boston, San Francisco, and Portland, Oregon, are three prominent cities that have adopted linkage programs. In these cities developers have lined up despite the fact that they are being forced to contribute some of their enormous profits to various civic projects. But even supposing that all of the deteriorated cities across the United States were ripe for the kinds of redevelopment that has been occurring in such geographical places as Chicago, Miami, and Santa Monica, it should be clearly understood that linkage money will not come close to providing enough of the necessary finances for public housing and other infrastructure projects. Such projects must be initiated and underwritten by governmental enterprise and social investment. As one of linkage's strongest proponents, Lawrence Dwyer, chairman of Boston's Neighborhood Housing Trust, has admitted: "Until the federal government gets back into the housing business, we're not going to see a solution" (quoted in J. Schwartz, 1988:47).

Affordable Housing Policy Alternatives

Historically, most developed countries have recognized the responsibility of government to provide housing to its citizens. How and to what extent governments should intervene in the housing markets, however, has been a matter of considerable debate. Karyd (1988:62) has characterized, even exaggerated, the two extreme (or pure) positions of this debate. Respectively, he identified the free market "believers" and the free market "opposers" as follows:

Almost every kind of services and goods are available on a market which means that there are sellers as well as buyers. There are markets for single-dwelling houses, condominiums and multi-dwelling houses. . . . The need for housing will be satisfied by the forces of the market—demand and supply. Compared to these real forces, the power of government is small. Because of its limited power and because the market is the best way to distribute housing, the role of government should be confined to lubricate and facilitate activities on the markets. If extremely high rents or sales profits are observed, this is not an indication of insufficient government control but a sign of improper market function. The reasons are often to be found in vainful attempts from the government to offset the market, e.g. by constraints on construction and supply.

Adequate housing is a basic human right, not a merchandise. The influence of markets over such an essential sector of human life should be removed or at least rendered harmless. Government should exercise control over physical planning, construction of new housing, rent levels and price levels. Although private-owned single- and multi-family dwellings may be tolerated, realized capital gains occurring at sale should be heavily taxed. For multi-family dwellings, prospective buyers should be subject to approval by the local tenant organization. The forming of condominiums should not be encouraged. In general, housing should be subsidized to prevent people from choosing inferior housing conditions in order to use money for other kinds of consumption.

My own position is that the eradication of homelessness in the United States will realistically require a vision that incorporates a mixture to these two ideological positions. In other words, the emergence and development of global capitalism can be adapted to meet simultaneously the housing needs of both privatization and socialization. Hence, if minimal levels of housing are to prevail for all people, residing both inside and outside this country, then some integrated and comprehensive approach must emerge to replace the privately based and inadequately supported present policy configuration.

The housing and homelessness policies presented in the three program proposals below capture the essence of an alternative housing program for preventing homelessness. These policy plans are very compatible with the values of social justice and the priorities of free market socialism.

The Francine P. Rabinovitz Plan

Like the other housing plans to be reviewed, Rabinovitz's plan is comprehensive in nature, addressing specific economic and social objectives. Like the others, it is also substantially more ambitious and more costly to achieve than are most current housing plans. The Rabinovitz plan involves programatic steps designed to upgrade the condition of the homeless over a ten-year period. Finally, as Rabinovitz (1989:12), a public administration professor and vice-president of Hamilton, Rabinovitz and Alschuler, Inc., policy and management consultants, has argued, the "first important policymaking principle is that homelessness can only be attacked if both public-sector actors and private-sector actors adopt a common purpose with complementary policies and objectives." Rabinovitz divides her objectives into those that will establish particular economic and social environments.

First, Rabinovitz (p. 13) calls for an economic environment in which:

- Money income for 90 percent of currently homeless households (or individuals) is at least at the poverty level, as set by federal standards.

- Employment at hourly rates equal to or better than the minimum wage is both available and rationally accessible for all the homeless who meet minimum standards of employability. ("Rationally accessible" means that neither deductions or earned income from public benefits nor the cost and complexity of transportation to and from any job site are so great as to make it an economically rational act to choose unemployment over employment.)

- Price levels of essentials, particularly housing, are consistent with prevailing average income levels for this population, whether the income is secured largely from public benefits or from employment, so that the phenomenon observable in some cities of people cycling each month from single room occupancy hotels to missions and shelters to the streets and back again largely disappears.

- The SRO housing stock where it still exists is preserved, rehabilitated, and supplemented by new facilities suitable for very-low-income people who are not necessarily beset by physical or mental disorders or dependencies and who, with provision of transitional services, are equipped to move on to better situations.

- There is no "street homeless" population upon whom the status is imposed by purely economic circumstances; nor must the sleeping accommodations of missions and other charitable shelters be supplemented by people sleeping regularly in chairs or chapel pews in order to avoid being forced into the streets.

Second, Rabinovitz calls for a social environment in which:

- A comprehensive and highly integrated array of public and private social services is available to all homeless people, both on demand and as a result of affirmative outreach programs to find those in need and make them aware of services available.

- Institutions that regularly deal with groups of particularly fragile homeless populations are sensitized to the special problems of that homeless subpopulation in dealing with the overall system and have special programs to make these adjustments.

- Personal security is enhanced, as evidenced by a reduction in the rate of violent crime in areas where the homeless are concentrated.

- There are decent and affordable—which in many instances means free—living facilities (both short- and long-term) and well-equipped treatment facilities (both emergency and maintenance) for all of the homeless with disabling mental disorders who are willing to make use of such facilities.

- In areas in which the homeless are concentrated, at least a rudimentary system of community infrastructure (for example, tenants' associations, recovery support groups) is in place for those who wish to take part.

- To the degree that it continues to exist at all, street homelessness is generally and accurately perceived to be a matter of choice, not necessity.

- It is possible to make a reasonable case that areas in which the homeless are concentrated have become places in which it is in the best interests of many low- and very-low-income adults to choose to live, even if they do not have the problems or dependencies now associated with residents of the area.

Institute for Policy Studies' Progressive Housing Program for America

The IPS Progressive Housing Program for America has been introduced and reintroduced in the House by Congressman Ronald Dellums (D-CA), beginning in 1989. As proposed legislation it has not left the housing committee. The act has contained five sections or titles, each with its own funding authorization: Title I—The National Tenant Protection and Private Rental Housing Conversion Act; Title II—The National Homeowner Protection Act; Title III—The Subsidized Housing Preservation Act; Title IV—The Social Housing Production and Financing Act; and Title V—Federally Mandated Local Housing Program. Such a program could cost as little as $29 billion and as much as $87 billion in its first year. But IPS has argued that it would save even more over the long term. IPS has also argued that its package of national housing legislation represents the first proposal to get to the root of the problem in comprehensive fashion. Finally, IPS has argued that its Progressive Housing Program for America is based on common sense: "It uses taxpayers' dollars wisely and cost-effectively to assure all Americans the right to homes they can afford, can live in with reasonable comfort, can count on staying in, and can control" (IPS, 1989:59).

The IPS housing program is founded on three fundamental principles that its supporters believe are absolutely essential for ridding the country of homelessness:

1. recognition of housing as a right rather than a commodity;

2. elimination of the role of private credit; and

3. promotion of social, nonprofit production and ownership of housing units (IPS, 1989:22).

According to the proposed plan, government action would be directed toward four complementary goals:

1. Expand the amount of housing under some form of social ownership, with residents controlling their housing.

2. Expand the amount of housing produced by socially oriented developers and increase democratic control over the housing production process and land use.

3. Expand direct public grants for financing housing production, rehabilitation, and ownership, and reduce dependence on privately controlled debt.

4. Provide adequate resources to meet housing needs and allocate housing resources on a equitable basis.

IPS has acknowledged that in the end the solution to low-income housing in America or the "creation of housing for use rather than profit, the replacement of private housing ownership, production, and finance with a system of social provision and protected occupancy" will not be an easy course to negotiate. Fundamentally for such a program to succeed, these policies will "require federal leadership and federal funding, as well as the capacity for decentralized implementation based on local resources and needs" (IPS, 1989:59).

As Chester Hartman (1988:191), a fellow at IPS and an expert on housing and urban planning, has maintained in a separate discussion regarding the IPS proposal, "if the goal of decent, affordable housing is ever to become a reality in the United States, a fundamental restructuring of the system by which housing is produced, financed, owned, and managed will be required that places housing rights above property rights and profits." Hartman argues that neither raising income nor lowering the housing costs or some combination of the two is feasible within the existing profit-making system. The former approach would require a massive income transfer and would inevitably produce severe inflation in the housing market, necessitating even greater income redistribution. The latter approach, while potentially resulting in small savings in costs, would most likely do so by reducing environmental and housing standards and by deteriorating work conditions and wage levels for construction workers. To bring about this radical structuring for providing the lowest possible costs in the production and maintenance of housing, the full IPS Platform reads as follows (Hartman, 1988:190):

- Proclaim decent, affordable housing as a *right* for all Americans, with a detailed timetable and action plan for attaining this entitlement.
- Create a strong, expanded "social housing" sector, capable of developing, rehabilitating, and managing large numbers of housing units at the local, neighborhood level.
- Provide outright capital grants for new construction and rehabilitation, to replace loans, with capital costs assumed by the government and not borne by occupants as part of their monthly payments.
- Transfer significant amounts of the existing housing stock, both owned and rented units, to the social sector, using government funds for permanent debt retirement.
- Provide subsidies (in the form of additional operating monies or housing allowances) to all occupants of social sector housing with incomes too low to afford operating costs (excluding repayment of capital).
- Create effective programs to retain and strengthen the existing stock of subsidized housing.

As Hartman spells out the philosophy behind the IPS housing proposal, one can appreciate how this program is grounded in both the principles of difference and the values of social justice. It is also consistent with the free-market socialist vision of community:

The programs proposed here are ways of spending large sums of tax money in order to effect a drastic and permanent decrease in housing costs for vast numbers of lower- and moderate-income people, the impact of which will spread throughout the full range of the housing market. A further benefit would be steady and guaranteed construction demand, which will be attractive to companies that build housing efficiently and construction workers who all too often are the victims of erratic construction cycles and uncertain and inadequate annual incomes (Hartman, 1989:198).

Schwartz, Ferlauto, and Hoffman's *A New Housing Policy for America*

Schwartz et al. (1988) have helped draft and enact state legislation. Their ideas and legislation on housing have been recognized nationally and internationally. Their New Jersey legislation in particular has provided models for other states. Referring to their landmark New Jersey legislation, Senator Bradley (D-NJ) (in Schwartz et al., 1988:xii) said it "has helped to expand homeownership opportunities, provide affordable rental apartments, and prevent homelessness for tens of thousands of New Jerseyans." Nevertheless, Schwartz et al. argue that without federal involvement, leadership, and partnership local and state efforts, such as the ones that they have been involved with, are only drops in the bucket that cannot possibly offer a viable solution to the crisis in low- and moderate-income housing in America. Consequently, they advocate a national housing program that includes, among other things, a federal down payment program, an employer-assisted home-ownership plan, mortgage interest rate buy down fund, shared equity mortgages, a National Housing Investment Corporation, and a Federal Housing Trust Fund for the construction of needed rental units. If such programs were put into operation during the 1990s, Schwartz et al. estimate that about 11 million new jobs would be created as a result.

These authors of *A New Housing Policy for America: Recapturing the American Dream* are convinced that the successful political adoption of these policies is dependent on the ability to link the aspirations of the middle class, particularly young families, with the needs of the poor and the homeless. Moreover, as Senator Bradley (p. xii) asserts in the foreword to their book:

We must all be concerned when a majority of America's 30 million tenants now live in dwelling units that our federal government acknowledges to be inadequate or overcrowded or cost-burdened. New policies must focus on the 10 million American families who are consigned to overcrowded or dilapidated homes and the 14 million more who pay much more of their incomes than they can afford for shelter.

More specifically, when it comes to stopping homelessness at its source and to preventing, treating, and curing the homeless in America, Schwartz et al. have advocated a threefold plan.

First, the authors call for a series of measures designed to avert the eviction of families on the verge of destitution. They argue that such a policy would not only stop the suffering from becoming homeless, but that there would be the added benefits of avoiding the social and financial expenses of emergency assistance. For examples, they point to state statutes in Maryland, New Jersey, and Pennsylvania that have addressed homelessness at the front end—before it happens. New Jersey's Homelessness Prevention Program provides temporary assistance as a last resort for those who have inadequate funds beyond their control and face imminent homelessness. For those who have a mortgage, loans are provided; for those whose rents exceed more than 50 percent of their income, grants are provided.

Second, there are the homelessness efforts such as the 1987 Urgent Relief for the Homeless Act. In addition to this act's provision of emergency shelters, transitional housing, and the rehabilitation of rental property, Schwartz et al. call for the establishment of group homes, halfway houses, congregate care centers, and multigenerational shared living arrangements. They also want to see that specialized medical and mental health services become integrated components of housing complexes. Such policy developments would facilitate the coordination of prevention and treatment for the homeless.

Third, as a backdrop to the specific programs above, these three housing analysts and activists call for a reversal in the social and domestic spending trends of the 1980s. Specifically, they want to see a restoration of federal cuts in income assistance to poor people, in disability payments to handicapped people, in Medicaid funds for sick people, in food stamps for hungry people, and in rental assistance to homeless-vulnerable people. Last and certainly not least, Schwartz et al. want the restoration of the once expansive construction subsidy program for low-income housing in America.

The policies called for by these three comprehensive approaches to the U.S. crisis in low-income housing and homelessness have been well thought out. And the United States is quite capable of fully engaging this alternative and progressive plan for confronting its problem of homelessness. The only question that remains is: do the federally elected members of the House and Senate have the political will to "do the right thing" for a group of people whose interests are perhaps the most politically vulnerable of any in this society?

HOMELESSNESS IN GLOBAL PERSPECTIVE

In global terms, most of the 5 billion persons who inhabit this earth live in the less-developed regions of the world where available resources in general and in housing in particular are problematic. In the Third World, the central governments or state apparatuses can simply not afford to subsidize housing for its poor. It is also in the developing countries of the world, especially where urbanization has taken place, that most of the globe's estimated 40 million homeless persons can be found (Bingham, Green, and White, 1987).

In Latin America, for example, in the largest cities of Mexico, Brazil, Colombia, and Venezuela, the homeless problems are all quite severe (Burns, 1987). Consider the data presented to convey the nature of the conditions faced by Brazil's youth:

According to Government figures, 36 million Brazilians under the age of 18—about 60 percent of the total—are "needy," and seven million of these have lost all or most links with their families and are "abandoned or marginalized." One-third of all children between 7 and 14—some eight million—do not attend school, and more than half the children under 6 years old are undernourished (quoted in Knight, 1987:261).

In Bogota, Colombia, things are no better for their youth. On July 27, 1990, ABC's "20/20" did a docu-news story on "street urchins," or homeless children, some as young as four and five years, who prefer living in the sewers beneath the streets of Bogota. In the sewers there is filth, waste, disease, and rats, but the youth feel relatively safe and secure in contrast with the various kinds of abuse and neglect that they experience on the streets of Bogota. They receive no government support whatsoever, very little private charity, and much harassment and physical abuse from citizens and police.

As this book has pointed out, the United States also has its share of homeless people, young and old, living in alleyways and beneath the city streets in sewers and subways. What is unusual, however, is the magnitude of the homelessness problem for a postindustrial nation. The only other postindustrial society in the world today that is experiencing both a rise in the number and in the rate of homelessness is Great Britain. Of course, it does not take a mental giant to see how the policies of Reaganism and Thatcherism have had similar negative social consequences. I also suspect that other traditional liberal democratic countries of Western Europe, in response to the competitive markets of global capitalism, will soon follow with their own repressive versions of austerity capitalism, complete with the emergence and development of their own new homeless classes. With respect to the United States, in any event, it seems that the basic "law of homelessness" for an advanced capitalist society applies: "If a society cannot provide affordable housing, for instance by subsidizing rents, the number of homelessness [sic] will increase" (Friedrichs, 1988:5). By the end of 1990 such was already the case in the newly capitalizing countries of Eastern Europe, for example, where previously subsidized and state-owned housing has been transferred to the private sector of free enterprise.

It seems to this author that if the United States can employ a myriad of every technique imaginable to subsidize the wealth of this society, then it ought to be able to afford the subsidies necessary for satisfying the fundamental human needs of its poor. And if because of the inhumane, irrational, and destructive domestic U.S. policies, there must be poverty in the first place, then the very least that this society could do would be to eliminate homelessness within its borders. Given this nation's material wealth, it is the only socially just course of action to take. In other words, give America's new homeless and near homeless the security and the well being of permanent housing. GIVE IT TO THEM NOW!

REFERENCES

Bingham, Richard D., Roy E. Green, and Sammis B. White, Eds., 1987. *The Homeless in Contemporary Society*. Newbury Park, CA: Sage Publications.

Broder, David. 1990. "Old World Crumbles, New Not Yet Born." *The Montgomery Advertiser*, May 3.

Burns, Leland S. 1987. "Third World Solutions to the Homelessness Problem." In R. D. Bingham et al., eds., *The Homeless in Contemporary Society*. Newbury Park, CA: Sage Publications.

Cockburn, Alexander. 1990. "Beat the Devil." *The Nation*, July 30/August 6.

Fain, Jim. 1990. "Homestead Could Stand Sprucing Up." *The Montgomery Advertiser*, July 23.

Friedrichs, Jurgen. 1988. "Affordable Housing and Homelessness: A Comparative View." In J. Friedrichs, ed., *Affordable Housing and the Homeless*. Berlin: Walter de Gruyter.

Gil, David. 1989. "Work, Violence, Injustice and War." *Journal of Sociology and Social Work*, 6, no. 1.

Harrington, Michael. 1989. *Socialism: Past and Future*. Berkeley: Arcade Publishing.

Hartman, Chester. 1988. "Decent, Affordable Housing for All." In Marcus Raskin and Chester Hartman, eds., *Winning America: Ideas and Leadership for the 1990s*. Boston: South End Press.

Henry, Stuart. 1991. "The Informal Economy: A Crime of Omission by the State." In Gregg Barak, ed., *Crimes by the Capitalist State: An Introduction to State Criminality*. Albany: State University of New York Press.

institute for Policy Studies Working Group on Housing (with Dick Cluster). 1989. *The Right to Housing: A Blueprint for Housing the Nation*. Oakland, CA: Community Economics, Inc.

In These Times. 1990. Editorial. 14, no. 32. (August).

Karyd, Arne. 1988. "Affordable Housing and the Market." In J. Friedrichs, ed., *Affordable Housing and the Homeless*. Berlin: Walter de Gruyter.

Knight, Rudolph H. 1987. "Homelessness: An American Problem?" In R. H. Bingham et al., eds., *The Homeless in Contemporary Society*. Newbury, CA: Sage Publications.

Naisbitt, John and Patricia Aburdene. 1990. *Megatrends 2000: Ten New Directions for the 1990s*. New York: William Morrow.

The Nation. 1990. Editorial, "Dead Souls." February 26.

Rabinovitz, Francine F. 1989. "What Should Be Done?" *Society*, May/June.

Reiman, Jeffrey. 1990. *Justice and Modern Moral Philosophy*. New Haven, CT: Yale University Press.

Ross, Robert J. S. and Kent C. Trachte. 1990. *Global Capitalism: The New Leviathan*. Albany: State University of New York Press.

Schwartz, David C., Richard C. Ferlauto, and Daniel N. Hoffman. 1988. *A New Housing Policy for America: Recapturing the American Dream*. Philadelphia: Temple University Press.

Schwartz, John. 1988. "Giving Something Back: A Growing Number of 'Linkage' Laws Forces Developers to Fund Public Works." *Newsweek*, September 5.

West, Cornel. 1990. "Michael Harrington, Socialist." *The Nation*, January 8–15.

Selected Bibliography

Anderson, Charles. 1974. *The Political Economy of Social Class.* Englewood Cliffs, NJ: Prentice-Hall.

Appelbaum, Richard. 1989. "The Affordability Gap." *Social Science and Modern Society,* 26, no. 4 (May/June).

Aulette, Judy and Albert Aulette. 1987. "Police Harassment of the Homeless: The Political Purpose of the Criminalization of Homelessness." *Humanity and Society,* 11, no. 2.

Barak, Gregg. 1991. "Homelessness and the Case for Community-Based Initiatives: The Emergence of a Model Shelter as a Short Term Response to the Deepening Crisis in Housing." In Harold E. Pepinsky and Richard Quinney, eds., *Criminology as Peacemaking.* Bloomington: Indiana University Press.

Barak, Gregg and Robert E. Bohm. 1989. "The Crimes of the Homeless or the Crime of Homelessness? On the Dialectics of Criminalization, Decriminalization, and Victimization." *Contemporary Crises: Law, Crime and Social Policy,* 13, no. 3 (September).

Bard, Marjorie Brooks. 1988. "Domestic Abuse and the Homeless Woman: Paradigms in Personal Narratives for Organizational Strategists and Community Planners." Doctoral Dissertation. Ann Arbor, MI: University Microfilms International (1989).

Bingham, Richard D., Roy E. Green, and Sammis B. White, Eds. 1987. *The Homeless in Contemporary Society.* Newbury Park, CA: Sage Publications.

Blasi, Gary L. 1987. "Litigation on Behalf of the Homeless: Systematic Approaches." *Journal of Urban and Contemporary Law,* reprinted in Robert Hayes, ed., *The Rights of the Homeless.* New York: Practicing Law Institute.

Blau, Joel S. 1987. "The Homeless of New York: A Case Study in Social Welfare Policy." Doctoral Dissertation. Ann Arbor, MI: University Microfilms International (1989).

Caton, Carol L. M. 1990. *Homeless in America.* New York: Oxford University Press.

Crystal, Stephen, Susan Ladner, and Richard Towber. 1986. "Multiple Impairment Patterns in the Mentally Ill Homeless." *International Journal of Mental Health,* 14, no. 4.

Dakin, Linda S. 1987. "Homelessness: The Role of the Legal Profession in Finding

Solutions Through Litigation." *Family Law Quarterly*, 31, no. 1 (Spring):93–126.

Devine, Deborah Judith. 1988. "Homelessness and the Social Safety Net." Doctoral Dissertation. Ann Arbor, MI: University Microfilms International (1989).

Elias, Robert. 1986. *The Politics of Victimization: Victims, Victimology and Human Rights.* New York: Oxford University Press.

Friedrichs, Jurgen. 1988. "Affordable Housing and Homelessness: A Comparative View." In J. Friedrichs, ed., *Affordable Housing and the Homeless.* Berlin: Walter de Gruyter.

Gil, David G. 1989. "Work, Violence, Injustice and War." *Journal of Sociology and Social Welfare*, 16, no. 1: 39–53.

Gorder, Cheryl. 1988. *Homeless! Without Addresses in America.* Tempe, AZ: Blue Bird Publishing.

Harman, Lesley D. 1989. *When a Hostel Becomes a Home: Experiences of Women.* Toronto: Garamond Press.

Hartman, Chester. 1988. "Decent, Affordable Housing for All." In Marcus Raskin and Chester Hartman, eds., *Winning America: Ideas and Leadership for the 1990s.* Boston: South End Press.

Hayes, Robert M., Ed. 1987. *The Rights of the Homeless.* New York: Practicing Law Institute.

Henry, Stuart. 1991. "The Informal Economy: A Crime of Omission by the State." In G. Barak, ed., *Crimes by the Capitalist State: An Introduction to State Criminality.* Albany: State University of New York Press.

Hoch, Charles and Robert A. Slayton. 1989. *New Homeless and Old: Community and the Skid Row Hotel.* Philadelphia: Temple University Press.

Hombs, Mary Ellen and Mitch Snyder. 1983. *Homelessness in America: A Forced March to Nowhere.* Washington, DC: Community for Creative Nonviolence.

Hope, Marjorie and James Young. 1986. *The Faces of Homelessness.* Lexington, MA: Lexington Books.

Hopper, Kim James. 1987. "A Bed for the Night: Homeless Men in New York City, Past and Present." Doctoral Dissertation. Ann Arbor, MI: University Microfilms International (1989).

Hyde, Margaret. 1989. *The Homeless Profiling the Problem.* Hillside, NJ: Enslow Publishers.

Institute for Policy Studies Working Group on Housing (with Dick Cluster). 1989. *The Right to Housing: A Blueprint for Housing the Nation.* Oakland, CA: Community Economics, Inc.

Kanter, Arlene. 1989. "Homeless but Not Helpless: Legal Issues in the Care of Homeless People with Mental Illness." *Journal of Social Issues*, 45, no. 3:91–104.

Karyd, Arne. 1988. "Affordable Housing and the Market." In J. Friedrichs, ed., *Affordable Housing and the Homeless.* Berlin: Walter de Gruyter.

Kozol, Jonathan. 1988. *Rachel and Her Children: Homeless Families in America.* New York: Crown Publishers.

Marin, Peter. 1987. "Helping and Hating the Homeless: The Struggle at the Margins of America." *Harper's Magazine*, 274 (January)112–120.

McKittrick, Neil V. 1988. "The Homeless Judicial Intervention on Behalf of a Politically Powerless Group." *Fordham Urban Law Journal*, 16:389–440.

Momeni, Jamshid A., Ed. 1989. *Homelessness in the United States*, Vol. I: *State Surveys*. Westport, CT: Greenwood Press.

National Coalition for the Homeless. 1983. *The Homeless and the Economic Recovery*. New York: National Coalition for the Homeless.

———. 1986. *National Neglect/National Shame: America's Homeless—Outlook Winter, 1986–87*. Washington, DC: NCH.

———. 1989. *American Nightmare: A Decade of Homelessness in the United States*. New York: NCH.

———. 1989. "The Interagency Council on the Homeless: An Assessment." Washington, DC: NCH (March).

———. 1989. "State Homeless Persons' Assistance Act of 1989: Model State Legislation." Washington, DC: NCH.

O'Conner, James. 1973. *The Fiscal Crisis of the State*. New York: St. Martin's Press.

Rader, Victoria. 1986. *Signal Through the Flames: Mitch Snyder and America's Homeless*. Kansas City, MO: Sheed and Ward.

Redburn, F. Stevens and Terry F. Buss. 1986. *Responding to America's Homeless: Public Policy Alternatives*. New York: Praeger.

Reiman, Jeffrey. 1990. *Justice and Modern Moral Philosophy*. New Haven, CT: Yale University Press.

Ropers, Richard H. 1988. *The Invisible Homeless: A New Urban Ecology*. New York: Human Sciences Press.

Ross, Robert J. S. and Kent C. Trachte. 1990. *Global Capitalism: The New Leviathan*. Albany: State University of New York Press.

Rossi, Peter H. 1989. *Down and Out in America: The Origins of Homelessness*. Chicago: University of Chicago Press.

Ryan, William. 1971. *Blaming the Victim*. New York: Pantheon.

Schwartz, David C., Richard C. Ferlauto, and Daniel N. Hoffman. 1988. *A New Housing Policy for America: Recapturing the American Dream*. Philadelphia: Temple University Press.

Snow, David A., Susan G. Baker, Leon Anderson, and Michael Martin. 1986. "The Myth of Pervasive Mental Illness Among the Homeless." *Social Problems*, 33, no. 5 (June).

Spitzer, Steven. 1975. "Towards a Marxian Theory of Deviance." *Social Problems*, 22, no. 5: 638–651.

Sutherland, Edwin H. and Harvey J. Locke. 1971. *Twenty Thousand Homeless Men: A Study of Unemployed Men in the Chicago Shelters*. New York: Arno Press and the New York Times. First published in 1936 by J. B. Lippincott.

Torrey, E. Fuller. 1988. *Nowhere to Go: The Tragic Odyssey of the Homeless Mentally Ill*. New York: Harper and Row.

Viano, Emilio. 1983. "Victimology: The Study of the Victim." *Victimology*, 1.

United States General Accounting Office. 1985. *Homelessness: A Complex Problem and the Federal Response*. Washington, DC: GAO.

Walker, Lee. 1989. *Homeless in the United States*. Lexington, KY: The Council of State Governments.

Watson, Sophie with Helen Ansterberry. 1986. *Housing and Homelessness: A Feminist Perspective*. London: Routledge and Kegan Paul.

Zarembka, Arlene. 1990. *The Urban Housing Crisis: Social, Economic, and Legal Issues and Proposals*. Westport, CT: Greenwood Press.

Index

About the Author

GREGG BARAK is professor and chair of the Department of Criminology and Criminal Justice at Alabama State University. He has published many articles on a variety of public policy issues, including the administration of criminal justice, domestic violence and sexual assault, media and crime, black on black crime, and governmental crime. He is the author of *In Defense of Whom? A Critique of Criminal Justice Reform* (1980) and the editor of *Crimes by the Capitalist State: An Introduction to State Criminality* (1991). Since 1986 he has served as book review editor of *Social Justice: A Journal of Crime, Conflict, and World Order*. He received his doctorate in criminology from the University of California at Berkeley.